the
dirty lowdown
press
presents...

Mexican Food in Austin

The Guide

by

Christopher Nelson

and

Allison K. Walsh

All rights reserved. No part of this book may be reproduced or transmitted in any form or by any means, electronic or mechanical, including photocopying, recording or by any information storage and retrieval system, without written permission from the authors, except for the inclusion of brief quotations in a review.

Copyright © 2004 by The Dirty Lowdown Press
Copyright © 2004 all photos
Copyright © 2004 all maps

ISBN, print ed. 0-9760349-0-5
First Printing: October 2004
Printed in the United States of America

Nelson, Christopher, 1976-
Mexican food in Austin : the guide / [by Christopher Nelson & Allison K. Walsh].
p. cm.
At head of title: Dirty Lowdown Press presents--
Includes index.
LCCN 2004096189
ISBN 0-9760349-0-5

1. Restaurants--Texas--Austin--Guidebooks.
2. Cookery, Mexican.   I. Walsh, Allison K. II. Title.
III. Title: Dirty Lowdown Press presents--

TX907.3.T42A97 2004   647.95764'31
QBI04-200367

Published by:
The Dirty Lowdown Press
Post Office Box 1972
Austin, Texas 78767-1972 U.S.A.
www.thedirtylowdownpress.com

Cover Design and Icons by Marc Ferrino
Layout by Chris Nelson
Photographs by Derek Hatley
Maps by Stephen Graham

For John Collier Hogg, III

foreword

I'm in heaven. That's Mexican food heaven, and my hat is off to this new guide. As a native Austinite, past President of The Austin Restaurant Association and acting President of The *Saveur* Texas Hill Country Wine and Food Festival, I thought I knew this town inside and out. Yet these writers have proven otherwise. They have provided great information, personal comments, restaurant characteristics and menu favorites North, South, East and West. In a city that's known for great things like the Austin City Limits Music Festival, South by Southwest, The Austin Film Festival and The Wine and Food Festival, most local residents and visitors alike always want to know where to get a great margarita and an awesome plate of Mexican food. This guide hits the nail on the head.

I've grown up going to my family's favorites like El Rancho, Güero's, Cisco's, Joe's Bakery and La Reyna. My parents took me to these places and now my 19-year-old daughter takes her friends as well. It's the stories that are passed down for generations and the families who run these restaurants that keep us coming back for more. Now that I've experienced this guide, my calendar is booked for numerous adventures, and I hope yours will be too.

The writers have candid views of these eateries and some restaurants have more than one review to give readers a difference of opinion. I love reading about the great hangover places or where to go if you DON'T want to be seen. Tips like these are rarely found within the typical review.

Whether you are a visitor, newcomer or old timer to Austin you will find this a great source of information. The city is broken down geographically with easy-to-read maps and tips. Please contact The Dirty Lowdown Press at www.thedirtylowdownpress.com with your opinions and experiences as we continue learning about all Austin has to offer in Mexican food heaven.

Kevin W. Williamson
Chef / Owner, Ranch 616 Restaurant and Bar
President, The *Saveur* Texas Hill Country Wine and Food Festival

acknowledgements

The Dirty Lowdown Press would like to thank:

...*all of the contributors:*
Jordan Actkinson, Kenneth Adkins, Catherine Bower, Jennifer Braafladt, John Buchanan, Kevin Burns, Shazza Calcote, Brady Dial, Todd Erickson, Jeff Fraley, Lucrecia Gutierrez, Chad Hamilton, Leanne Heavener, Juliana Hoffpauir, Paul Jacobs, Aaron Kirksey, Shelly Lamont, Clay Langdon, Stephen LeVay, Stephen Malina, Wes Marshal, Kevin Martin, Pat McIntyre, Cile Montgomery, James Moody, Christopher Nelson, Will O'Connell, Cory Plump, Doug Prince, Jesse Proctor, Boutros Puchachos, Amy Rogers, Tomas Salas, Gracie Salem, Tony Sanchez, Edmund Schenecker, Scott Staab, Stacey Stoddard, Trent Tate, Michael S. Thomson, Caroline Tinkle, Ann Tucker, Fay Wallace, Shayna Weeden, Fleetwood Wilson, and Virginia B. Wood

...*these special venues for their support:*
Vespaio Restaurant, Ranch 616, The Elk's Lodge BPOE #201, Little Blanco Farm, Walsh Station and Moody's house for purveying the ridiculous amounts of beer, wine and Hennessey necessary for the DLP team meetings; Michael's Restaurant in Fort Worth, Wet Salon, and Favorite Liquor for agreeing to peddle this book sight unseen; and to the Longbranch Inn for both.

...*the inimitable team:*
Christopher Nelson, Ann Tucker, Susan Shields, Scott Staab, Leanne Heavener, Patricia Campos, Lucrecia Gutierrez, Marc Ferrino, Stephen Graham, Moxy Castro, James Moody, Derek Hatley, Cile Montgomery, Fay Wallace, Bill Steubine, and Slick McJ

...and my mom and dad.

- Allison K. Walsh, Publisher
The Dirty Lowdown Press

editor's note

They say do what you love. So I did.

I moved back to Austin, gathered my friends and started eating copious amounts of Mexican food — sometimes several times a day. The plan was to create a simple yet passionate, guide to my favorite cuisine in my favorite town. A year and half and many pounds later here we are.

What has become clear is that Austinites have a unique relationship with Mexican food. Is it a love affair or a socially-acceptable addiction? Either way, the places that provide us with our beloved victuals are ubiquitous. The hope is to reacquaint you with Austin through this subculture, to introduce you to some new favorites, to enlighten and to entertain.

Truthfully, I am not a food writer, but more a food enthusiast. Similarly, most of the contributors are just everyday people with an opinion and passion for the food. The reviews as such are honest and impartial. With this in mind, we look forward to your feedback.

Buen Provecho...

- Allison K. Walsh

editor's note

This book was so much fun to write, I don't know where to start. First, I'm fatter. The publisher kept telling me that nobody would buy a book on Mexican food from a skinny (in the face) person. Second, we tried to approach all the restaurants with an open mind. We thought that if they're open, somebody likes something there and it is our job to discover it. Suprisingly few restaurants were complete disappointments, but it is entirely possible that we ate the wrong dishes at those. Third, please write us with your reviews, experiences and favorite dishes. When you want the 'dirty lowdown' you gotta take it to the streets. Eventually, I would like to see this book written by the unique residents of Austin who support and love the many Mexican food restaurants in this town. So if you have an opinion or bone to pick, by all means, send it in.

Also, none of the writers have PHDs in Comparative Gastronomy from the Universidad de Mexico. Some have sharper palettes and pens than others, but we all love the simple pleasure of Mexican food and the reviews reflect that simplicity of taste. After reading many of the reviews, you might notice that hangovers and boozing are mentioned with the same frequency as 'enchilada' and 'and'. Well, the Dirty Lowdown Press is a salty bunch, many of whom have livers more sinful than the Boston Diocese and lifestyles that necessitate heavy and frequent doses of migas. Such is life in the DLP.

Finally, I would like to thank all the contributors whose effort and generosity have made this book a truly collaborative project. Many selfless hours were spent eating and writing and it is greatly appreciated. I hope that readers find the book informative, entertaining and ultimately helpful in their quest for incredible Mexican food.

"Vaya con Dios, Bodhi" [1]

- Christopher Nelson

[1] *Point Break*, 1991

Please Don't Ignore

Disclaimer about not being aggravated:
We have gone to great lengths to be as accurate as possible with all of our information prior to going to press. Please note that restaurants are constantly opening and closing, as well as changing their policies, hours of operation, and/or menus. To be safe, it is recommended to phone the intended establishment to avoid any aggravation.

Disclaimer about disagreeing with us:
Know that it is the nature of small, independent Mexican restaurants to be hit or miss. If you find our review way off the mark, nine times out of ten you can go back the next day to discover a completely different experience. Or you may find a harsh review of one of your favorites. Clearly there is no one expert opinion on the subject. For this reason we have tried to include multiple reviews, kind and not so kind, for some of the more popular and thus more hotly-debated restaurants. Be aware that some reviewers have chosen to use humor and satire in order to express their opinions. The reviews do not reflect the opinion of the Dirty Lowdown Press.

Disclaimer about racy language:
Though few and far between, some contributors have chosen to use expletives and mild vulgarities in their reviews. This language is meant for emphasis and is written with humor to punctuate where needed and represent the vernacular of today. The DLP apologizes if this type of language is found offensive for that is not the intention.

Disclaimer about being an ass:
We do not condone drinking and driving. Don't be an ass.

Contact Us
Please remember that this guidebook is only our first attempt and that your feedback is essential to the pursuit of the dirty lowdown. Visit us and share your ideas and comments at www.thedirtylowdownpress.com. Or write to us at: The Dirty Lowdown Press, PO Box 1972, Austin, TX, 78767.

legend

The DLP Seal of Approval
It is the holy grail of every ambitious restauranteur and equal to twelve Michelin stars. It is to the enchilada what the Nobel Prize is to a scientist.

Hangover Worthy
Does it stop your throbbing, unwelcome headache? Is its grease sublime enough to soak up the stale scotch in your belly? Will it bring you back to life for round two?

Little English/No English
Wild Card. This means you might have to gesture wildly and make grunting noises if you no habla. It most likely means the place is good, but it's no guarantee.

Beer/Wine
This is the lighter side of the alcohol spectrum, much like dipping your toe in the pool.

No Alcohol
Some of these places are bare-bones operations, some are waiting for their license and some might be considered breakfast-only places even though they also serve dinner.

Full Bar
Jackpot. Margaritas.

UT Friendly
Whether you're a UT student, parent, football fan or just want to relive your glory days as water boy for the Flatpoint Donkeys, these places provide ample collegiate atmosphere.

Outdoor Seating
Sitting outside, sipping a margarita in Austin in the springtime is as close to heaven as many of us will get.

Fast Food
These places are not necessarily chains and not all the food is processed. This merely means that it is quick.

legend

Vegetarian Friendly

Sometimes vegetarians can feel like outcasts when looking for Mexican food that caters to their specific culinary needs. It's not that Mexican restaurants hate vegetarians, it's just that they love animal flesh. There are, however, a few places that have vegetarian items and menus. Most of these places are not exclusively vegetarian, so don't expect them to handle the poblanos with separate gloves.

Credit Cards
We didn't specify here between AMEX, Visa, Mastercard, Discover, Carte Blanche, Penny's, Exxon, or Home Shopping Network. If you are credit card person, you probably have more than one. If you're not, then the one you do have is probably maxed out.

Hours of Operation, Address
We've done our best here. Getting accurate information took countless nerve-racking hours. It ain't all in the phonebook—trust me. Church, personal problems, dentist appointments, parole hearings and the lottery are just some of things that can cause a restaurant to open late or close early, so call if you're concerned about the time.

Prices
This is Mexican food. Not French cuisine. You will receive no handmade chocolate at the end of your meal and there will be no desert wine to accompany that last tortillas chip before you pay at the counter. The only really expensive place is Fonda San Miguel and it's worth every penny. Otherwise, a dish on the high end will run $9-10 and $3-5 on the low end. If you're in a pinch, check the back of the book for our list of best restaurants for your money, or just go to Arandas. Either way, you'll be more than satisfied.

Ratings
The DLP does not support or condone any rating system. Every thing and every experience is unique, especially when it comes to Mexican food. If you want chile pepper stars, you've come to the wrong place. This is not a competition and there is no first prize. Hey — if they're still in business then they must be doing something right.

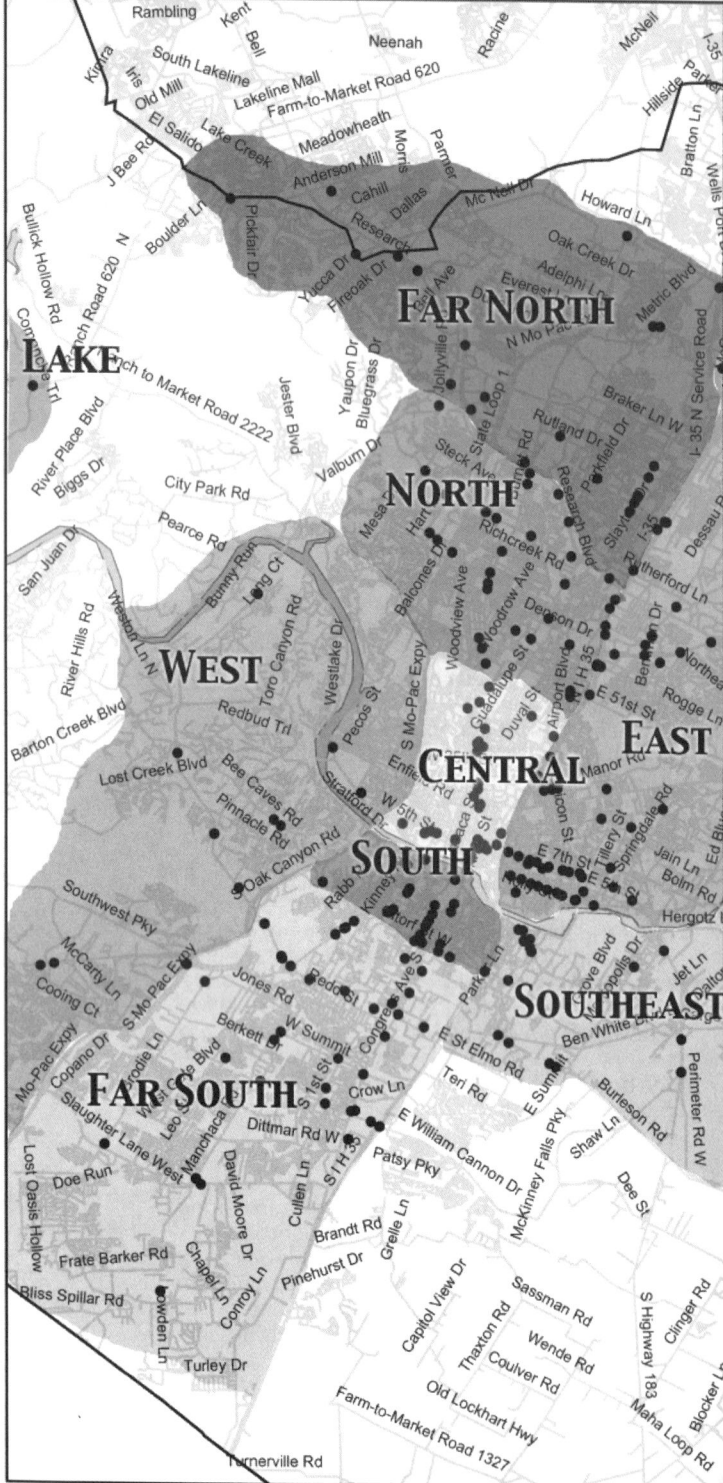

Foreword v
Acknowledgements vi
Editor's Note vii
Disclaimer ix
Legend x

zones

CENTRAL 1

EAST 37

SOUTHEAST 81

SOUTH 97

FAR SOUTH 127

WEST 143

NORTH 157

FAR NORTH 183

LAKE TRAVIS 205

indexes

Best Dishes 212
Helpful Phrases 219
Glossary 221
Contributors 233
Restaurant Index 244
Order Form 252

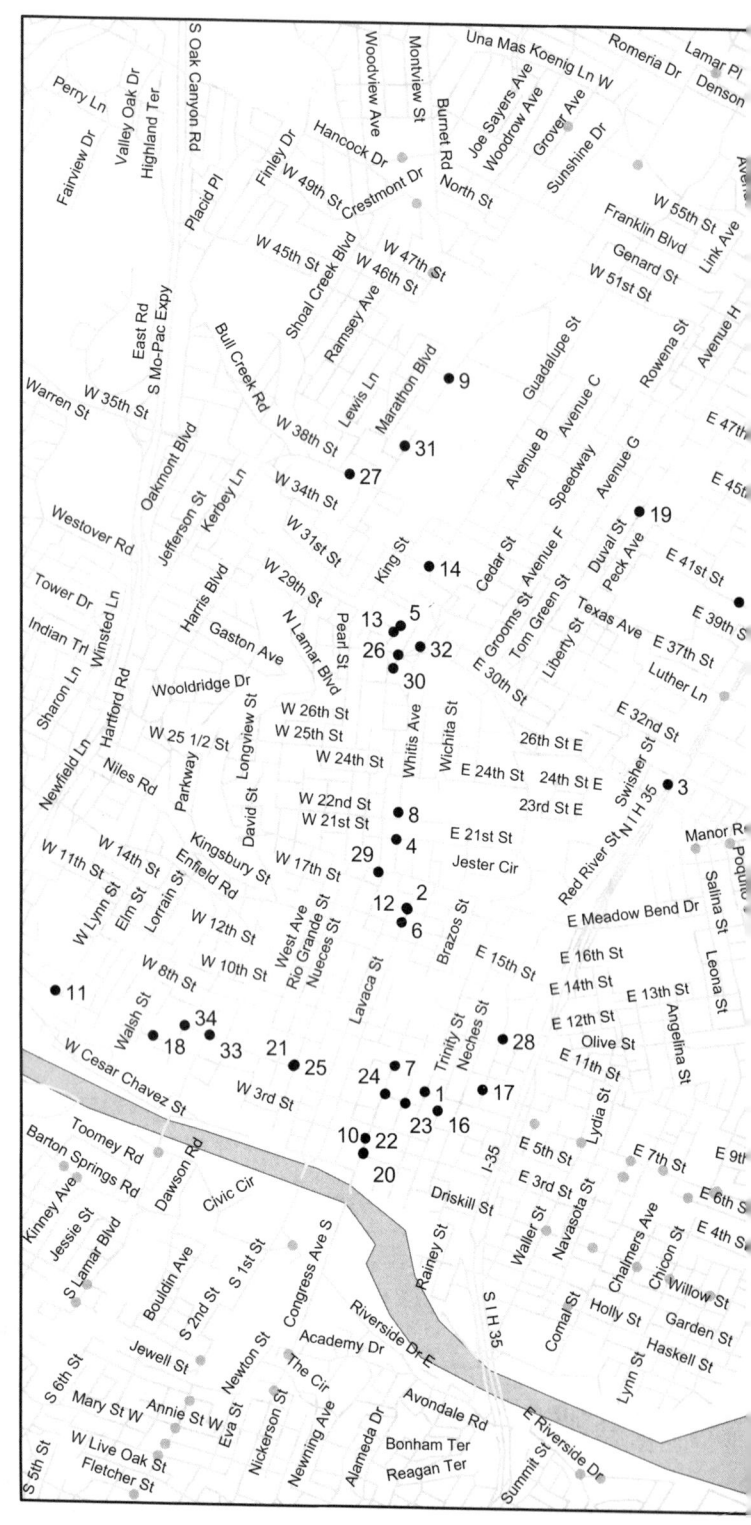

mexican food in austin

Central Austin is the heart of the city. In its center, downtown continues to grow with new loft buildings, office towers, restaurants and entertainment districts. Once busy only during the day with businessmen and Capitol workers, downtown now bustles at night with 6th Street bars, Red River music venues, upscale Warehouse District watering holes and developing urban neighborhoods. Immediately surrounding downtown are cozy, historic neighborhoods like Clarksville, Old Enfield, and Pemberton. Minutes away, heading north, is The University of Texas with over 55,000 students and large swaths of land dedicated to higher learning, student housing and adolescent fun. Just above UT is the Hyde Park neighborhood whose eclectic residents give the area great flavor and an unmistakably Austin feel.

1 Ancho's
2 Arturo's Bakery Café
3 Aus Tex-Mex Café
4 Baja Fresh
5 Chango's Taqueria
6 Chaveros Chicken Bowl
7 Chipotle
8 Chipotle
9 Chipotle
10 Copa
11 El Arroyo
12 El Mercado
13 El Patio
14 Foodheads
15 Freebirds
16 Iron Cactus
17 Jaime's Spanish Village
18 Juanita's
19 Julio's
20 Las Manitas
21 Mama Ninfa's
22 Manuel's
23 Marisco Grill
24 Pancho's Express
25 Ranch 616
26 Ruby's BBQ
27 Santa Rita Tex-Mex
28 Serrano's
29 Taco Cabana
30 Taco Shack
31 Taco Shack
32 Trudy's Texas Star
33 Whole Foods
34 Z Tejas Grill

dlp

Ancho's Restaurant

700 San Jacinto Blvd. 78701
Phone: (512) 476-3700
Mon-Fri 6:30am-2pm
5:30pm-10pm
Sat-Sun 7am-2pm
5:30pm-10pm
Credit Cards

The only thing authentically Mexican about Anchos is its name. Located in the Omni Hotel building, Anchos is the culinary anchor for this chain hotel whose nostalgic décor elicits memories of the 1980's with a soul-crushing color palette of Regurgitated Aubergine, Corporation Gray and Flayed Pumpkin. Anchos' saving grace is its breakfast buffet. All the standard breakfast items are laid out in a serve-yourself, spit-guarded environment and paid for by weight. So, you can load up on bacon (which is light), eggs, fruit and biscuits for the price of a Starbucks latté. It's one of the best breakfast deals downtown.

- Chris Nelson

Arturo's Bakery & Café

314 W 17th St. 78701
Phone: (512) 469-0380
Mon-Fri 6:30am-3:30pm
Sat 7:30am-1:30pm
Credit Cards

Imagine the West Village in NYC. You have just discovered the most incredible taco joint / sandwich shop / espresso bar in the world. You envision your increased popularity and perhaps a write-up in *The Post* as a local hero to all of the Texan transplants. Arturo's kinda feels like that. Near the capitol, this much overlooked café must be good if the local politicos stomach the blaring Pixies and modest digs. I'm a fan of anything they make with spinach—quesadillas, tacos, sandwiches whatever. Though they have various salads and some Mediterranean and Thai selections, their ample use and perfect combination of cheese and grease make it a Tex-Mex hangover wonderland. Their seated section is an adjacent basement—dark and quiet—a hip hideout.

- Allison Walsh

mexican food in austin

AUS TEX-MEX CAFÉ

2804 N IH 35 78705
Phone: (512) 479-0288
Mon-Sat 7:30am-9pm
Sun 7:30-2:30pm
Breakfast till 11:00 M-F
Breakfast all day Sat & Sun
Credit Cards

Though the drug runners jamming up I-35 are too nervous to notice and their semis too huge to pull in anyway, this corridor is a hot zone of good Mexican food. The chef of this one-room outfit, Jorge Arredondo, is so proud of his creations that he touts his name on the marquis, the menu and the promotional handouts (which include a handsome photo). Perhaps this is some sort of tricky political strategy? His masterworks are his two special sauces, a red and a green, which smother most everything. The chips were crispy and hot—a nearly lost art—and the guacamole was the right color. This is a nice, friendly place of proud Tex-Mex—no matter any looming political aspirations.

- Allison Walsh

BAJA FRESH

2100 Guadalupe St. 78705
Phone: (512) 322-0100)
Sun-Thurs 11:00am-9:00pm
Fri & Sat 11:00am-10:00pm

No microwaves, no can openers, no freezers, no lard, no MSG. That's the motto of this new arrival to Austin. Californians have been eating this unprocessed grub for decades, but I guess it took us Texans awhile to reckon' Mexican food doesn't have to be swimming in grease and render you paralytic afterwards. (Don't get me wrong, I like to get my nap on just like the next guy — it's just nice to have choices.) The important thing to remember is that this chain has taken over the West Coast and is literally sweeping the nation only because it tastes good. We no longer have to insult our taste buds, much less our intelligence, with flavorless crap for the sake of our health. Taco Cabana has been proudly serving us freshly prepared, unprocessed food from fresh ingredients for years, but unfortunately the marketing guys probably figured that no one would eat there if they promoted any sort of health aspect. My how times are a changin'. Their menu is comprehensive including various types of shrimp and fish tacos which are a welcome addition to the local fast food offerings. Honestly, as far as fast food chains go this is first rate: consistently clean, well run, friendly and damn good. Since it's hard to find parking, their location on the Drag is kind of a pain, but at least you never have to eat at the Dobie food court again. But don't forget Taco Cabana — she's still 24 hours and serves beer.

- Allison Walsh

INSIDERS TIP: There is a sign for the staff behind the counter that reminds them to say "Of course we could do that!"

CHANGO'S TAQUERIA

3023 Guadalupe St. 78705
Phone: (512) 480-8226
Daily 11am-10pm
Credit Cards

Chango's is inexpensive, speedy, healthy and damn good. I go to the Guadalupe location all the time and have never had a bad experience. The menu is not very extensive; just the basics, but it gets the job done. The flour tortillas are made fresh with each order. I can have a gigantic burrito and a beer for less than eight bucks and be out of there in twenty minutes. Even when there is a long line, they crank the food out without compromising the quality. The place is casual, clean and simple. The people are friendly and efficient. Go there.

Families?	Yes
Romantic?	No
Price?	Cheap
Alcohol?	Beer

- Cory Plump

Other Locations: South

Chavero's Chicken Bowl

1610 Lavaca St. 78701
Phone: (512) 474-9003
Mon-Fri 7am-4pm
Closed Sat-Sun
Breakfast all day
Credit Cards

Aside from a very obvious identity crisis: Is it Chavero's Restaurant or The Chicken Bowl? A hamburger joint or a Chinese restaurant? This little downtown Tex-Mex eatery does have some merit. The seven-year-old Chicken Bowl offers a curious mix of Mexican dishes and teriyaki bowls. Frightening, I know. The one friend who opted for fried rice gave it two enthusiastic thumbs down. The tortilla soup was a tasty appetizer, as was the chile con queso, both flavorful and perfect in consistency. The cheese enchiladas were a solid choice and came adorned with always delicious, grated government cheese. Crispy tacos were a disappointment only because of stale shells; the meat filling, however, was good and spicy.

They ran out of green sauce so we were unable to sample their green chicken enchiladas, and they had apparently also had a run on guacamole, as they were out of that, too. But our conscientious waiter sent someone to the store for avocados to slice up in lieu of the guacamole salad. The Chicken Bowl earns big points for their friendly, accommodating service. The day we were in, a young man took the initiative to wait on our table, although it was apparent you are to order at the counter. The UPS driver seated near us ordered a hamburger and fries, which our waiter informed us was an off-the-menu special from time to time. If they are not too busy, they'll almost always make it for you if you just ask.

Two flagrant fouls were the tortillas and salsa: the former being unremarkable and approaching stale, store-bought status, and the latter being exceedingly watery. If you are looking for ambience, keep looking, because you won't find it at The Chicken Bowl, but if, on the other hand, your goal is a quick, ultra-affordable, downtown standard Tex-Mex lunch with friendly service, add Chavero's Chicken Bowl to your roster.

- Amy Rogers

dlp

CHIPOTLE MEXICAN GRILL

2230 Guadalupe St. 78705
Phone: (512) 320-0238
Fax: (512) 320-9951
Open 7 Days 11am-10pm
Credit Cards

801 Congress Ave. 78701
Phone: (512) 391-1668
Mon-Fri 11:00am-8:00pm
Sat. 11:00am-6:00pm
Credit Cards

4400 N Lamar 78756
Phone: (512) 419-9898
Open 7 Days 11am-10pm
Credit Cards

This fast-food chain, owned by McDonald's, is a carefully choreographed experience. You go through a burrito assembly line, directing the burrito builders beyond the sneeze guard to include the fillings you want. To make things even easier, there are only four meat choices: beef, chicken, pork and barbacoa. The extras are more varied and include black beans, rice (note: it's white rice), grilled peppers and onions, pico de gallo, corn pico, cheese, sour cream and for $1 extra, guacamole. You've got to be quick and direct with the burrito builders. They can slip into auto-pilot, standing and scooping all day long.

INSIDER'S TIP: Chipotle's margaritas are made with real tequila. While other chains try to substitute white wine, this outfit understands its clientele and has splurged for a liquor license. Impressive.

- Ann Tucker

Other Locations: Far South, West, Far North

"I love Nuevo Leon for its snapper Vera Cruz and with it waitstaff; I will always split the regular dinner at Maudie's, and the carne guisada; and then there's Guero's on Sunday for the music, tacos al pastor and Santa Fe enchiladas with the fried eggs."

- Bob "Daddy-O" Wade
Artist

mexican food in austin

Copa Bar & Grill

217 Congress Ave. 78701
Phone: (512) 479-5002
Fax: (512) 479-5094
Mon-Fri 11am-2pm
Credit Cards

central

The next time you are waiting in line at Las Manitas take one large step north to find an alternative called La Copa, (previously known as Palmeras). This oft overlooked lunchtime spot has put a lot of effort into their renovations and has turned out quite a handsome, well-appointed establishment. The menu is straight-up, true-blue Tex-Mex. The real treat is the walls and walls of exposed brick, some with the original painted advertisements…cool old Austin. It's nice and dark for the hangover with a much more blue-collar crowd than its neighbor. NO actors, NO politicos and NO ex-boyfriends—this place is safe. Perhaps, you've ventured into its upstairs late-night personality Buzios Room. We hear it's a great space with a bar and dance floor offering a Brazilian night on Fridays and House music on Saturdays.

- Allison Walsh

photo by Derek Hatley

dlp

EL ARROYO

1624 W 5th St. 78703
Phone: (512) 474-1222
Fax: (512) 474-9769
http://www.ditch.com
Mon-Wed 11am-10pm
Thu 11am-11pm
Fri 11am-12am
Sat 10am-12am
Sun 10am-12am
Breakfast all day & weekends until 3pm
Credit Cards

"Body by Queso" is silk-screened on the back of the wait staff's t-shirts. And what with the hard-bodied waitresses, it's difficult not to enjoy the irony here. In addition to hotties, El Arroyo has earned its place in the pantheon of Austin's Mexican food institutions by cooking consistently great Tex-Mex in a location that's hard to beat. Multi-level decks offer outside seating under ancient, overgrown oaks that shade and assuage the diverse clientele. All of this takes place over the eponymous arroyo where the restaurant was built, inspiring dishes like the "Ditch Enchiladas." Driving down 5th Street you can't miss its sign that features up-to-date messages and news like "It's Tuesday, another excuse to drink."

- Chris Nelson

Other Locations: West, North

EL MERCADO RESTAURANT

1702 Lavaca St. 78701
Phone: (512) 477-7689
Mon 10:30am-10pm
Tue-Thu 10:30am-10:30pm
Fri 10:30am-11pm
Sat 9am-11pm
Sun 9am-10pm
Credit Cards

The wait staff at El Mercado definitely have their green cards. Not only that, they most likely have a love for rock-n-roll, piercings, tattoos and black clothing. Don't let their hipster image fool you — they're nice. They'll take your order, bring some margaritas, and rock the shit out of your ceviche before it hits the table. All this in the friend-

mexican food in austin

liest of ways. El Mercado is a Gringo eating establishment that makes damn fine Mexican food. Their vegetarian menu is extensive, but I wouldn't know anything about that. There might be an Emo rocker waiter that could help you out with that one.

- Chris Nelson

Other Locations: South, North

EL PATIO RESTAURANT

2938 Guadalupe St. 78705
Phone: (512) 476-5955
Mon-Sat 11am-9:45pm
Credit Cards

Upon receiving the assignment to check out El Patio, I cringed. Having gone there before, I was fearful of another trip. I resolved to try something different than what I had ordered before, chicken enchiladas, but I was let down once again. I ordered three beef tacos with guacamole and a coffee. All three were terrible. The tacos were flat, fried shells lathered with greasy beef and even greasier guacamole. I could only finish one and a half before I slid the goop off the taco shells and just ate them alone. I also ordered a small bowl of queso which never arrived. To make things worse, the whole place was filled with people that really seemed to be enjoying themselves even though I could see they were eating bad food. Also, all the waiters wore really dirty red jackets with holes and stains. I felt like I was in a bank.

- Aaron Kirksey

INSIDERS TIP: There's no patio at El Patio, though there is an abundance of crackers and butter upon request.

"I opened a Tex-Mex restaurant in Paris in 1981, really the first one. It was called the Studio and was similar to Julio's on 45th. In Austin, my favorites include Las Manitas, where they used to have barbacoa, which I now have to get at El Sol y La Luna. I do love Las Manitas for the beans: nice, fresh lard. And the enchiladas rojas, which are thick and smoked perfectly. For a hangover, go to El Azteca and have the cabrito plate, although it's seasonal. And try Azul Tequila for the conchinita pibil."

- *Claude Benayoun,*
  Co-owner, Vespaio

THE AUSTIN HOT SAUCE FESTIVAL

by Brady Dial

Coffee fanatics will tell you that drinking coffee on a hot day will make the weather seem cooler by raising your internal temperature. If that's true, then thousands of people should be experiencing a cold front at the end of every August, as they gather to eat fiery homemade salsas in Waterloo Park, courtesy of the Austin Hot Sauce Festival. Founder Robb Walsh must have pitched the first modest gathering in 1991 to *The Chronicle* as the exact opposite of the Polar Bear Club.

Since those humble beginnings at the Travis County Farmer's Market, the event has ballooned into a cutthroat culinary competition. Restaurants and commercial bottlers come from around the state to burn your face off. But most of those products you can get off-the-shelf and are merely a "warm up" — the real action is the amateur competition. Hundreds of entries, divided into three categories: red, green and "special," all ready for sampling by the public. Where does a spice girl (or boy) begin? Here are a few words of wisdom from a festival veteran:

1) Bring your own chips. For years, the festival was sponsored by a chip company that shall remain nameless out of respect for their charitable intentions, but their low-calorie product was never meant to cradle salsa. Also, although the fest does an admirable job of keeping chips available, nothing is worse than having only tortilla shards left when there's dipping to be done. Go for a less greasy, light and crispy chip, since you'll be eating a lot of them. El

dlp essay

Milagro makes an excellent *totopo* chip that's just right. (*Totopo* is the Spanish word for baked tortilla or tortilla chip).

2) Be prepared for the heat. That means internal and external. There's just no quick way to get people through the sampling lines, so be prepared to stand in the sun for quite a while — lots of water is a good thing. On the other hand, water will be useless on a habanero-scorched tongue. Dairy products are the best way to neutralize the heat, but unless you feel like toting around a jug of milk (some people do) or scrambling back and forth to the ice cream stand, the next best thing is to chew up a couple of dry tortilla chips and let the paste sit on your tongue between samples. Sure, it sounds a bit gross, but this is no time to be squeamish – you're here to eat the heat.

3) Come early, have a plan. By the end of the first hour, the place is packed and the lines are long. Get in early, hit the commercial samples while they're setting up the amateur competition, then jump in line ASAP. The red salsas get the biggest lines, so if you want to start sampling fast, hit the greens or "specials". A word of caution, though: "special" can mean anything from beet-rutabaga salsa to chipotle peanut butter. This may be the closest real-life experience to trying one of Harry Potter's "Every Flavor Beans". Some are great, others...not so much.

After that, just grab a beer, take a stroll through the mist sprayers, find some shade and listen to live music the rest of the day - it's a hot paradise (coincidentally, the same name of the best bottled salsa available there). People watching is great, there are other foods to sample and it's the perfect place to just "chill."

Foodheads

616 W 34th St. 78705
Phone: (512) 420-8400
Mon-Sat 8am-4pm
Credit Cards

Foodheads is not a Mexican food place but it does serve gourmet breakfast tacos. The ingredients are fresh and interesting and the eggs are cooked over hard instead of the defacto scrambled. Other things on the Foodheads menu are equally as good, like the sandwiches, salads, etc. One of the best things is that they deliver. So if you live in the Campus/Central area, wake up, crack a beer and get some tacos delivered for breakfast because damn it, you're still drunk.

- Chris Nelson

INSIDERS TIP: At time of press, Foodheads was in the process of acquiring a beer and wine license.

Freebirds World Burrito

1000 E 41st St. Ste. 260 78751
Phone: (512) 451-5514
Daily 11am-10:30pm
Credit Cards

Freebirds focuses on one thing and does it well — the burrito. Stand in line to have a custom steak, chicken or veggie burrito made in front of you at lightning speed by minimum wage college students sweating pico de gallo. The sizes come in Regular, Monster and Super Monster with your choice of rice, beans, cheese, cilantro, onions, pico, hot sauce, jump kicks, donkey broth, etc. The portions are massive. A Super Monster burrito could feed a small village or cause a serious case of gout. Freebirds is a chain that started in College Station for Texas A&M students and has been expanding throughout Texas. The burrito is more common in north Texas, New Mexico and Colorado. I suppose this makes it a specialty dish in the Hill Country but I wouldn't go that far. It's essentially fast food but I would put it in a category well above Taco Bell because, hey, Freebirds is pretty damn good.

- Chris Nelson

mexican food in austin

IRON CACTUS RESTAURANT AND MARGARITA BAR

606 Trinity St. 78701
Phone: (512) 472-9240
Fax: (512) 472-5283
Sun-Thu 11am-10:30pm
Fri 11am-11pm
Sat 12pm-11pm
Music as scheduled
Credit Cards

Located in the heart of downtown, the Iron Cactus is a place to be seen, or not to be seen, depending on your age and the company you keep. Sporting a kick-ass rooftop patio that overlooks Sixth Street, it will surely delight any post-college drinker who's looking to resurrect that certain Spring Break *je ne sais quoi* on a Tuesday night. On the weekends, it's brimming with hotties, which makes the Cactus the perfect place to take your old college roommates when they roll into town wanting to see Austin at its plastic finest. The beer is cold, the eye candy abundant and the patio is worthy of its own reality show. They tell me they serve food there, but I'd stick to the beer and Jger shots…when in Cancun. Have fun and bring your I.D.

- Jeff Fraley

Other Locations: Far North

photo by Derek Hatley

JAIME'S SPANISH VILLAGE

802 Red River St. 78701
Phone: (512) 476-5149
Mon 11am-2pm
Tue-Thu 11am-9pm
Fri-Sat 11am-11pm
Credit Cards

Jaime's is a veritable Austin institution and the Number One restaurant for University of Texas fans. Before football games you'll find the place packed with co-eds looking good, getting drunk and filling up on some of the best Tex-Mex in town. The walls of Jaime's are covered in pictures of students having a good time as well as posters of the delicious UT Pom Pom squad. Jaime's is huge with inside and outside seating, earning its name as the Spanish Village (even though you're not allowed to light fireworks in the central plaza). Its location across from Stubb's also makes it a great place to eat before a big show. Everything on Jaime's menu is surprisingly good, so it's impossible to go wrong. Warning to minors: Jaime's has a big sign on the front door that spells out the alcohol laws so don't expect to get served.

- Chris Nelson

JUANITA'S TACOS

1120 W 5th St. 78701
Phone: (512) 708-1179
Mon-Fri 7am-2pm
Sat 8am-2pm
Sun 9am-1pm
Breakfast all day

The very small parking lot is a good first sign; a brisk eight steps takes you to the very small door of the very small caboose that is now Jaunita's Tacos. You squeeze yourself through the door and meander past the three very small tables and grab a small menu looking for something to satisfy your large hunger. Leaning down to a small window you will notice the three very small women in a very small kitchen scurrying around. One of them stops to take your order and gets right to business—no small talk. The decoration on the walls is from even smaller people thanking Juanita for a "yummy"

mexican food in austin

breakfast; many wishing simply that their mothers could cook as well as Juanita.

Almost everything about this place is small. It's easy to miss on Fifth Street (on the corner of Walsh Ave.) with all the large buildings of Downtown and the many billboards overwhelming the small, simple signage. The food however is a completely different matter. The "Loco Taco," accurately named that since it's not really a taco at all, is one of the menu highlights. A large burrito stuffed with sautéed mushrooms, onions and perfect chicken-breast meat. It is covered in a spicy, cheese sauce and served with beans and rice. I told myself I would not finish the whole thing and would save some for later. (I too am trying to get smaller). That, however, did not happen.

I devoured all of it. A few days later I came back for more—adding a fajita beef taco to the order. The taco was small, perfect in every way, very tasty and not overwhelming—just the way they should be and I'm glad. Because I know I will be going back many times and I need to keep my waist, well... small.

- Scott Staab

"My favorites are the chalupas at Las Palmas, the al pastor torta from La Mexicana and Trudy's for their top-shelf margaritas."

- Courtney Cline,
Owner of the dog Buck

The best thing about Juanita's is that there is never a line, and as a result, the tacos are always hot and fresh. It's a tiny place on the corner of 5th and Walsh where you can hide out for an unbothered breakfast in the dimly lit red caboose or just out back on the small patio. It's nice to have places like this up your sleeve, where you can relax without the hustle; like home only they fill your coffee and do all the cooking. The potatoes are mixed in with the eggs and cheese making a nice ball of food that is made perfect with their homemade, traditional style, Mexican hot sauce on top (both verde and rojo). There is a migas taco here that differs from Maria's. It has more of a fresh chopped jalapeño flavor that goes well with the cilantro-laden hot sauce. Muy delicioso. (Note: Cash only again, I'm beginning to notice a trend here.)

- Stephen Malina

Reprinted with permission from INSite Publications.

dlp

Julio's Restaurant

4230 Duval St. 78751
Phone: (512) 452-1040
Breakfast till 11:30
Cash Only

On Duval, squeezed between a cleaners and a laundromat, is Julio's Café. Given its neighbors, it's no surprise that the food tastes clean—not something many Mexican restaurants can claim. While it's not health food, the guacamole is fresh, the produce crisp and the chips are never stale. Julio's is best known for its chicken, freshly roasted daily and served up in every possible way. The chalupas and flautas are excellent and the caldo de pollo is a guaranteed cure all. But the true stand out is the chicken taco. Taco purists may balk at Julio's flour tortilla only policy, but Julio's first warms the tortilla just enough to melt a handful of cheese. The sliced roasted chicken, lettuce and tomato are then loaded on. This position shift from cold cheese on top to hot on the bottom makes all the difference. Julio's serves the standard sides of rice and beans (both well seasoned) with chopped tomatoes, onions and peppers. But, their best side of all is the nugget ice scooped up out of the ice machine behind the cash register. It makes coca-cola taste sweeter and the margaritas even stronger.

- Ann Tucker

INSIDERS TIP: Every now and then Julio's runs out of chicken and closes early.

Las Manitas Avenue Café

211 Congress Ave 78701
Phone: (512) 472-9357
Mon-Fri 7am-4pm
Sat-Sun 7am-2pm
Credit Cards

mexican food in austin

As you walk through the kitchen to get to the patio in this Congress Avenue institution, you can't help but feel as if you're in Old Mexico. Charming to the point of mocking other self-proclaimed "authentic" Mexican food joints, Las Manitas is the real deal all the way around. The food is traditional, gloriously fresh, and I've never had a dish short of outstanding. Specifically, it's my favorite place for breakfast in town. For the more adventurous, the delicious menudo and chicken pozole will not only cure any hangover, but will also make any self-respecting breakfast taco hang its head in shame. I recommend the simple, yet divine, plato de chorizo con huevos to kick-start your AM with a smile on your face. Get out of bed, pop some aspirin and get to Manitas—you won't regret it!

- Jeff Fraley

Las Manitas is popular and deservedly so! The ladies at Las Manitas have perfected delicate and delectable Mexican dishes. The guacamole is so fresh and tasty, I could eat mounds of it. The beans have plenty of pork fat to make them creamy and smooth. If you stop in on the weekend, don't miss their luscious mole, which has a subtle a hint of spice and sweetness. Las Manitas is only open for lunch and breakfast: the portion size reflects it. You will have no problem cleaning your plate 'till it shines.

- Shazza Calcote

This popular eatery is, in my opinion, the most over-rated restaurant in Austin. The service is so legendarily bad that it is comical. Pity the poor patron who speaks no Spanish as it is not uncommon to get waiters who do not understand basics such as "water" or "orange juice."

I have never understood the attraction to Las Manitas. My last experience was no better or worse than a usual visit. I can say it is consistently inconsistent. The one constant is the table top metal containers that include salsa that sits at room temperature all day. As best as I can tell these containers are constantly refilled but never washed. Provecho.

- Caroline Tinkle

dlp

The best. I have to start by saying that Las Manitas is the best, the most authentic Mexican cuisine and admirable small business eatery in Austin! I have dreams about the bacon-lard refried beans that cling to my heart strings. If your not one for meat-laden ecstasy, then their black beans will rival any you have ever tried.

I have been going to this restaurant for 15 years, and now that I live in San Marcos it is the only place I drive into town for. I have literally tried everything on the menu and the specialty menu. Breakfast is excellent; especially the Juevos con Hongos (mushrooms and eggs) or the authentic Chilaquilles with either green or red sauce. But it is the specialty lunch menu that is astronomical. Every day of the week offers different specialties of which any are well worth your ordering. Like the Uchepos, peppers stuffed with corn and black beans. Las Manitas has created their specialty menu around Mexico's regions and traditions. Enchiladas Zacatecanas (green enchiladas w/ sour cream and tomatillos), Potosinas (potatoes and orange sauce), and Friday's Camarones are of the most amazing. My personal favorite is on the regular menu, the Michoacan, either chicken or cheese with an acidic red sauce, cabbage, beans, carrots, with rice and refried beans. The measure of a good Mexican restaurant is in their staples—and Las Manitas has the best refried beans, vegetarian black beans, veggie steamed rice, Mexican rice, salsa, and homemade flavored waters or "Aguas" (watermelon, tamarind, strawberry, melon, horchata). Also, the tortillas rock! Every time I eat one my Aunt Maria rolls in her grave wishing she could make such a delicacy.

The hot sauce is for the professional Mexican food lover. This may not be a place for the faint of heart. The pace is fast during the rush, and there is a counter in the main dining area a la 50's lunch counter (where I always sit). Local art is displayed, and all of the servers are from the South of Texas. The owners are sisters with an impeccable work ethic who will most likely come to your table and ask "how everything was" unassumingly. If you love authentic cuisine, appreciate hard working dreamers, like to experiment with food, and want to see rock stars and movie stars in the know, treat yourself to this little diner.

- Catherine Bower

mexican food in austin

Mama Ninfa's Mexican Restaurant

612 W 6th St. 78701
Phone: (512) 476-0612
Fax: (512) 476-0242
www.mamaninfas.com
Sun-Thu 11am-10pm
Fri-Sat 11am-11pm
Credit Cards

The famed Coyote Café from Santa Fe came to Austin, built a million-dollar restaurant, and brilliantly fizzled because, it seems, Austinites aren't willing to shell out $30 for chipotle-infused rabbit haunches or green chile flan. In its abandoned shell, the Ninfa's chain set up shop and has successfully continued ever since. The food at Ninfa's seems to have learned lessons from the past tenant, and so it sticks to the basics and does it well. The fancy setting is what really sells Ninfa's and makes it a good place to bring an out-of-town business associate or someone who bristles at sight of plastic booths or paper napkins. WARNING: Do not park in Katz's Deli parking places! Though Ninfa's and Katz's are next door to each other, Katz's guards these places as if they are a birthright and will absolutely tow you.

- Chris Nelson

UPDATE: Cursed! One day after closing the exterior of the building began falling apart. The next owner better get an exorcist.

Other Locations: North

"For a quick lunch on a mild day, Taco Deli has the best scallop tacos on Thursdays and delicious queso any day of the week. For Sunday dinner, I say Matt's El Rancho for a couple of margaritas, the Bob Armstrong Dip and the green chile chicken enchiladas, que rico! My favorite Saturday morning stop is Cisco's on east 6th: the migas are God's remedy for a vicious hangover. It has a truly historical atmosphere, historically lousy service and great food. Don't expect to sit in the front room unless you live in the neighborhood. And finally, on Thursday night it's got to be Güero's: The Don, The Don, The Don and maybe another Don after that. It's a great place to drink with a group of people. Just make sure you are somewhat inebriated before ordering. Although, I do really like the Queso Flameado."

- Kevin Burns,
urbanspace Realtors
www.urbanspacerealtors.com

dlp

MANUEL'S DOWNTOWN

310 Congress Ave. 78701
Phone: (512) 472-7555
Fax: (512) 418-8807
Mon-Thu 11am-10pm
Fri-Sat 11am-11pm
Sun 11am-9pm
Music as scheduled
Credit Cards

Manuel's has been an Austin staple for outstanding, affordable interior Mexican cuisine for nearly twenty years, yet I know many people who fall in the category of, "Yeah, I know of it, but I haven't tried it." Well, I'm telling you right now, no one should be apathetic about trying this gem. Located in the belly of downtown, the atmosphere lands somewhere between old Austin and a Flock of Seagull's video set from the 80's. Perhaps the dated decor has deterred some folks, but I promise you won't be served by the Thompson Twins. Instead, you'll find an attentive, knowledgeable wait staff serving such dishes as yellowtail ceviche (best in Austin), authentic Suiza enchiladas that are filled with succulent chicken, and pork tenderloin with a pineapple or avocado and pumpkin seed salsa. If that's not enough, I believe they serve the best house margarita in town. So everybody Wang Chung tonight and mosey on down to Manuel's for a meal that never seems to disappoint. Excellent spot for a happy hour as well.

- Jeff Fraley

Plainly, Manuel's offers a more sophisticated menu for more sophisticated prices. Most importantly, they do it very well. A nice break from my "everyday" Mexican food, I enjoy doing it up a bit when it's worth it. With twenty years experience the recipes have been honed and perfected including some award-winning selections like their enchiladas de mole and their margaritas. The quality of the food, as well as the service, is outstanding—virtually unrivalled in this culinary field. I must admit that even if I wasn't hungry, I would have no qualms about bellying up to the bar for the most delightful concoction to ever pass through my lips—their fresh-pressed watermelon margarita. How I wish they were open for breakfast.

- Allison Walsh

Other Locations: Far North

dlp essay

THE LANGUAGE OF TEQUILA

by Edmund Schenecker

Reprinted with permission from The San Antonio Express-News. Originally entitled: "Heart of tequila lies in careful harvesting; aging" Copyright © 2004

Tequila, like any fine spirit, has a language all its own. As with other spirits, such as cognac and Champagne, tequila is named for a region — Tequila, Mexico — and government laws strictly regulate its ingredients and distillation process. Here, drawn in part from Jose Cuervo Distillery information, is a list of tequila terms:

Agave azul/blue agave: A prehistoric plant that looks like a cactus, but is related to the lily family. Only the blue agave (which actually looks blue-green) is used in making tequila. The plant takes up to 10 years to mature properly and yields a pineapple-type heart, the piña. Tequila must be produced from no less than 51 percent reducing sugars from the blue agave with the remaining content from other natural sugars.

Aguamiel: Pronounced "ah-gwah-mee-el," this translates as "honey water" and is the sugary, unfermented solution used to make tequila. It is obtained by crushing the steamed piñas in a mill. This sugar is then extracted by repeatedly washing the resulting plant fibers. If done properly, 98 percent of the agave's sugars can be extracted.

Añejo tequila: Pronounced "an-yay-ho," this means "aged." The aging takes place in small barrels made from American or French oak. Rules require that

dlp essay

tequila be aged a minimum of one full year to earn this coveted designation. Typically, this is the most costly tequila to produce.

Blanco/white tequila: White or silver unaged tequila less than 30 days old. Just off the still, tequila is combined with distilled water, bringing it to drinking proof. It is then set aside for 15 to 20 days to marry with the water. Besides filtration, no other processing is done.

Caballito: Pronounced "ca-ba-yee-toh," this is a tall, thin Mexican shot glass used for tequila.

Gold tequila: Young tequila that develops an amber hue from the oak casks in which it is stored.

Horno: Pronounced "orno," this is the traditional oven used to cook agave piñas.

Jalisco: Pronounced "ha-lees-coh," this is the state in Mexico where the majority of all the tequila in the world is produced.

Jimador: Pronounced "heem-a-dor," this is the skilled laborer who harvests the agave plants. Normas: Any legitimate tequila produced under the Normas must carry the letters NOM (Norma Official Mexicana) on the label. The NOM indication will always have an official number assigned by the government that corresponds to the tequila distillery from which it was made.

Laid to rest: This term describes the date the barrel was put into storage to age.

Maguey: Pronounced "mah-gay," this is the name given to the agave plant by Spanish explorers and is still used in Mexico as a generic description of agave plants.

dlp essay

Margarita: The margarita is the most requested drink in bars and restaurants. Margaritas are traditionally made with tequila, lime juice and triple sec. The margarita accounts for more than 60 percent of tequila consumption in the U.S.

Mezcal: This is not the same as tequila — the two should not be confused. Mezcal is similar to tequila in that it is distilled from the agave (once, as opposed to twice for tequila), but it is unregulated and can be made from any species of the plant in any part of Mexico.

Mosto muerto: The aguamiel after fermentation is completed.

Ordinario: The first-run distillate when making tequila.

Pencas: The spiny, broad, cactuslike leaves of the agave plant, used by early Indians as needles and paper. In cultivating the agave, these leaves must be cut on the proper angle. If they are cut too short, the weight of the piña could be lost; if they are too long, the plant could become difficult to handle.

Piña: Pronounced "peen-yah," this is the pineapple-shaped heart of the blue agave plant that averages between 40 to 70 pounds, but has been known to weigh in at 150 pounds. The hearts are cooked in traditional brick ovens or modern autoclaves and then shredded or ground into a pulp. The juice from the piña is then distilled.

Reposado tequila: Reposado, pronounced "ray-po-sah-doh," means "rested."

A tequila must be "rested" in wood barrels, typically

dlp essay

white oak, for a minimum of two months, but no longer than a year. This is a requirement of the Mexican government.

The "resting" mellows and refines the tequila, producing a combination of superb smoothness and great taste.

Sangrita: The traditional Mexican apertif that is usually served chilled alongside a shot of tequila. Sangrita should not be confused with the popular Spanish fruit and wine elixir, Sangria.

Sangrita is traditionally blended with the following ingredients: fresh lime juice, fresh orange juice, onions, salt and hot chiles. Some people also use tomato juice.

Tequila (the town): Both the region and the town that gave the spirit of tequila its name. This town in central Mexico was settled in 1656 and named after its early residents, a local Indian tribe.

Tequila means "lava hill" in the Mexican Indian language, and the agaves are grown in soil rich in volcanic ash.

Tequilero: Pronounced "tay-keel-air-oh," this is the title of the tequila distiller or anyone experienced in the production of the spirit.

Worm: Make no mistake about it — there are no worms in legitimate tequila. The worm is often included in bottles of mezcal as a marketing gimmick. The production of mezcal is very lightly regulated by the Mexican government and the result often is a harsher taste.

mexican food in austin

MARISCO GRILL

211 E 6th 78701
Phone: (512) 458-9440
Mon-Thu 9am-10pm
Fri-Sat 9am-12pm
Sun 11am-10pm
Credit Cards

This place is for seafood maniacs. Consistent, spicy and downright pleasurable, Marisco serves all the specialties one would expect with a name like theirs. The Veulve a la Vida will certainly bring you out of your hangover and prime you for their generous seafood soup or grilled octopus. Both locations maintain a high standard, but the 6th Street location is my favorite. Like "the purloined letter" it is hidden smack dab in the middle of the infamous strip of bars and consequently not known as a place to go eat. This makes Marisco perfect because you never have to wait to get seated and it's close to the action for going out afterwards. For those who work downtown and get tired of Las Manitas, Marisco makes a great addition to your vocabulary of downtown lunch spots.

- Chris Nelson

Other Locations: North

PANCHO'S EXPRESS

609 Congress Ave. 78701
Phone: (512) 236-0029
Fax: (512) 236-1078
Mon-Fri 7am-3pm
Closed on weekends
Breakfast 7:00am-11:00
Credit Cards

Don't get excited. This is not Pancho's Mexcian Food Buffet—this is the little sister Pancho's Express. But how is it possible? I have been a huge fan of their buffet chain since childhood. Not for the food so much, as for their ridiculous all you can eat price of $3.99 and their Mexican flag concept. See, after you have loaded up down the assembly line and paid, the restaurant becomes full service. Pancho had the brilliant idea of placing small Mexican flags on individual flagpoles on each table. So when needing another Dr. Pepper, or another plate of enchiladas, or 39 more tacos, just raise the flag and your waitress will come over and take care of you. Oh the kitsch, the memories and the ridiculously full bellies that always manage to save room for the sopapillas. Always a big hit. These buffets are still scattered around Texas though I couldn't tell you about the food — it's about the experience. I even have my own set of commemorative Pancho's drinking glasses. So I don't want to go without the ceremonious flag…call me a purist.

- Allison Walsh

UPDATE: Booyah! The Pancho's empire has just graced the Austin city limits with one of their buffet restaurants—Monterey Oaks at 290.

RANCH 616

616 Nueces St. 78701
Phone: (512) 479-7616
Fax: (512) 479-5979
http://ranch616.citysearch.com
Mon-Fri 11am-2:30pm
Sun-Thu 5:30pm-10pm
Fri-Sat 5:30pm-11pm
Music Tues and Thurs
Credit Cards

Ranch 616 is as excellent as it is unique. Though not traditionally thought of as Mexican cuisine, Ranch 616 has successfully blended southwestern fine dining with some of our favorite Mexican staples. Affectionately known as Ranch, it is also simply just one of the best restaurants in town—for food, drinks, but also just to have a lot of fun and hangout (if you're lucky enough to score a barstool and have a little extra money to spend). Usually packed, reservations are recommended, but they are soon to open an adjacent late night watering hole, The Rattle Inn, with bar menu, so hopefully more out and abouters, young, Austin sophisticates, stargazers and true booze swillers will be able to nosh on their famous fried oysters, (voted best in the South,) and sip expertly-prepared cocktails.

Chef and owner Kevin Williamson's menu specials, including the lunchtime quesadillas and tamales, change daily, so sit tight while your waiter gives you a culinary soliloquy—quite a performance. And the waiters are all super cute and will treat you with as much Southern

mexican food in austin

charm as the menu calls for. If heading here mainly for Mexican influenced dishes, the Angus ribeye atop their enchiladas of the day is sublime. Or for something lighter start with caldo de pollo. Chef Antonio Vidal's flair for spice is certainly a South-of-the- border influence found in their many jalapeño accents, their poblano mashers or their own tampiquena blend of peppers and onions. You really can't go wrong … and I promise you'll be back.

- *Allison Walsh*

INSIDERS TIP: Check out their Tequila Tuesday for dinner — a *prix fixe* menu paired with a chilled shot of tequila.

Ruby's BBQ

512 W 29th St. 78705
Phone: (512) 477-1651
Daily 11am-12pm
Credit Cards

Living, as I do, on a strict diet of barbecue and Tex-Mex, Ruby's saves me all the trouble of figuring out which I'm going to eat for my next meal. Ruby's brings the world's two greatest culinary traditions together in a divinely simple concept: the brisket taco. America might have its hamburger, but the national dish of Texas should be the brisket taco. Go over to Ruby's and you'll figure it all out. I'm sure they sell something else, but, hell, I can't be bothered to figure it out. The tacos are just too good.

- *Tony Sanchez*

central

dlp

Santa Rita Tex-Mex Cantina

1200 W 38th St. 78705
Phone: (512) 419-7482
Sun-Thurs 11:00am-10:00pm
Fri & Sat 11:00am-11:00pm

Trying a new restaurant is very much a gamble. Sometimes they've got it totally together and it's a winner. Sometimes you wonder if they put any thought into it at all. Unfortunately, Santa Rita needs a little more time to work out the kinks. The restaurant has gone through major cosmetic renovations and the patio is great, but maybe go for drinks and eat somewhere else. Our server, who told us that he used to be a sous-chef, should have stayed in the back of the house. I think that he came around to ask us if we were ready to order about 69 times in the first half hour we were there. The tortilla soup was lukewarm with a ball of guacamole in the middle creating a sort of green slime on top of the chicken fat broth, and there was a lot of discussion with our waiter on whether the avocado slices could be left off of or put on the side of my companion's fish tacos. When our entrees arrived, it was apparent that the lengthy avocado discussion had been forgotten entirely. The 71st time he came back to our table, he asked my friend how the fish tacos were because he had never tasted them before and were we ready for the check. I had a combination plate that was wholly inedible and cold. Santa Rita has a lot of expensive plasma televisions in the bar and some bright new paint, but they need to work on the real reason a restaurant should exist.

- Leanne Heavener

"We started going to Nuevo Leon when it was on east 7th in the little house. There were only like 12 tables and there was always a line and so I started having Sunday dinner, earlier and earlier to avoid the crowds. I have always loved the place because they know what I want to eat, what I drink. I always have Shrimp Saltillo. We have always had the same waitress, Grizelda, who was a teenage busser when we started going every Sunday. She always worked harder than everybody and we've watched her grow up. It's simply my favorite Mexican spot in town."

- Scott Bolin,
Co-owner, Vespaio

mexican food in austin

Serrano's at Symphony Square

1111 Red River St. 78701
Phone: (512) 322-9080
Fax: (512) 322-0182
Sun-Thu 11am-10pm
Fri-Sat 11am-11pm
Credit Cards

While I really enjoy the wonderful variety of Mexican food available these days, sometimes I get a craving for some good old traditional Tex-Mex. Give me a plate of enchiladas covered with cheese and chili gravy with some homemade corn tortillas on the side and a cold cerveza or a margarita "perfecto" and you'll see one happy hombre. Serrano's fills this niche with room to spare. If it's Texas-seasoned mesquite grilled meats, chicken, seafood and vegetables you're hankering for, well it's bonus time baby! Founded back in the mid-eighties by the Gonzales brothers, with the help of grandma's recipes, Serrano's has enjoyed a long run of prosperity in the Austin metro area. Now with eight locations, you can't swing an armadillo without hitting one. One of the best features of any Serrano's restaurant is the genuine desire to please the customer. Don't be afraid to ask for anything on or off the menu, done any way you like it. You'll find them very obliging. Moderately priced and easily accessible, remember Serrano's the next time you need that Tex-Mex comfort food fix.

- Pat McIntyre

Serrano's has been one of my favorite Tex-Mex restaurants because of two things: the beef enchiladas with their Tex-Mex chili sauce and the "la Perfecta" margarita. You never hear someone rave over beef enchiladas, but as far back as I can remember they are how I've judged Tex-Mex restaurants and I keep coming back to this place. I know there must be some of you out there who feel the same. So come out of the beef enchicloset, choose one of the several locations (I like the one downtown at Symphony Square,) and kick back with one of Serrano's signature big ass "la perfecta" margaritas.

- Will O'Connell

Other Locations: West, South, North, Far North

Taco Cabana

517 W Martin Luther King Blvd. 78701
Phone: (512) 478-0875
Open 24 hours
Breakfast 11am-11pm
Credit Cards

Well, all I can say is you can't find anything better for $2.14. What more could one want in a black bean burrito? Fresh tomato, lettuce, rice and beans. You Atkins groupies can suck an egg. Folks have been eating this stuff for centuries.

The taquería began in 1978 in a little town better known for its mission ... no, Tonto not Bracketville, but San Antonio. It seems that the enterprising owner had problems with after hours vandalism, so a 24/7 gastonomic experience was born. Twenty-six years later there are 123 of these places scattered around the US. There are at least ten in Austin.

All of you omnivorous types will equally enjoy the various carnes, grilled on-sight. Tortillas are also made on premises. The salsa bar, another brilliant concept, allows you to create your own flavors. Try the salsa fuego or the pineapple chipotle. It seems almost everything is homemade ... except the suds. So order out or order up and partake of your favorite adult beverage.

Sí, El Guapo, you have a plethora of piñatas.

- Edmund Schenecker

Other Locations: All over the damn place

SHAYNA'S RECIPE FOR A TASTY MICHELADA

By Shayna Weeden

Michelada, roughly translated means "my cold beer".

Having lived in the mountains of Taxco, Guerrero Mexico for the past 10 years, I have tasted many, believe me, many micheladas and this is my tried, true and favorite way to make a michelada. It's a real thirst quencher on a hot afternoon!

Juice from a 1/2 lime
Coarse salt
3 dashes Worcestershire sauce
2 dashes Tabasco sauce
2 dashes of Maggi seasoning
Ice
12 ounces of the Mexican beer of your choice.

(I prefer it with a lighter beer like Dos Equis or Sol for daytime sippin' or a darker beer like Negra Modelo or Victoria for nightime slurpin'.)

Squeeze the juice from the lime and put to the side. Salt the rim of a chilled mug by rubbing it with the lime and dipping it in coarse salt. Fill mug with ice. Mix lime juice and all of the sauces and seasonings together in the glass. Pour in beer, stir and serve, adding more beer as you sip or slurp away!

www.shaynajewelry.com

dlp

TACO SHACK

2825 Guadalupe St. 78705
Phone: (512) 320-8889
Mon-Fri 6:30am-2:30pm
Sat 7am-1pm
Cash Only   UTICON

4412 Medical Pkwy. 78756
Phone: (512)300-2112
Mon-Fri 6:30am-2:30pm
Sat 7am-1pm
Cash Only

4002 N Lamar 78756
Phone: (512) 467-8533
Mon-Fri 6:30am-2:30pm
Sat 7am-1pm
Cash Only

Maybe you can't judge a book by its cover, but generally speaking, the outside of a good Tex-Mex place will tell you all you need to know. It should still have its original paint job, colorful but faded, modest and slightly dumpy at first glance—the smaller the better. Why, you ask? Because it means that the place has been in business for awhile, the owners have spent their money on good ingredients rather than glitzy signage and customers have been led inside by their noses and tummies rather than their eyes. And the small size, well, that means people are coming for the food, not to hang out and eat chips and salsa. That said, when you first see Taco Shack's original Burnet Road location, you'll know you're in for a treat. The diminutive building lives up to its name and any lingering doubt will be erased by the line that generally trails out the door. Never fear – the service is fast and friendly and you'll be back on the road in no time. As for the food, they built their reputation on their breakfast tacos, and the signature "Shack Taco," filled with eggs, chorizo, potato and cheese, won't let you down. For a spicy wake-up call, the "El Niño" is the way to go. If you're the type that likes to eat on the way to work, get the 10-inch Burnet Road burrito. Sitting in a traffic jam never tasted so good. For lunch, just go with the special – either the beef taco plate or cheese enchiladas, depending on the day. You can't go wrong.

- Brady Dial

Possibly the oldest shack for tacos in Austin, Taco Shack still does everything right. They mix all their ingredients to make a nice pile of breakfast wrapped in a tortilla, and all of their tacos are perfect. The Shack Taco is the specialty that probably everyone has heard of by now. It is in scope with Maria's Migas taco but is wholly different. What's in the Shack Taco, you ask? I believe it goes something like this: chorizo, potato, egg and cheese. Yes, that's it. They just opened a Taco Shack at Brazos and 4th Street, but the original location is the one off Medical Arts. Cash only here and it's not really a restaurant, sit down style affair, so just walk, ride, or I guess drive if you have to, over to one of their four locations for breakfast some time. I'm sure you will like.

- *Stephen Malina*

Reprinted with permission from INSite Publications

UPDATE: There's a new location in the recently-constructed Frost Bank tweezer tower. It seems that the Taco Wars' battlefield has made it downtown.

Other Locations: North, Far North

Trudy's Texas Star

409 W 30th St. 78705
Phone: (512) 477-2935
Fax: (512) 477-1805
www.trudy's.com
Mon-Fri 7am-2am
Sat-Sun 8am-2am
Credit Cards

For a great weekday happy hour or weekend lunch, catch up with friends out on the tree-covered, outdoor deck at Trudy's—it doesn't get much better than this. Order up Mexican martinis and Tex-Mex grub, sit back and you'll find yourself reminded why Austin is the best town around. Check out the green salsa and a full range of appetizers, from Tex-Mex egg rolls to various quesadillas, at a good value. To get you up the learning curve, know this: two Mexican martinis is the limit, and the watchful staff is unlikely to be fooled by crafty ploys like switching seats to try to get that 3rd 'tini. Also know that the happy hour rates may end at six, so go early to get a

dlp

good groove going. Parking is sufficient at a free lot across the street. If the weather is rough, there's plenty of space inside and the bar area adjacent to the deck is primo.

- Todd Erickson

INSIDER'S TIP: Happy Hour all night on Mondays.

Other Locations: South, Far North

"Hungover? Most definitely stumble to one of two places — Polvo's for the outstanding black sauce, for which they are best known, an amazing red sauce and the Papas Monterrey, which will soak up and save any morning-after stomach. And the other best choice is by far Curra's, if only for a great cup of Oaxacan coffee, an equally great red sauce and a dreamy avocado margarita — so smooth. But perhaps a third choice is El Sol Y La Luna for the melt-in-your-mouth spinach-chipotle enchiladas — go easy on the mushrooms."

*- Chris Payeur,
Sound Engineer*

WHOLE FOODS MARKET

601 N Lamar Blvd. Ste. 300 78703
Phone: (512) 477-4455
Daily 8am-10pm
Credit Cards

Better known for its health food and hippie watching, Whole Foods does indeed serve tacos. Luckily there are no wheat grass or carrot tacos, though tofu is a choice. You might as well be in Boston because having a taco made by a health food nut is like having a donkey fix your car. What they give you is more California wrap than anything resembling Mexican food. Whole Foods is, however, in a fortunate location where few Mexican restaurants reside. I understand the need for a quick taco, but exercise caution on this one. It's fine and dandy for a vegan to play dress up and think they're eating a taco, but no sensible person should fall victim to this bait and switch.

- Chris Nelson

Z Tejas Grill

1110 W 6th St. 78703
Phone: (512) 478-5355
Mon-Thu 11am-10pm
Fri 11am-11pm
Sat 10am-11pm
Sun 10am-10pm
Music as scheduled
Credit Cards

As one of the few semi-upscale Mexican restaurants, Z Tejas draws an eclectic crowd — from Westlake couples to bootylicious blonds. It's a tree house of sorts with seating outside, on the screened-in porch and along the catwalk overlooking the street. The whitewashed walls and comfortable wooden furniture make the interiors light and airy. The food reflects the ambiance—gourmet yet casual, traditional yet modern, expensive but not impossible. The fish tacos and chicken fried steak are some popular items along with their powerful margaritas and other mixed drinks. Lunchtime sees a big business crowd while dinner is a date destination. Translation: do business to get paid and take ladies to get laid. I hear brunch is also good, but I haven't seen brunch since puberty.

- Chris Nelson

Other Locations: Far North

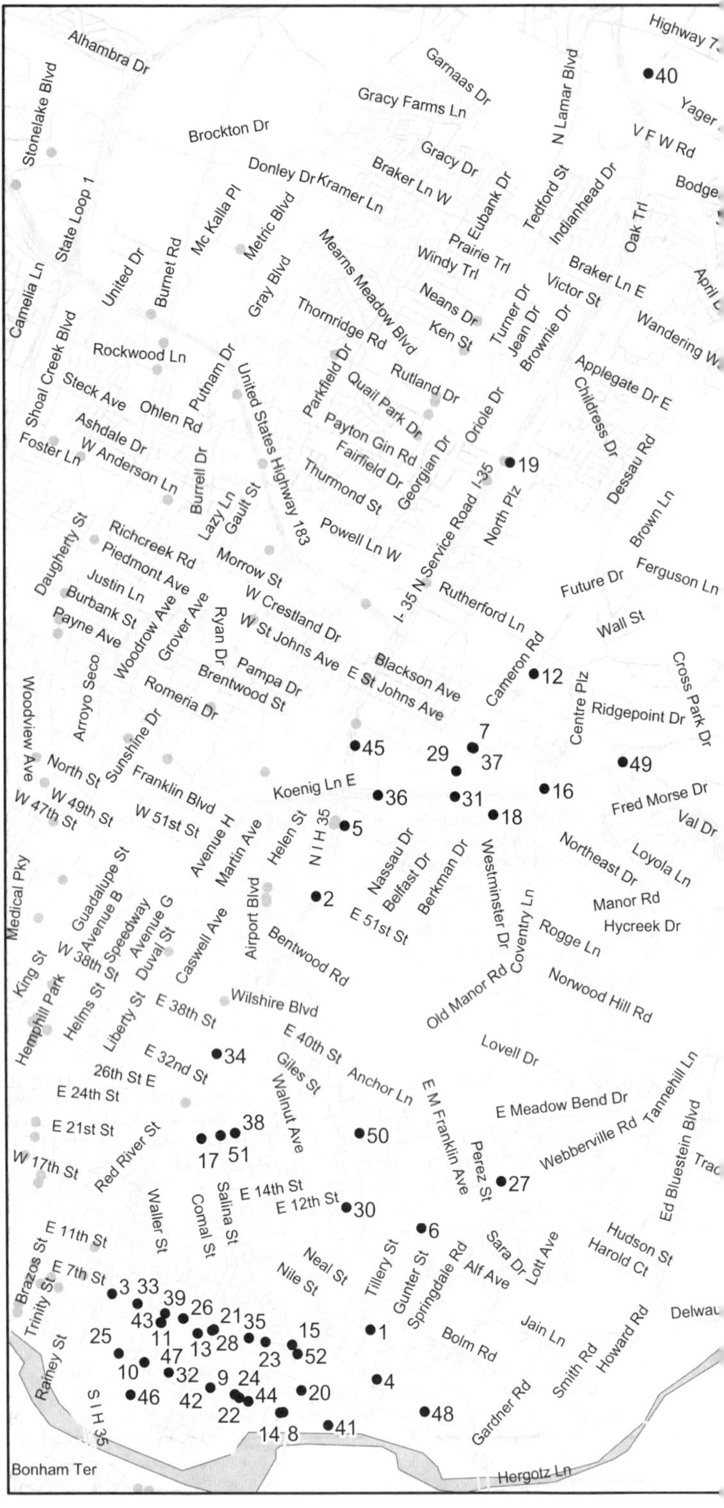

Highway 7
40
Alhambra Dr
Garnaas Dr
N Lamar Blvd
Gracy Farms Ln
Yager
Stonelake Blvd
Brockton Dr
V F W Rd
Gracy Dr
Donley Dr
Kramer Ln
Braker Ln W
Eubank Dr
Tedford St
Indianhead Dr
Bodge
State Loop 1
Mc Kalla Pl
Metric Blvd
Oak Trl
Prairie Trl
Windy Trl
Braker Ln E
Camelia Ln
United Dr
Burnet Rd
Gray Blvd
Mearns Meadow Blvd
Victor St
April
Neans Dr
Turner Dr
Thornridge Rd
Ken St
Jean Dr
Brownie Dr
Wandering W
Shoal Creek Blvd
Rockwood Ln
Parkfield Dr
Rutland Dr
Putnam Dr
United States Highway 183
Applegate Dr E
Steck Ave
Quail Park Dr
Childress Dr
Ohlen Rd
Oriole Dr
Ashdale Dr
Payton Gin Rd
Georgian Dr
Foster Ln
W Anderson Ln
Burrell Dr
Fairfield Dr
19
Dessau Rd
Thurmond St
I-35
Gault St
Lazy Ln
North Plz
Daugherty St
Richcreek Rd
Powell Ln W
I- 35 N Service Road
Brown Ln
Piedmont Ave
Morrow St
Justin Ln
Ferguson Ln
Future Dr
Rutherford Ln
Burbank St
Woodrow Ave
Grover Ave
W Crestland Dr
Payne Ave
Ryan Dr
W St Johns Ave
Wall St
Cameron Rd
Blackson Ave
Cross Park Dr
Pampa Dr
12
Arroyo Seco
Brentwood St
E St Johns Ave
Centre Plz
Woodview Ave
Romeria Dr
Ridgepoint Dr
Sunshine Dr
7
45
29
37
49
North St
Franklin Blvd
Koenig Ln E
16
36
31
W 49th St
W 47th St
W 51st St
Fred Morse Dr
18
Val Dr
Avenue H
Helen St
5
N I H 35
Martin Ave
Nassau Dr
Belfast Dr
Berkman Dr
Westminster Dr
Northeast Dr
Loyola Ln
Medical Pky
Guadalupe St
Airport Blvd
2
Manor Rd
Avenue B
Speedway
Avenue G
E 51st St
Coventry Ln
Hycreek Dr
Caswell Ave
Rogge Ln
W 38th St
Duval St
Bentwood Rd
King St
Hemphill Park
Helms St
Liberty St
Old Manor Rd
Norwood Hill Rd
E 38th St
Wilshire Blvd
E 40th St
Lovell Dr
E 32nd St
34
Giles St
Anchor Ln
26th St E
Walnut Ave
E M Franklin Ave
Tannehill Ln
E 24th St
E Meadow Bend Dr
E 21st St
38
Red River St
50
Webberville Rd
Ed Bluestein Blvd
17
51
W 17th St
Perez St
27
Trac
Waller St
Salina St
E 14th St
E 12th St
30
Comal St
E 11th St
6
Hudson St
Neal St
Tillery St
Sara Dr
Lott Ave
Harold Ct
Brazos St
E 7th St
Nile St
Gunter St
Springdale Rd
Alf Ave
3
33
39
26
21
35
Trinity St
43
Delwau
Jain Ln
Howard Rd
25
11
28
15
1
Rainey St
13
Bolm Rd
47
23
52
Smith Rd
10
32
9
24
4
S I H 35
46
42
44
20
Gardner Rd
22
48
14
8
41
Bonham Ter
Hergotz Ln

mexican food in austin

East Austin's character runs deep, illustrating the long history of Austin through its diversity of landmarks and people who inhabit this part of town. France's Embassy to the Republic of Texas was built atop the hill overlooking the city along with many old mansions in the neighborhood around it. The construction of Interstate 35 segregated the Eastside from the rest of the city and so it has developed largely on its own. With rising rents in other parts of town, young people and artists have flocked to the East Side for more affordable housing and the thriving communities are largely untouched by corporate chains and development. Though feelings among the residents about the continuing gentrification is mixed, the East Side is quickly becoming a destination in itself for its plethora of great restaurants, new art galleries and refurbished bars.

1 Abarrotes
2 Amaya's
3 Angie's
4 Arandas #1
5 Arandinas
6 Arturo's Taqueria
7 Arturo's Taqueria 2
8 Bejuco's
9 Chapala Jalisco
10 Chulita's
11 Cisco's
12 Costa del Sol
13 Dario's
14 Dos Hermanos
15 El Azteca
16 El Charrito
17 El Chile
18 El Regio
19 El Regio
20 El Tripaso
21 Fonda del Sol
22 Innocente's
23 Joe's Bakery & Coffee Shop
24 Juan in A Million
25 La Bahia
26 La Casita
27 La Cocinita
28 La Michoacana
29 La Michoacana
30 La Morenita
31 La Palapa
32 Las Cazuelas
33 Las Palmas
34 Los Altos
35 Los Comales
36 Los Jaliscienses
37 Luvianos
38 Mi Madre's
39 Mi Rey
40 Moe's Southwest Grill
41 Morelia
42 Mr. Natural
43 Nuevo Leon
44 Papa Pancho's
45 Pappasito's
46 Porfirio's
47 Rico's Tamales
48 Taco Sabroso
49 Tres Amigos
50 Un Rincon de Mexico
51 Vivo
52 Zunzal

Abarrotes Mexicanos

901 Tillery
Phone: (512) 926-1709
Mon-Sat 5am-3pm
Sun 7am-1pm
Credit Cards

This charming little corner store serves cold drinks, chips, ice cream, candy, bus tickets to Mexico and fresh, homemade food. Abarrotes is a cross between a convenience store and taquería with an ambiance that is all family. In addition to great breakfast tacos, they serve lunch specials like carne guisada and pollo asada. When the crowd slows down, you'll see members of the family sitting down at one of the small tables, peeling potatoes and quietly discussing the day's events.

- Chris Nelson

Amaya's Taco Village

5405 N IH 35 78723
Phone: (512) 458-2531
Mon-Thu 7am-9pm
Fri-Sat 7am-10pm
Sun 8am-9pm
Breakfast all day
Sat 7am-3pm
Sun 8am-4pm
Credit Cards

Tucked into a cookie cutter strip shopping center lies a Mexican restaurant with food about as significant as its architectural surroundings. Amaya's is bland. The fluorescent lighting made me think I had walked into a fly-by-night telemarketing center, but instead of a phone I was brought chips and salsa. The salsa and fresh tortillas are the best things about Amaya's. The salsa is hot, tangy and highly addictive. The tortillas are delivered piping hot and ever so soft. We had the carne asada and beef fajitas, which both fell flat. Situations like this beg the question: Is it Nature or Nurture? If Amaya's had stucco walls and piñatas galore, would the food taste better? This teleological quandary is far above the head of a simple Mexican food lover like me. I can only tell you that my next visit to the shopping center will be for auto parts and not tacos.

- Chris Nelson

mexican food in austin

Angie's Mexican Restaurant

900 E 7th St. 78702
Phone: (512) 476-5413
Mon-Thu 7:30am-4pm
Fri 7:30am-9pm
Closed on Tuesdays
Breakfast all day
Credit Cards

I know a New Orleans chef who was visiting Austin and ate lunch at Angie's. As he and his brother were driving away after their meal, they both looked at each other, smiled and turned the car around to go back for more. Angie's is awesome. It is authentic Tex-Mex cooked with the freshest ingredients. Located in an old house that overlooks downtown, Angie's décor and service is like their food — swift, simple and good. The lunch crowds are big but the line moves quickly. I especially like ordering a six pack of beer which they bring to your table iced down in a metal pail.

- *Chris Nelson*

Arandas Taqueria #1

3518 E 7th St. 78702
Phone: (512) 389-3834
Daily 8am-2am
Credit Cards

With over six restaurants and more in the works, Arandas is well on its way to Mexican food domination in central Texas. Though every Arandas has its own intangible character, the service, banquettes and signature menu are the same. Once you visit #1, you realize where the die was cast and how their wildly successful template was perfected. #1 is on East 7th Street, the strip which houses some of the tastiest places in town, and it competes with the best of them. All food groups are represented here — the enchilada, the taco, the carne asada and much, much more. Arandas is famous for their tortas cubanas, which are large sandwiches made on Mexican semi-baguettes and filled with whatever meat or vegetable suits your fancy. Lettuce, tomato, sour cream and many other condiments are available. The botanas and grilled onions make excellent appetizers or additions to guarantee a wonderful meal. No margaritas will be found at

dlp

Arandas, which I suppose is for the best, considering they're open until 4am for the late night post-bar crowd (However, some locations do close earlier). Anytime of day is good for Arandas wherever you might be — and there's probably one close by.

- Chris Nelson

Other Locations: South, Far South, North, Far North

east

ARANDINAS TAQUERIA

1011 Reinli St. 78723
Phone: (512) 454-2210
Sun-Thu 6am-12am
Fri-Sat 6am-1am
Breakfast all day
Credit Cards

Please see review on page 83

Other Locations: Southeast, North

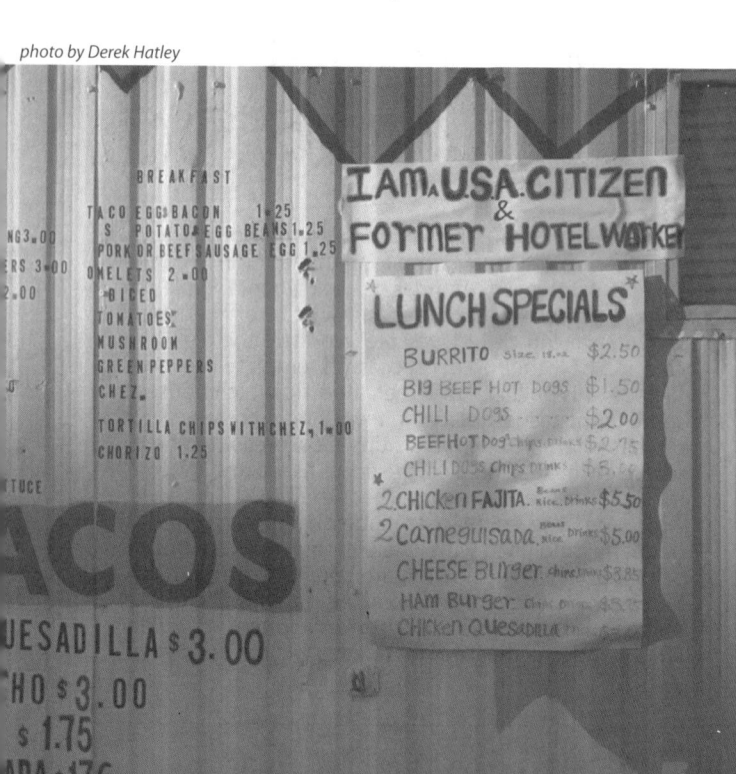

photo by Derek Hatley

mexican food in austin

ARTURO'S TAQUERIA

3306 Oak Springs Dr. 78721
Phone: (512) 926-8474
Daily 7am-10pm
Breakfast all day
Credit Cards

7210 Cameron Rd. 78752
Phone: (512) 451-5318
Daily 7am-10pm
Breakfast all day
Credit Cards

If there is one thing I've learned from my extensive research, it is that if there is a buffet to be had then go with the buffet. The only off the menu exception is caldo. Not being a made-to-order item, it simmers all day anyway. I have deduced that the restaurant has put their best and least expensive efforts into the buffet and, in their eyes, for anyone not to take advantage of the all you can eat, miracle of life, deal of the century, is crazy and a pain in their "hey, eat off the buffet" ass. The menu that is offered during buffet hours is a mere courtesy in order to check out beer and soda prices and, of course, the various caldos. This is just a theory substantiated by the throngs of locals forgoing the even brief sit-down for drink orders and heading straight for the stacks of buffet plates.

- Allison Walsh

"Arandas #5 has great service, consistent, super fresh corn tortillas and fantastic salsa. The beauty of the salsa is the fresh ingredients. Depending on the weather, if it is hot outside, the avocado tostado and if it's cold, the menudo or the cheese enchiladas. Visually I love the the yellow cheese with the red sauce and the white cheese with the green. And I want to say that I hate to be nickel and dimed over chips and salsa. I go to Guero's for the frozen margaritas cause they're real; Fonda San Miguel for the mango margarita and Dos Hermanos for the tacos al pastor and a bowl of bacon."

- Johnny Walker
Artist, Art Teacher, Carpenter, Skateboarder

`dlp`

Bejuco's Restaurant

2711 E Cesar Chavez St. 78702
Phone: (512) 476-7878
Mon-Fri 7am-12am
Sat-Sun until 2am

Bejuco's #1 is what I am unofficially calling the most extensive Mexican/American/seafood menu ever. And, what makes this so beautiful is that they have carefully photographed and laminated every food choice available from the jelly packages for your toast to the chicken mole; from the club sandwich to the strawberry shake; from the oysters on the half shell to the ... you get the idea. The décor is Mexican minimalist in a brightly lit, seemingly temporary building with barren walls and picnic tables. It was only after having ordered that it dawned on us that the photographs were a makeshift language decoder — a truly ingenious idea. It was really hard to believe that this small, empty restaurant was going to be able to procure all of the items that it boasted, so we ordered ten of the most outrageously incongruent items available, and felt more than confident that we could stump them, but with no luck. Honestly, I don't think we had a lot of faith in Bejuco's at the onset, but we became believers.

Bejuco's #1 at the time of review was BYOB (though several kinds of beer bottles had posed for their picture) but a kind gentleman offered to send someone next door to Sam's Discoteca while our sweet waitress brought us great fresh salsa. The chicken mole was scrumptious and the shrimp el diablo spicy. My friend was not as happy with the cheese enchiladas, but that had more to do with the Mexican versus American cheese controversy. It never ceases to amaze me how they can give you such generous portions all for under ten dollars. Bejuco's is a wonderment that will have to be reexperienced. I will be returning to the "Cathedral del Marisco". Who says you can't find love in a double wide?

- Allison Walsh

Other Locations: Southeast

TEQUILA! CENTURIES OF TRADITION FLAVOR MEXICO'S FAMED LIBATION

by Edmund Schenecker

Reprinted with permission from The San Antonio Express-News. Copyright © 2004

About an hour's drive west of Guadalajara, Mexico, in the state of Jalisco, is a little town called Tequila. That's right, Tequila. Long before any of us had our first margarita, there was the town of Tequila. And prior to the town, there were Tiquila Indians, who lived in this verdant mountain region long before Hernán Cortés set foot in Mexico. The Tiquila took their name from the Nahuatl word that describes the distinctive volcanic soil of the region, and they produced a fermented beverage for use in religious rituals that was made from the same plant that tequila is made from today. The conquistadors, however, were unimpressed with this home brew and sought to improve its palatability with a process they picked up from the Moors. So they distilled the drink of the Tiquilas to produce their own concoction. They called it Mezcal wine and it was consumed almost exclusively in Mexico until, in 1795, King Ferdinand IV granted Don Jose Maria Guadalupe de Cuervo the first commercial license to produce what we now know as tequila.

Since international popularity of the spirit has grown so dramatically over the last two centuries, the Mexican government established specifications in 1978 to preserve this national treasure. Normas, similar to the French wine regulations known as appellation controlée, dictate certain aspects of the produc-

dlp essay

tion of tequila. To be classified tequila, a product must be made from 100 percent natural ingredients, have 38 percent to 40 percent alcohol by volume, be produced only from blue agave grown in the Mexican states of Jalisco, Guanajuato, Michoacan, Nayarit and Tamaulipas, have fermented juice that is distilled twice and, as a final product, have no less than 51 percent reduced sugars from the blue agave.

My itinerary to Tequila included not only a visit to the spiritual epicenter of the Tiquila tribe but also an invitation to visit La Rojeña, owned by the descendants of Jose Cuervo and the oldest distillery in the Americas. To prepare myself for my visit, I sampled a wide assortment of tequilas at watering holes in and around Guadalajara. Among my choices were La Distilleria, an establishment that proudly proclaimed it served 87 different brands of tequila, and La Feria, a local cantina whose offerings not only included an ample selection of tequilas but various folkloric performers: singers, mariachis, dancers and charros doing rope tricks. I opted for the rope tricks and took a taxi over to La Feria with a fellow devotee. Once there, my companion and I ordered a tequila blanco, a Sauza. I also requested a sangrita, a little shot of tomato and orange juices with a distinct presence of chile that the locals use as a palate cleanser, and a tequila congelado, served chilled. Oddly enough, only one brand, Jose Cuervo Tradicional, was served in this refreshing manner. Because of its smoothness, I sipped on this Tradicional the rest of the evening.

Shortly after our drinks arrived, however, I learned a sad truth about my close friend: he has a drinking problem. Not the usual sort of malady, but one whose side effects were particularly unwelcome at a tequila bar. As the night progressed and singers and charros paraded on and off the stage, he would stand up, applaud and speak a Spanish no one could comprehend. Without fail, he would also bump our table. For some reason, only my tequila would tumble over. And despite the fact that it was my compadre who wasn't

dlp essay

handling his tequila — or mine — very well, our waiter kept giving me the eye.

Although I had thought myself somewhat familiar with Mexico's national treasure, the variety and complexity of tequilas is mind-boggling. A thorough tutorial at La Rojeña the following afternoon helped explain the intricacies of crafting tequila. The folks from Cuervo were celebrating the bottling of their 1800 Millennium tequila, and they insisted that my tour begin not at their ancient distillery but in the agave fields. The jima (harvest) takes place year round with jimadores trimming the long spiny leaves of the agave every day, forcing the sugars to develop in the hidden heart of the agave. After a decade of this, give or take a year or two, the agave is ready to be harvested. This is when the jimador cuts off the pencas, the leaves that give the agave its distinct appearance. All that remains is the pineapple-looking heart, the piña, that weighs anywhere from 80 to 175 pounds.

Truckloads of piñas are taken to La Rojeña where they are first split, then baked in huge ovens for 24 to 36 hours. Cuervo still uses traditional hornos to bake the piñas, though many other houses use high-pressure autoclaves to hasten the cooking process. A day or so later, the golden, honeyed piñas are removed from the ovens and allowed to cool, their starches now converted to sugars. Then comes the crushing and the shredding. Water is added to dissolve the sugars. This aguamiel, or honey water, is collected in tanks where fermentation takes place. Yeast is introduced, the tanks are heated, and, depending on the preference of the tequila maker, fermentation lasts as little as 36 hours and as long as 10 days. According to the Normas, this mosto must be distilled twice, a process that is virtually identical to the alhambic process that was brought to the New World by the Spaniards nearly four centuries ago. After the first distillation, the alcohol level reaches 20 to 30 percent, climbing to 55 percent after the second. (Thanks to the addition of distilled water, the final product has an alcohol con-

continued on page 67

dlp

CHAPALA JALISCO

2101 E Cesar Chavez St. 78702
Phone: (512) 320-0308
Mon-Thu & Sun 7am-11pm
Fri-Sat 7am-12am
Credit Cards

This cheery Eastside café doesn't mess around. The menu spells it out with a simple list of choices. This is a no-frills, straight-up joint, no hype. I ordered a couple of breakfast tacos and a chicken burrito from my sweet-as-tamarind "no speakey English" waitress while I inhaled their homemade salsa. My food appeared in seconds and was perfect. Great flavor, nothing fancy but extremely tasty. My waitress checked on me often and was quick to bring two more bowls of salsa to me. Chapala is a sunny, bright place with festive yellow walls and piñata colored window trims around the requisite protective iron bars. They have painted murals of Lake Chapala to help transport you and your taste buds to the motherland. At this place you've got satellite TV, a Tejano jukebox, a smattering of domestic and imported beers, nice-as-can-be waitresses, and dirt cheap breakfast specials before 11:00AM. I'm thinking Tuesday mornings to recover from Monday Night Football.

- Allison Walsh

"At Maria's Taco X-press I go for the migas tacos, the tamarind agua fresca, and the cheese enchilada.. When I take in Curra's I go for the enchiladas chiapas, the conchinita pibil and the homemade soups. At Guero's it's the queso flameado. Taco Cabana has the best fast food. The beef burrito ultimo is a "work of art for $2.45."

- Mark Addison
Music producer/President, India Records
Amateur chef

CHULITA'S MEXICAN CANTINA

1510 E Cesar Chavez 78702
Phone: (512) 499-8488
Daily 12pm-12am
Sat 12pm-1am
Fri & Sat DJ
Music as scheduled
Credit Cards

Restaurant by day and cantina by night, Chulitas is a welcome addition to the Cesar Chavez strip. I suggest ordering a beer immediately, because it takes awhile for the food to arrive. Once you taste the food you'll know why — each dish is individually and lovingly prepared and will surprise the hell out of you. The Weta's Plate is out of this world. When the sun goes down, Chulitas is transformed into a raucous bar with a loud Tejano jukebox, pool tables and a rough and tumble crowd. I think this place is here to stay.

- Chris Nelson

CISCO'S RESTAURANT BAKERY & BAR

1511 E 6th St. 78702
Phone: (512) 478-2420
Daily 7am-2:30pm
Breakfast all day
Credit Cards

Three Lone Stars, two Margaritas, three more Maker's on the rocks, a cab ride home and your head hits the pillow. As you rise to the inevitable fog the next morning, your mind slowly ambles to thoughts of Cisco's. The Eastside staple has always been big with the local politicos and UT students. Most claim LBJ put it on the map, but Rudy "Cisco" Cisneros catered to all celebrities and always took care of the locals.

The crowd has shifted since Rudy passed on in 1995. The celebrity watching has dwindled, and now most who enter are trying to remember stories from the night before. The service is fast and unobtrusive; the fare is the perfect hangover cure. Everything from the Ranchero Steak to the Migas contains just the right amount of grease your body is yearning for. Not as odd as most think, this Tex-Mex staple is also famous for its buttermilk biscuits—the exact amount of bread to soak up three Lone Stars, two Margaritas, three more Maker's on the rocks.

- Scott Staab

Costa Del Sol Restaurant

7901 Cameron Rd. #4
Phone: (512) 832-5331
Mon-Thu 9am-9pm
Fri-Sun 9am-10pm
Credit Cards

Specializing in Salvadoran and Mexican dishes, this little gem has nothing going for it but great food. Housed in what looks to be an old Golden Chick, this slightly renovated joint sits adjacent to a strip center overlooking the traffic of 183 and Cameron Road. Now I wouldn't drive *way* out of my way to go here, but if I were close and very hungry I would totally pull in for the camarones a la plancha and some fried plantains. The pollo encebollada was really, really, really good. It seemed kinda pricey (around 10 bucks for a huge plate) but well worth it.

- *Allison Walsh*

Dario's Mexican Food Restaurant

1800 East 6th St. 78702
Phone: (512) 479-8105
Fax: (512) 472-3835
Closed Mondays
Tue-Wed 7am-4pm
Fri-Sat 7am-11pm
Sun 7am-3pm
Music Fri & Sat Evening
Breakfast all day
Credit Cards

Much like a belly being filled with Mexican food, Dario's has slowly expanded for the past twenty years into a large restaurant seating over a hundred hungry patrons. The busiest part of the day is lunch when they sell between 250 and 300 cheese enchilada plates with their special chile con carne sauce. This dish is somewhat of a religious experience and will rekindle one's faith in the almighty enchilada. The green chicken enchiladas will also make you genuflect with juicy pieces of spiced chicken that melt into your mouth. For the boys in blue, try the Dink Special, named after Officer Dink who apparently would make this dish for himself back in the kitchen. All of this washes down nicely with some of the

mexican food in austin

strongest frozen margaritas in town. Live Tejano and Classic Rock on the weekends.

- Chris Nelson

DOS HERMANOS MEXICAN FOODS

2730 E Cesar Chavez St. 78702
Phone: (512) 474-9655
Mon-Sat 7am-8pm
Sun 7am-6pm
Breakfast 11am-3pm
Credit Cards

east

Dos Hermanos (Spanish for "two brothers") has been cooking up tasty Mexican food and tortillas from their charming location here in Austin on East Cesar Chavez for at least ten years. Aside from a good glass of horchata (or agua de horchata as some know it), they offer a great array of authentic Mexican food. Personally I've always been a huge fan of their tacos. From the carne asada to the chicken and beef fajita they make a scrumptious lunch. What few people know is that they also mix up one of the best salsas in this fine city. They don't normally bring it out with the rest of your fare; so you have to ask for it by name, "Excuse me could I get some of that green salsa?" At least I always have to ask for it, but they probably take one gander at this gringo and figure it would send me to the Seton Emergency Room. It's that hot. It's a bright green salsa, which is not necessarily tomatillo based as most salsa verde is. No, the green salsa of Dos Hermanos is more of a fresh jalapeño purée, and it tastes as such. So if you're a connoisseur of things that glow in the night this is the salsa you don't want to miss. Its bright green color and fresh taste will always keep you coming back again and (once you recover) again.

- Douglas L. Prince

oto by Derek Hatley

dlp

EL AZTECA RESTAURANT

2600 E 7th St. 78702
Phone: (512) 477-4701
Mon-Sat 11am-10pm
Closed Sundays
Credit Cards

Seriously in-the-know Austinites have been frequenting El Azteca since 1963 for the best chips and salsa around and, surprisingly for an Eastside establishment, an entire vegetarian selection. Everything is excellent. I even have a friend who, when craving red meat, foregoes the chop houses around town and heads here for the steak. The décor is simple and Mexican: family photos, ceramics, shiny, doilied placemat streamers and mauve walls enhance the collection of warrior artwork, curios and Quetzalcoatl calendars. Look directly under the framed black and white photos of Abraham Lincoln and Benito Juarez and you will usually see Guerra family members convening with their hawkeyed matriarch/sometimes-checkout lady. Even though there is a tiny bar area, I wouldn't dig in for a slew of margaritas — just a couple will do. I swear, come here for the food and lots of it.

- Allison Walsh

INSIDER'S TIP: Do not decline the sherbet or cookie... or both.

EL CHARRITO RESTAURANT

7100 E Hwy. 290 78723
Phone: (512) 467-9394
Daily 7am-10pm
Cash Only

As you drive by El Charrito you likely wouldn't go inside a smallish, dilapidated green building adjacent to a fleabag hotel out on East 290. But as you enter, the place offers a new promise—counter seating accompanies the eight or so tables, a jukebox where an accordion is required to get your disc inside and a small TV playing Mexican soap operas. These are usually indicators of good things to come from the kitchen. The menu consists of your standard Tex-Mex enchiladas, fajitas, nachos and tacos. Things started off well with some spicy salsa that was full of garlic. Things started moving the other direction when the nachos came fresh out of the microwave with processed cheese. The chicken fajitas, while somewhat tasty, were about as much to look at as the bad reception on the television. The chicken enchiladas with verde sauce (the true testament to Mexican food in this reviewer's estimation) were average at best, not to mention the bones I found in the pulled chicken. All in all I'd give El Charrito two stars. I'm just not sure that the five star scale is the correct measure.

- Chad Hamilton

El Chile Café y Cantina

1809 Manor Rd. 78722
Phone: (512) 457-9900
http://www.elchilecafe.com
Mon-Thu 5pm-10pm
Fri-Sat 5:30pm-10:30pm
Sunday 11am-4pm (Brunch only)
Credit Cards

What a great new spot on the trendy Eastside! It will be hard to keep up with all of the newcomers as the Eastside begins to cater to its growing hip constituency. The restaurant has an almost California feel with soothing tangerine, lavender, and sunshine yellow walls coupled with an innovative eclectic Mexican cuisine. There is a large outdoor deck for dining or sipping their out-of-this-world sangria or the irresistible prickly pear margaritas. They even supply Mexican blankets for our cooler months. The menu is a far cry from your average greasy Eastside eatery. Here the focus is on tone and taste. The guacamole is refreshing and the perfectly spiced ceviche is sublime. They offer several Platos del Asadero — sizzling skillets of various grilled meats. Or try the mouthwatering tacos callejeros. Per our waiter's suggestion we shared the pollo a la poblano con hongos — tangy; original and we gobbled it up as if we'd just emerged from the desert. I'm nominating their flour tortillas for Best in the World.

- Allison Walsh

dlp

El Regio

6615 Berkman Dr. 78723
Phone: (512) 933-9557
Sun-Thu 10am-10pm
Fri-Sat 10am-11pm
No inside seating, pickup only
Cash only

9437 N IH 35 78753
Phone: (512) 836-5892
Sun-Thu 8am-10pm
Fri-Sat 8am-11pm
No inside seating, pickup only
Credit Cards

Please see review on page 86

Other Locations: Southeast, Far South

El Tripaso Taqueria

408 N Pleasant Valley Rd. 78702
Phone: (512) 476-2852
Hours: Whenvever they feel like it

I really want to like El Tripaso. From the outside, it's one of those tiny Eastside taquerías with enough charm and character to choke a horse. A sweet Dona greets you and takes your order as brightly colored paint slowly peels from their sign and cinder-block building. The drive-thru window is very convenient for morning taco runs, on-the-go guisada pick-ups and laid back afternoon cruising. Sadly, the book does not live up to its cover. All of the meat tacos come with just meat and nothing else. No cilantro, no lettuce no chopped onions — nothing. They also tend to be over-cooked, chewy and dripping with grease. I'm all for fatty, greasy tacos but a 70/30 meat to fat ratio on a barbacoa taco is the threshold. Here, it comes close to 50/50. I write these words with pain (and as some constructive criticism) because I could see myself being a regular El Tripaso. Character is one of the hardest ingredients to come by and they have it in spades. Once you have character, the rest should be cake.

- Chris Nelson

dlp essay

FAST FOOD MISCEGENATION

by Boutros Puchachos

Austin is home to some ungodly number of Mexican food restaurants, most of which are pretty damn tasty. When it comes to selection, some decisions require little thought: If you live northeast of downtown and you're filthy drunk, I'd advise eating migas at Tamale House every morning, literally. They're like inter-temporal, anti-booze and they will cure your hangover. If you like your margaritas to donkey-punch you in the liver, (i.e. you're not some kind of communist) then I'd recommend going to Trudy's and trying your wiliest to exceed the three drink maximum. It's sort of a battle of wits.

At times, though, it can be almost problematic to have so many good taco venues in one city. Many of the restaurants in Austin are of such equally superior quality that if you're of an indecisive ilk (or high off sizzurp), you can end up vacillating between Mexiplaces until long past closing time. If this ever happens, cut your losses, head to Taco Cabana and get crocked on frozen margaritas.

A better solution, though, is to devise a new barometer for restaurant quality, and I prefer to judge based of quantities of Latina pulchritude. Ask yourself, "How foxy is my taco mistress?" You should be able to answer, "Quite."

This strategy works well and I have practiced it religiously for years. For a long time it brought me to La Michoacana. There was a cashier who was the most beautiful creature I'd ever seen. She looked like Pocahontas from the Disney movie and I often dreamed of having a "Lady and the Tramp" moment,

dlp essay

where we started on opposite ends of a cabrito taco and ended in a passionate kiss. Then she'd say, "Ay ... Cuerpo de hombre mío, persisteiré para siempre en tu gracia." And I'd be all like, "Um ... what, baby?"

Sadly, my love affair came to an end. You see, one of the lady-chefs, who was far less fetching, took a fancy to The Boutros and soon there was a love triangle in taco town. Hell hath no fury like a woman's scorn. And jealousy sours a taco. So, I stopped going to La Mich for a spell. When I finally returned, I found my erstwhile love had married a cockfighter.

Sad though it was, the experience taught me that one of the few things that enhances Austin's already extraordinary Mexican food is a little harmless miscegenational romance from afar. So, if you're a gringo, lust after someone of Latino descent this evening; if you're Kazakhstani, chase some Côte d'Ivoirian tail and likewise. At the very least, this will foment racial harmony and understanding. At best, we'll all get laid and humanity will evolve into some sort of jumbled, mixed-up race of super-babies ... which is good.

Harmony should always be strived for. So, if you want to change the world, there is no better place to start than your corner taco stand.

Fonda Del Sol Mexican Buffet

1912 E 7th St. 78702
Phone: (512) 279-4383
Mon-Fri 11am-3pm
Sat-Sun 10am-3pm
Cash Only

Have you ever been driving around and said to yourself, "I need to buy some Tejano CDs, a Brazilian soccer jersey and eat a $5.99 all-you-can-eat lunch buffet."? If the answer is yes, fear no more, Fonda del Sol is one-stop shopping for the hungry, Norteño-loving soccer enthusiast. The buffet is extensive — with hot plates full of tacos, quesadillas, enchiladas, fajitas, chile relleños and much, much more. After filling up, walk through the side doors into the music store and get some soccer apparel in addition to Jalisco bumper stickers and blinged-out belt buckles. It's one thing to leave a restaurant feeling better, but looking better is icing on the cake.

- Chris Nelson

Innocente's Café

2337 E Cesar Chavez St. 78702
Phone: (512) 479-0218
Sun-Thu 7am-8pm
Sat 7am-10pm
Breakfast all day
Credit Cards

After I ate at Innocente's, I vowed that I would bury them with a blistering review of how they put horse meat in my tacos, spit in my eye and dragged my mother's name through the gutter. Instead, I will tell the truth. Innocente's is awful. The ambiance is that of a funeral parlor. Half of their menu is unavailable. The stew had zero charisma, and the Budweiser was warm. I hope that they are not supporting an invalid grandmother with proceeds from the restaurant. Her days may indeed be numbered.

- Chris Nelson

Innocente's is easy to miss on Cesar Chavez, a street lined with at least ten other Mexican restaurants. One reason to visit this traditional, family-owned restaurant is the very spicy green salsa served up with tortilla chips when you arrive. It is not for the faint of heart, so order a Mexican bottled soda right away to put out the fire. They serve breakfast, lunch and dinner very affordably, with breakfast specials for early risers from 7 to11am. The menu consists of the usual fare, but honorable mentions go to the huevos borrachos, scrambled eggs with serranos, onions, tomatoes and cheese and the ladies plate, which is meant only for the hungriest of ladies. You can order every imaginable combination plate and they have a covered patio in front with picnic tables. The family is usually milling around at tables near the back of the restaurant, and if you're lucky, you'll catch a glimpse of Innocente himself.

- Jennifer Braafladt

JOE'S BAKERY AND COFFEE SHOP

2305 E 7th St. 78702
Phone: (512) 472-0017
Tue-Sun 7am-3pm
Closed Mon
Breakfast all day
Credit Cards

If a diner and a Mexican bakery had a child, Joe's would be it. Breakfast is the order of the day with both tacos and biscuits on the menu as well as pork chops and pork skin eggs. The large photo of Henry Cisneros nicely complements the lunch counter and plastic yellow booths stripped from a Waffle House. You can listen to the Tejano jukebox while waiting to order a vast array of cookies, empanadas and sweet rolls. Ask them what Cisneros eats and you'll be off to an ambitious breakfast feast.

- Chris Nelson

"The white fish ceviche and ribeye with mole at Polvo's is to die for. I feel as if I am back in Tulum, Mexico—a true Mexican experience."

- Eric Massey,
Stylist, Wet Salon

Juan in a Million

2300 E Cesar Chavez St. 78702
Phone: (512) 472-3872
Fax: (512) 472-5626
Sun-Wed 7am-3pm
Thu-Sat 7am-9pm
Breakfast all day
Music begins mid summer
Credit Cards

Juan in a Million has something in common with the Mexican town of San Miguel de Allende; they are both places where gringos travel long distances to bask in the native Mexican culture with other like-minded gringos. I cannot explain why so many white people travel to the Eastside to this particular place other than it is damn good. The food tends be be on the Tex Mex side, but authentic items such as machacado pop up throughtout the menu. Breakfast on the weekends is very popular and lasts well into the afternoon as hungover folks get happy with Juan's great food.

- Chris Nelson

I have to drive 30 miles from the quiet solitude of my country home to get to Juan in a Million. It's worth every mile. When I walk through the door, I can never decide which makes me happier: the gracious welcome of owner Juan Meza or the mouth-watering aromas. For over twenty years, Juan has been making each happy customer feel like they are the most important person on earth with a handshake, an endearing smile and scrumptious food. He also serves my favorite breakfast in Austin. Juan in a Million's Con Queso Breakfast ($6.25) is two eggs smothered in delicious queso sauce with a side of carne guisada as good as Mom used to make. Add to that smoky and rich refried beans, small cubes of tasty fried potatoes and a couple of tortillas to soak up the delicious gravy and cheese. Wow!

-Wes Marshall

As soon as you walk in the front door you will receive a warm welcome, which is nice to see. Everyone is welcomed and treated with respect, an old fashioned but very effective business practice. That alone is something that will keep you coming back for reasons other than the food. But luckily they do the food well too, so you don't have to lie to yourself when you want to go there.

There's almost always a crowd, but generally you don't have to wait long for a table; I'm not sure how they manage that. The Don Juan is the breakfast taco to get at Juan in a Million. I say breakfast taco, but it's more like a plate of eggs, potato, bacon and secret ingredients served with as many tortillas as you need to finish it. It too is a spectacle. The Don Juan and some hot coffee is a delectable breakfast.

- Stephen Malina

Reprinted with permission from INSite Publications

LA BAHIA SEAFOOD AND MEXICAN RESTAURANT

1208 E Cesar Chavez 78701
Phone: (512) 542-9955
Tue-Sun 9am-10pm
Closed Monday
Breakfast Tue-Sun 9am-12pm
Credit Cards

I relocated to Connecticut from Austin almost two years ago. If you have never been to New England, I should point out that I have not had Mexican food in over a year. I am not sure why there is no good Mexican food in New England, but I have a theory: I think that Mexicans got there and realized how insanely cold it gets and headed back down south ASAP! So, by the time I landed at Bergstrom I was salivating. I ran through the airport like O.J. (back in his pre-murderous everybody-loved-him days).

We headed from the airport to a new joint on Cesar Chavez called La Bahia Seafood Mexican Restaurant. To our horror we realized that the restaurant was so new that they hadn't gotten their beer license yet. The girls ordered appetizers and John and I ran across the street to the Texaco for a twelve pack of tall boys. On the walk we overheard a man and a woman negotiating sex for money. It is nice to know that the price of love is still affordable at $20. Upon our return, we were welcomed with some chips and salsa, bean and cheese nachos and ceviche.

The guacamole salsa snapped my pretentious head out

of judging the decor to reaching for my tall boy to put out the fire in my mouth. It was spectacular. Not too hot to stop eating but hot enough to make you take a breath. The bean and cheese nachos were yummy. The cheese was oozing just the way it should when served and the beans had that nice salty flavor that I love. I cannot say enough good things about their ceviche. Ceviche can be a little scary looking when served and is often very tart and salty. This ceviche was everything I wanted ceviche to taste like; it was the bomb. By the time I got through the appetizers I was into my third beer. I ordered several items to get a good mix from the menu. The waitress/owner was really helpful while we were ordering. She recommended her favorites and I could tell by her smile how much she liked certain dishes. I went with her recommendations and added a few other items.

I started with the seafood soup. It was very hearty and they didn't skimp a bit on the goods. The soup temperature was perfect as well, so we could all dive right in. Thumbs up so far, and I had three more plates of food in front of me. The next dish I had was the "fish Veracruz" and let me tell you something, those boys in Veracruz are using the right bait. It was delicious and the spices were awesome. The next plate was the "Shrimp chile relleño" This was my overall favorite. Once again it had all the right spices and the shrimp were perfectly prepared. The final dish I had was "Shrimp La Bahía". This was the owner's favorite and my main dish. The taste was unique. I can't say in all my Mexican food experiences this was the first time I had this taste. It was very delicious and had a completely different after taste than your first impressions. Eat this dish slowly and ride the flavor coaster. All the dishes were served with a good amount of white rice and refried beans. The prices were very reasonable, and the staff was friendly; you won't leave this restaurant hungry broke or disappointed. I won't be surprised to find La Bahía lasting a long time in Austin and becoming a town favorite. Everyone had a similar experience that day, I just hope they get their beer permit before I go back on my way to the airport on Monday!

- Kevin Martin

La Casita

1614 E 7th St. 78702
Phone: (512) 469-0105
Sun-Thu 7am-10pm
Fri 7am-8pm
Closed on Saturdays
Breakfast all day
Credit Cards

Ok, so Fajita Xpress went out of business and La Casita moved in. Not only that, but Maggie the Clown lives above La Casita. That's right, there are clown offices above a Mexican food restaurant. I can't really say I know too much about the effect of a clown on Mexican food, but it does not seem positive. La Casita's food is not nearly as good as Fajita Xpress and there's no beer. Later that night I had nightmares about clowns who twist enchiladas into dog shapes and paint smiles on children's faces with guacamole and beans. The horror!

- Chris Nelson

La Cocinita

4140 E 12th St. 78721
Phone: (512) 927-9066
Daily 7am-2pm
Breakfast all day
Credit Cards

Fours walls, a table, a chair and some carne asada. That's what you need to know going in. Munch down, fill up, and head out — that's what La Cocinita delivers. Their no frills approach makes it great lunch spot with daily specials clocking in at under $5. The most popular item and the one that draws the loyal breakfast crowd is their famous burrito—so large and brimming with eggs that it looks like a beached whale on your plate, beconing you to take it out of its misery, out of this world and into your stomach. This ain't no manatee love story. This is true life Tex Mex.

- Chris Nelson

mexican food in austin

LA MICHOACANA

1917 E 7th St. 78702
Phone: (512) 473-8487
Mon-Fri 8am-9:30pm
Sat-Sun 7am-9:30pm
Credit Cards

6908 Cameron Rd. 78752
Phone: (512) 451-9404
Daily 8am-9:30pm
Credit Cards

You can get everything at La Michoacana. It's a grocery store, butcher shop, bakery, lunch counter and jewelry store (bling available only on weekends). It is the Central Market of the Eastside with most all products and services bearing the mark of Mexico. The lunch counter has at least ten different dishes under heat lamps that one may order as tacos, gorditas or tortas. Whether it's fajitas, carnitas, tripas or cabrito, your serving will be generous and lovingly prepared by the ladies behind the counter. The tacos come with chopped onions, cilantro and sliced key limes. The gorditas and chile relleño are also not-to-be-missed house specialties. Pay at the checkout first and take your receipt to the counter to order your food. It might be wise to learn a few Spanish phrases before you go, but then again, a friend of mine seems to do just fine by pointing and salivating. I have to say that everything is awesome at La Michoacana — from the food to the prices to the ambiance of this Eastside gem.

- Chris Nelson

photo by Derek Hatley

dlp

LA MORENITA MEXICAN RESTAURANT

2944 E 12th St. 78702
Phone: (512) 472-4841
Mon-Sat 7am-3pm
Cash only

In a perfect East Austin location stands a small pink concrete diner connected to an old church decorated with childlike paintings of various combination plates on the windows and furnished with collapsible table and chairs — the dive of dives but somehow exquisitely charming. At first, this is one of those places that an Austinite dreams of discovering in order to impress unflappable friends. Unfortunately, the food was not in keeping with my aspirations. However, if your parents were the kind to load up the freezer with El Charrito Mexican dinners before they went out of town, then you're in luck because this was a culinary trip down memory lane.

- Allison Walsh

LA PALAPA MEXICAN RESTAURANT Y CANTINA

6640 E Hwy. 290 78723
Phone: (512) 459-8729
Sun-Wed 11am-10pm
Thu-Sat 11am-11pm
Breakfast Sat-Sun 11am-3pm
Live music Tue-Thu
Karaoke w/ Big Jim Fri & Sat
Saturdays Nights Fajita Buffet
Credit Cards

People love to discover the out-of-the-ordinary: like finding a great bottle of wine that you can only buy in Portugal or being the first to a great estate sale when you figure out that crazy neighbor had traveled all over the world and had great taste in addition to her 16 cats.

The first visit to La Palapa brought about those same feelings — entering the dark, very empty restaurant felt like we had stumbled into a cantina near the border. The Tilapia a la Diablo in a simple vegetable broth was one of the best pieces of fish I have had in all of Texas. The roasted vegetable appetizer had perfect consistency and that touch of smoky favor that did not overpower the natural favors at all. I thought I had found one of those favorites that you love to turn friends on to and keep to your own little private group.

The second trip brought me quickly back to reality. The 9-to-5 crowds gathered in a now brightly lit room on long tables. Buckets of beer were being served, and one waitress scurried about trying to take care of everyone. The Bob Seger 45 spun into Steve Miller; combine that with the neon lights of the many beer signs pushed the atmosphere away from my imagined cantina towards a local happy hour bar. After a decent wait for the obviously overworked waitress, I stuck with seafood and ordered the Cameranes a al Vercuzana, tasty but the sauce was much heavier this time and seemed more "packaged".

My friend had the spinach and mushroom enchiladas, commenting that they were, "pretty good, but maybe too much cheese". Hmmm, maybe that sums up the second visit quite well. Since the food did not hit me "Like a Rock" I will give La Palapa one more chance. They have karaoke on Friday and Saturday night, and I bet I can pull off a great Bob Seger.

- Scott Staab

Las Cazuelas Mexican Restaurant

1701 E Cesar Chavez St. 78702
Phone: (512) 479-7911
Open 7 days a week 7am-2am
Breakfast all day
Friday Night Norteño Band
Cash only

People who arrive from Mexico at the bus station two blocks from Las Cazuelas are likely to feel swindled by the bus company if they eat there first. That's because the food is so authentic that they'll think they never left Mexico. The interior is something you'd find two blocks away from a bus station in Mexico with large signs displaying the names of every Mexican dish under the sun. Freshness is the main ingredient at Las Cazuelas. You can

dlp

see them make the salsa up front and judging by the exquisite taste and length of time it takes to make a grilled chicken, I wouldn't be surprised if they kill it just after you order.

- Chris Nelson

LAS PALMAS RESTAURANT

1209 E 7th St. 78702
Phone: (512) 457-4944
Mon-Thu 11am-10pm
Fri-Sat 11am-11pm
Closed Sundays
Friday Evening guitar player
Breakfast all day
Credit Cards

You may remember Las Palmas as the old location for Nuevo Leon. Certainly many people have entered its doors thinking just that. Whatever anyone thinks going into it, they have surely left content with the quality of the food sitting neatly in their belly. Their enchiladas are recommended by the banner across the patio reading, "Famous Enchiladas." The sampler plate gives you enchiladas rojas, verdes and sour cream. Our taste test revealed the rojas to be the winner with its smoky undertones and rich afterburn. Margarita specials tend to involve whatever tequila they need to liquidate from their inventory at the time. I recommend the frozen margarita with a shot of Chambord — the closest thing to an alcoholic frozen Skittle.

- Chris Nelson

photo by Derek Hatley

mexican food in austin

Los Altos

3301 N IH 35 78722
Phone: (512) 236-1219
Daily 7am-11pm
Credit Cards

Small, quaint and authentic describes this eatery on I-35's access road. The two small dining rooms are adorned with the requisite Mexican flags, Bud Lite posters and a jukebox with Selena's numerous hits. A small television in the corner runs Mexican soap operas that attract the staff like flies to honey. Commercial breaks are for taking orders and bussing tables. Don't think that this degrades the quality of the food. It is excellent. The enchiladas are the pride of the house and for good reason. Many of their dishes seem standard fare until put into your mouth. Barbacoa takes on a different character when swathed in their spicy adobada a la Jalisco sauce served up with cilantro and chopped onions. The salsa is salty, spicy and freshly made that day. Sadly there were no margaritas, but perfection is hard to achieve. If you are passing through Austin via I-35 and want to stop for a bite, this is the place.

- Chris Nelson

Los Comales Mexican Restaurant

2136 E 7th St. 78702
Phone: (512) 480-9358
Mon-Thu 10am-10pm
Fri-Sat 10am-12am
Sun 9am-10pm
Mariachis Fri-Sat 9pm-12am
Credit Cards

The grill is king here. Anything thrown upon Los Comales grill — fresh onions, jalapeños, carne asada — is recommended. The simplicity and honesty of the grilled dishes are pure, flavorful and rewarding. If man could put his sins on the Los Comales grill alongside a family of jalapeños, there would justice for his soul. Their expansive dining room sometimes reaches full capacity during lunchtime with businessmen and laborers all dining in what is obviously a favorite place. The patio outside is nice in the evenings, especially with a cold margarita, which tends to be stronger than the average. Salsa at Los Comales is rich, red and spicy—all of which are seldom found together. The dinner crowd during the week can be thin, but come Friday night, a mariachi band can be found serenading the patrons. Try it. Love it.

- *Chris Nelson*

LOS JALISCIENSES

6201 E Hwy. 290 78723
Phone: (512) 452-3332
Mon-Fri 7am-11pm
Sat-Sun 7am-12am
Evenings (Norteño Music)
Credit Cards

Los Jaliscienses is heavenly. This hidden gem is a secret favorite of many a seafood lover in Northeast Austin. Attached to an EconoLodge and housed in a 1960's inverted-bannana-ish building, it looks like some sort of Barbarella pleasure dome. Inside it's all Mexi-pleasure food. In addition to their top-notch seafood soups and plates, their green habanero sauce is perhaps some of the tastiest in town. If *Travel & Leisure* listed Mexican food getaways for couples, this would top the chart. So get a room at the EconoLodge, put on some Keith Sweat, order up some shelled aphrodisiacs and get your Mexi freak on 'till the early morn. "Does that feel good, baby? *Ooh*, I thought so."

- *Chris Nelson*

"The most interesting aspect in the evolution of Mexican restaurants in Austin over the last thirty years is the culinary diversity. First there was just Tex-Mex in the mainstream. Then with the advent of Fonda San Miguel in 1975, the general restaurant public began to develop an appreciation for more complex interior dishes. These days, we not only have restaurants that serve plenty of old-fashioned Austin Tex-Mex, we also have a few West Texas Tex-Mex places, and some San Antonio Tex-Mex joints. And while Fonda still reigns supreme on the Interior side, we have an explosion of small Interior Mexican restaurants that boast the cuisines of their native areas of Mexico, as in "estilo Potosino," or in the style of San Luis Potosi; "estilo DF," or in the style of the federal district (Mexico City) or "estilo Norteno," in the style of the Northern states of Mexico. It makes Austin Mexican food heaven, as far as I'm concerned."

- *Virginia B. Wood,*
Food Editor, The Austin Chronicle

TEQUILA! continued from page 45

tent of about 38 to 40 percent). The final production step is aging, a process that gives each tequila its designation as blanco (white), plata (silver), reposado (rested) and anejo (aged), dictated by the length of aging. White tequilas are aged less than 60 days.

Our tour of La Rojeña concluded in the magnificent cellar where the Cuervo family keeps its own stash. The almost medieval setting includes a stone staircase and a lot of wrought iron. Our host, Juan Domingo Beckmann, is the 10th generation of his family to work for the firm and among his responsibilities are new ventures such as the Cuervo 1800 Single Barrel. He believes that "through the use of special aging techniques and imported woods, tequila can be as smooth and complex as the finest Cognac or (other) brandy." Thanks to my intensive studies of the past few days, I was just the person to test his theory.

Call it one of life's more memorable moments: Juan Domingo taking a long-handled cup, dipping it down into oak barrels that bear his family's name, and beckoning his masterpiece into welcoming snifters. Truly this would be the highlight of my tour, and a heady blend it was — rich with woody flavor, a seductive nose and a bigger body than any I had enjoyed. I quickly realized that Juan Domingo's own tequila had never been off the barrel and was stronger than any that reaches the market here in San Antonio. Instinctively I gripped my precious snifter and cast my gaze around the cellar. Who knows how I would have reacted if that compadre of mine had spilled even a drop of this nectar. But after I spied him talking with Juan Domingo's tequilero, I closed my eyes and took the snifter back to my nose. No rope tricks on this night.

Margaritas Tropicales
1 1/2 ounces (3 tablespoons) tequila
1/2 ounce (1 tablespoon) lime juice
1/2 ounce (1 tablespoon) Triple Sec
Tropical fruits, such as mango, tamarind or hibiscus

flower, for garnish

Combine tequila with lime juice and Triple Sec. If desired, substitute margarita mix using one part tequila to 3 parts of mix. Put in glass; garnish with fruit as desired.
Makes 1 drink.

Source: Jose Cuervo Distillery

Sunburn Margarita
1 1/2 ounces (3 tablespoons) tequila
1/2 ounce (1 tablespoon) lime juice
3 ounces (6 tablespoons) cranberry juice
Splash of Grand Marnier

Combine all ingredients.
Makes 1 drink.

Source: Jose Cuervo Distillery

1800 Sunsets
Shot of 1800 Reposado or other good tequila
Drop of grenadine
Champagne

Pour tequila and grenadine into champagne glass. Fill with champagne.
Makes 1 drink.

Source: Jose Cuervo Distillery

1800 Martini
1 1/2 ounces (3 tablespoons) tequila
Splash of amaretto
Orange twist, for garnish

Combine tequila and amaretto. Serve straight up in chilled glass with sugared rim, garnished with orange twist.
Makes 1 drink.

Source: Jose Cuervo Distillery

LUVIANO'S

7213 Cameron Rd. 78752
Phone: (512) 458-1439
Open 7 days a week 7am-10pm
Fri 7am-Midnight
Breakfast all day
Credit Cards

Volleyball anyone? With games starting nightly around seven, it is now possible to gorge yourself with the heavenly Tex-Mex and work it off without leaving the premises. And if volleyball isn't your game then grab a beer and throw a few rounds of darts. The backyard is an immense garden full of trees and outdoor tables; perfect to enjoy your dinner and watch the game. Of note were the camarones rancheros grilled with onions, bell peppers and mushrooms topped with gobs of melted cheese. The tomatilla sauce con queso with the enchiladas verdes was also fantastic. This place also offers a nice selection of combination plates so you can really sample their menu but never spend more than six dollars. Luviano's is also one of the few joints I know of that serves menudo all week long. Bring your appetite and your sneakers.

- Allison Walsh

MI MADRE'S

2201 Manor Rd. 78722
Phone: (512) 480-8441
Mon-Sat 6am-2pm
Closed Sunday
Breakfast all day until 2pm
Credit Cards

Mi Madre's went above and beyond the requirements of a good Mexican restaurant. I had the migas plate which costs about $5.50 with coffee. The plate was of gargantuan proportions: chips, tortillas, beans, eggs with chorizo and salsa. I couldn't finish it and left in a gluttonous stupor that was both painful and pleasant at the same time. It was the only food I ate all day long. I am going to return there but I am going to save it for a time when I am really hungry.

- Aaron Kirksey

MI REY RESTAURANT

1505 E 7th St. 78702
Phone: (512) 476-4211
Daily 7:30am-3pm
Breakfast until 11:30am
Credit Cards

Ay, Mí Rey. Mí lunchtime bomba. Mí Jefe de fajitas. Mí amor de sabor. You are the one. Your gorditas gave me the loving. Why did you not call? I came in the night for you. And you had closed your shutters. The lunchtime specials were so special, Mí Rey. Is there another in your life? Another who you give the special loving? There were many others eating when I smothered your chile onto my relleño. Do you love them more? Tell me, Rey, am I your favorite? You are mine for the special noontime. Besos. Besos para siempre.

- *Chris Nelson*

"I like Maudie's on Lake Austin Boulevard for their fajita tacos and I drink my margaritas at Z-Tejas. It's Taco Shack for breakfast tacos."
- *Matt Luckie,*
Owner, Lucky Lounge, Red Fez and Oslo

MOE'S SOUTHWEST GRILL

500 Canyon Ridge Dr. Ste L 78753
Phone: (512) 997-9200
www.moes.com
Sun-Thu 11am-9pm
Fri-Sat 11am-10pm
Credit Cards

Fresh ingredients (they brag they don't have a freezer) and rock and roll are the trademarks of this fast food chain found mainly in the Carolinas and in Georgia. It's interesting to see the convergence of Moe's and the Californian Baja Fresh closing in on Taco Cabana/Chipotle territory. The Bell had better step up and realize that the new health conscious Mexican food addicts are not only watching their carbs, but are demanding the highest quality in food preparation, recipes from scratch, and definitely no lard. To separate him from the rest Moe's has given everything on the menu kitschy, pop culture names like the Pinky Tuscadero, the Triple Lindy or the Seinfeldian Art Vandalay and Close Talker. Run assembly line style, everything is made in front of your eyes. No room for error- fast and good with a cheerful pop open of your beer from the cashier as you pay. Stylized portraiture of Rock and Roll legends adorns the wall complete with more catchy titles and puns- this Moe must be some kind of card.

- Allison Walsh

Morelia Taqueria

105 Tillery St. 78702
Phone: (512) 385-8002
Daily 6am-10pm
Breakfast all day
6am-12pm on request
Music seasonally
Credit Cards

Ever crave Mexican food after a few days out of town? Want to avoid the traffic and relax outside with a cold beer and some botanas? Exit Caesar Chavez from 183 coming from the airport and right on the corner is the modest taquería Morelia. We were treated like royalty, where even the cook made a cameo to ask how we wanted our meat prepared. This place is charming. Consider Morelia's your pit stop on the way home for authentic Mexican dishes. Or, before 10:00 am, load up on their breakfast tacos, $2.75 for three.

- Allison Walsh

Mr. Natural

1901 E Cesar Chavez St. 78702
Phone: (512) 477-5228
http://www.mrnatural-austin.com
Mon-Sat 8am-7pm
Credit Cards

Please see review on page 121

Other Locations: South

NUEVO LEON

1501 E 6th St. 78702
Phone: (512) 479-0097
Fax: (512) 474-4611
Sun-Mon 11am-9pm
Tue-Thu 11am-10pm
Fri-Sat 11am-11pm
Breakfast all day
Friday Mariachi
Saturday live music
Credit Cards

I know a guy who eats at Nuevo Leon every Sunday night, without fail at 6:00 with a different group of friends each time. He's been going for years. And he always has the same waitress, Griselda, who when he stared frequenting the place, was a teenage busser. The huge restaurant, on the south side of 6th street as you head East, is always manned by Kevin at the front door, welcoming you right on in. Former Governor Ann Richards was dining the last time I went. The menu is huge with favorites being Shrimp Saltillo, grilled shrimp with two cheese enchiladas with sliced raw jalapeño and white onion, the old fashioned tacos, double-shelled and fried, and the tortilla soup, a meal of its own. The margaritas are great whether shaken or frozen and there is always attentive, lovely service. It always feels like UT just won a home game in here.

- Gracie Salem

UPDATE: New Location open for breakfast tacos at San Jacinto and 15th.

PAPA PANCHO'S

2401 E Cesar Chavez 78702
Phone: (512) 691-9265
Tue-Sun 7am-5pm
Closed Mondays
Breakfast al day
Credit Cards

Papa Pancho's is on the right track. It's like a phoenix rising out of the ashes of another failed restaurant, but has yet to take flight. It needs beer to help its wings spread and a liquor license to put wind beneath those wings. All the other bases are covered. The food is delicious. The menudo is some of the best around, and they serve barbeque on Saturdays. I'm excited about the patio/party facility they're building in the back, complete with stage, Christmas lights and stations where kegs will hopefully be tapped. During our visit, Papa Pancho went around to each table, introduced himself and asked about the meal. With personal attention like that, I'm faithful that Papa Pancho's will take to the air quite soon if that license comes in as planned.

- Chris Nelson

PAPPASITO'S CANTINA

6513 N IH 35 78752
Phone: (512) 459-9214
Mon-Thu & Sun 11am-11pm
Fri-Sat 11am-12am
Credit Cards

This outfit, along with its Cajun sister Pappadeaux's, is a well-oiled conglomeration found mainly on freeways near motel/hotel chains throughout Texas. This corporate duet makes few mistakes by answering to the franchise god of routine. These restaurants are built on systems that are well defined, practiced and choreographed down to a science. No matter which location you visit, there will never be any variance of service, presentation, flavor or portion size. This methodology acts as a beacon to the business traveler, large family birthday gatherings, secretarial happy hours and the uninventive out on their first date. Conversely, it acts as more of a lighthouse to others warning of the hackneyed operations within.

Now with all of this said, I have to admit, begrudgingly, that our food rocked and not in a tawdry simple-food-for simple-people kind of way. I thought the flavors were clever and bold. The Morelia tacos made quite an impression, as did the jumbo shrimp Diablo. The margaritas were straightforward and limey. And, thankfully, our server wasn't full of that fraudulent eagerness and jovialness that is so annoying. I will look forward to being lost in Marietta, GA and returning to this establishment.

- Allison Walsh

dlp essay

THE DIABLO MARTINI

A lip-tingling twist on an old favorite

by John Buchanan

Ingredients:

1/4 shot	*Olive juice*
1/2 shot	*Lime juice (freshly squeezed)*
4-6 drops	*Cholera Hot Sauce (This amount varies wildly depending on your level of heat tolerance. Be sure to try your favorite hot sauce.)*
4 oz.	*Vodka (Tanqueray Sterling works very well with this recipe.)*
1	*skewer jalapeño stuffed olives*

Fill cocktail shaker with ice (less ice if the vodka is chilled). Add olive juice and lime juice. Add drops of hot sauce. Top with vodka and shake vigorously. Strain into a chilled martini glass. Add the olive skewer.

Porfirio's Tacos

1512 Holly St. Ste B 78702
Phone: (512) 476-5030
Mon-Sat 6am-1:30pm
Closed Sundays
Breakfast 6am-11:30am
Cash only

This is a bare-bones outfit with three locations in the city. The bulk of the business is done in the mornings with work crews picking up breakfast tacos and loading up on coffee. The favorite on the lunch menu is the carne guisada plate which is served with fideo, a Mexican spaghetti. I would, however, stick to the breakfast tacos, if you know what I mean. No dinner.

- Chris Nelson

Other Locations: Southeast

Rico's Tamales

1701 B E Cesar Chavez 78701
Phone: (512) 477-7207
Daily 7am-10pm
Breakfast all day
Cash only

This adorable diner has ventured into rare Mexican food restaurant territory by giving its customers a view into their modern, well-kept kitchen. I guess the secret to melted, uncongealed cheese really is the microwave. But despite these tricks of the trade, Rico's serves up deliciously inexpensive, mouth watering meals. Homemade salsas round out their simple menu which isn't all about the tamale. Grab a seat at the counter, hang out and swivel round to enjoy the view of their incredibly well landscaped exterior. We had the chicken dinner smothered in their spicy green salsa and a couple of breakfast tacos to share. Just perfect. With an order of just made jalapeño-and-cheese tamales to go, at six bucks a dozen, it was a very pleasant way to wait out a not-so-pleasant hangover.

- Allison Walsh

dlp

TACO SABROSO

5100 E 7th St. 78702
Phone: (512) 247-3333
Mon-Tue closed
Wed-Thu 11am-9pm
Fri-Sat 11am-11pm
Sun 11am-9pm
Music Saturdays
Credit Cards

Heading out East 7th Street toward the airport, Taco Sabroso is the last outpost for Mexican food. Conversely, it's the first place you hit coming from the airport. For a Mexican food lover, Taco Sabroso is the equivalent of a last meal before entering prison (flying to a place with no tacos) or, the first meal on release from prison. Any which way, their tacos are authentic Mexican served on small tortillas with chopped cilantro, onions and lime. Choose from an array of salsas before getting locked up or tasting freedom. I've heard that this place is a favorite of Governor Rick Perry, but please don't hold it against them.

- Chris Nelson

photo by Derek Hatley

mexican food in austin

TRES AMIGOS

7535 E Hwy. 290 78723
Cross Street: Hwy. 183
Phone: (512) 926-4441
Fax: (512) 926-7455
Sun-Thu 11am-10pm
Fri-Sat 11am-11pm
Breakfast all day
Credit Cards

Please see review on page 154

Other Locations: Far South, West

UN RINCON DE MEXICO RESTAURANT

2039 Airport Blvd. 78722
Phone: (512) 320-1551
Daily 7am-10pm
Credit Cards

"A Corner of Mexico" is how the name translates and where you are transported at this roadside eatery. The owners of the place are from D.F. (Federal District/Mexico City) and offer traditional regional dishes like birria and pozole. Birria is a lamb stew that comes piping hot with cilantro and diced onions to be added at will. The dish is a refreshing departure from the standard Mexican offerings which also appear on the menu. Breakfast tacos there are good and cheap (three for $1.99) and perfect for picking up on your way out to the airport. The interior of Un Rincon is a spartan gathering of plastic tables and chairs but the telenovelas being played on the TV put some added flavor into the room. I really enjoy Mexican TV and being able to watch it while slurping authentic Birria is a lovely, simple pleasure.

- Chris Nelson

Vivo Cocina Mexicana

2015 Manor Rd. 78722
Phone: (512) 482-0300
Mon 11am-3pm
Tue-Thu 11am-10pm
Fri-Sat 11am-10:30pm
Credit Cards

This new Eastside eatery is a much welcome change of pace in that it has successfully bridged Mexican food with a more sophisticated atmosphere. Vivo, meaning alive, emphasizes fresh, healthy ingredients without the usual taste sacrifice. Though I never tell the wait staff what I am up to, invariably, true to the Austin sense of hospitality, I receive some sort of special treat. Vivo was kind enough to bring out a fourth sauce accompanying the trio offered as an appetizer. They were all unique without the usual abandoned weak link. Their claim to fame is the puffy tacos filled with their own special concoctions which seem to be catching on due to favorable write-ups in the local paper. I enjoyed my Mexican food with a little ambiance. Somehow, the loveliness prevented me from gorging and left me feeling satiated, yet not sleepy.

- Allison Walsh

UPDATE: For the summer the outdoor deck at Vivo has morphed into a lush tropical oasis. Beautifully planned and well tended, this is the perfect spot to unwind and soak up some greenery while sipping margaritas and listening to the tranquil fountain. They have been known to give a long stem rose to the ladies upon departure—a nice gesture which does brighten your day.

Zunzal

642 Calles St. 78702
Phone: (512) 474-7749
Sun-Thu 8am-10pm
Fri 8am-11pm
Beer only
Breakfast upon request
Vegetarian meals upon request
Credit Cards

El Zunzal is not your typical Tex-Mex restaurant due to the fact that it specializes in Salvadoran fare. For those not familiar with Salvadoran cuisine its a lot like Tex-Mex but with the plantain and the yucca being big players on the menu. My dinner date and I decided to start off with the tamales and the pupusa. The two varieties of tamales (pork and chicken) were absolutely fantastic with a masa casing and steamed in banana leaves rather than the Mexican corn husk. At $2 a pop they were an absolute bargain. The pupusa is a Salvadoran specialty — round corn meal dough stuffed with meat or cheese and topped with a vinegar-based slaw. The cheese variety that we sampled was delightful. Due to the fact that this was my first foray into Salvadoran food in Austin, I have completely forgotten the name of my entree; however, the flavor of this dish can not escape me. Two chicken breasts were lightly fried and served on a bed of cucumbers and slaw and topped with a ranchero sauce. The entire plate was encircled in fried plantains. The presentation alone would rival Austin's best fine dining. And the taste certainly does beat many of Austin's fine dining establishments. This dish immediately earned a spot on my top five favorite plates of food in Austin. So when you go to El Zunzal ask for the pollo frito something or other that is near the bottom of the Salvadoran section of the menu. Other entrees included a carne asada and a fried snapper. All dishes were accompanied with the aforementioned slaw. My dinner date took the safer route going with the chicken fajitas from the Tex-Mex page of the menu and they did not disappoint — very flavorful pieces of chicken with your typical fajita fixin's, but I say when in El Salvador go with the chicken dish whose name the Gringo can't recall. El Zunzal is on the Eastside and our waitress didn't speak of lick of English which showed me exactly how poor my Spanish has gotten. We were able to order via a combination of my Spanglish, her Spanish and lots of pointing and staring. I'm not much on rating places on star system, but I'll be going back to El Zunzal very soon.

- Chad Hamilton

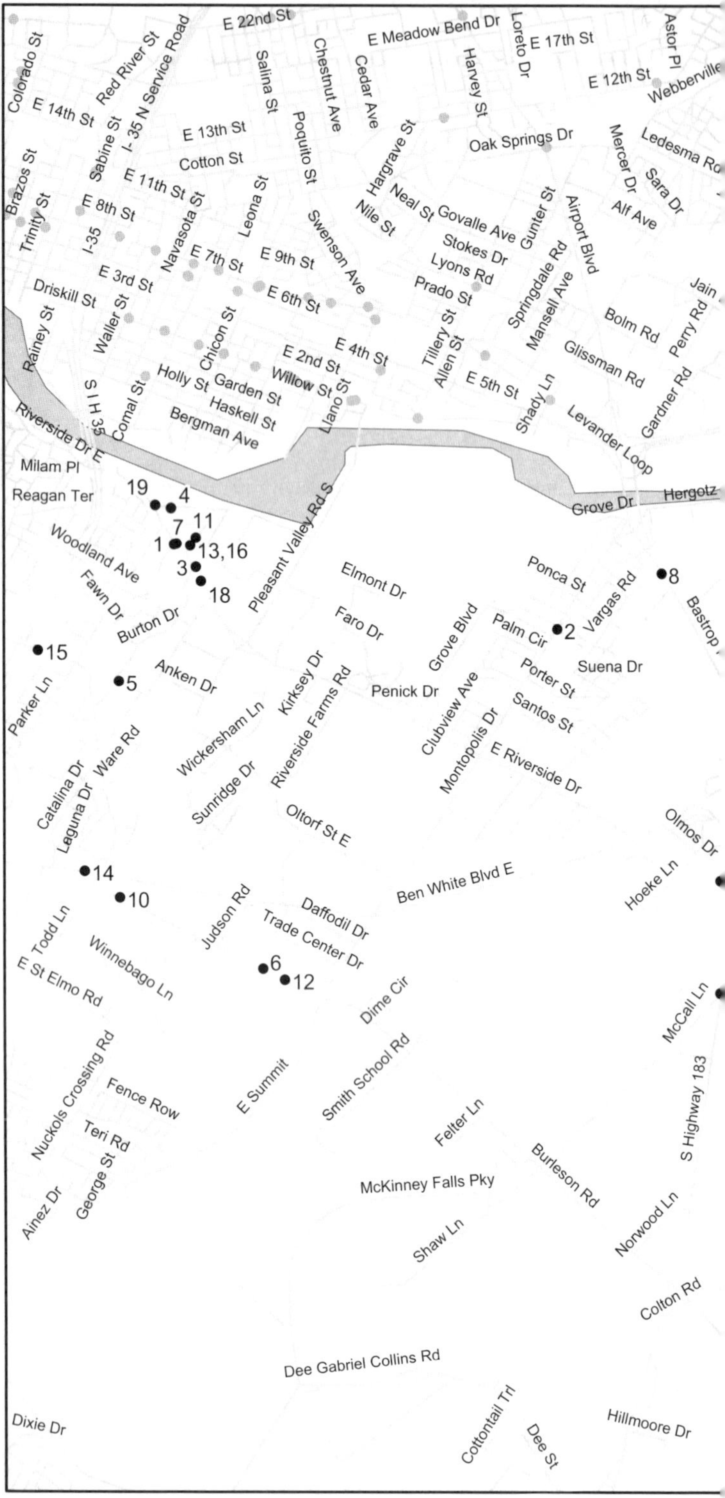

E 22nd St
E Meadow Bend Dr
Loreto Dr
E 17th St
Astor Pl
Colorado St
Red River St
I- 35 N Service Road
Salina St
Chestnut Ave
Cedar Ave
Harvey St
E 12th St
Webberville
E 14th St
Sabine St
E 13th St
Poquito St
Hargrave St
Oak Springs Dr
Mercer Dr
Ledesma Rd
Brazos St
Cotton St
E 11th St
Leona St
Sara Dr
Trinity St
E 8th St
Navasota St
Neal St
Nile St
Govalle Ave
Gunter St
Airport Blvd
Alf Ave
I-35
E 7th St
E 9th St
Swenson Ave
Stokes Dr
Lyons Rd
Springdale Rd
E 3rd St
E 6th St
Prado St
Mansell Ave
Jain
Driskill St
Perry Rd
Rainey St
Waller St
Chicon St
Tillery St
Bolm Rd
E 4th St
E 2nd St
Allen St
Glissman Rd
S I H 35
Holly St
Garden St
Willow St
Llano St
E 5th St
Gardner Rd
Comal St
Haskell St
Shady Ln
Riverside Dr E
Bergman Ave
Levander Loop
Milam Pl
19
4
Reagan Ter
Pleasant Valley Rd S
Grove Dr
Hergotz
7
11
1
13,16
Woodland Ave
3
Elmont Dr
Ponca St
Vargas Rd
8
18
Fawn Dr
Bastrop
Faro Dr
Grove Blvd
Palm Cir
2
Burton Dr
15
Suena Dr
Anken Dr
Kirksey Dr
Porter St
5
Penick Dr
Parker Ln
Riverside Farms Rd
Clubview Ave
Santos St
Wickersham Ln
Ware Rd
Montopolis Dr
E Riverside Dr
Catalina Dr
Sunridge Dr
Laguna Dr
Oltorf St E
Olmos Dr
Ben White Blvd E
14
Hoeke Ln
10
Judson Rd
Daffodil Dr
E Todd Ln
Trade Center Dr
Winnebago Ln
E St Elmo Rd
6
12
Dime Cir
McCall Ln
Smith School Rd
Nuckols Crossing Rd
S Highway 183
Fence Row
E Summit
Felter Ln
Teri Rd
Burleson Rd
George St
McKinney Falls Pky
Ainez Dr
Norwood Ln
Shaw Ln
Colton Rd
Dee Gabriel Collins Rd
Dixie Dr
Cottontail Trl
Hillmoore Dr
Dee St

mexican food in austin

Southeast Austin might seem small, but East Riverside offers a wealth of Mexican food eating that can easily keep one busy for days. It is a place where many UT students live in inexpensive, behemoth apartment complexes with collections of surrounding neighborhoods also supporting the bustling street. Many of the roads will take you through winding, hidden paths and make you feel like you're in the country. With the large lots and an abundance of greenery it's not uncommon for neighbors to keep chickens, goats or other animals that have a tendency to end up on the dinner table.

1 Al Pastor
2 Alonzo's
3 Arandinas
4 Baby Acapulco
5 El Jacalito
6 El Meson
7 El Regio
8 El Sumbido Grill
9 Hacienda
10 Happy Taco
11 Janitzio
12 La Casuelita
13 La Regiomontana
14 La Tapatia
15 La Terrazza
16 Mariscos Seafood
17 Porfirio's Dos
18 Taco Cabana
19 Vallarta Jalisco

AL PASTOR RESTAURANT

1911 E Riverside Dr. 78741
Phone: (512) 442-8402
Daily 8am-10pm
Beer only
Breakfast all day
Credit Cards

What a find! The unassuming Al Pastor restaurant sits humbly in a strip mall on East Riverside minding its own business and it is *fantastic*. Well at least the salsa, guacamole and the tortilla soup. Try to refrain from plowing through basket upon basket of chips and salsa before your food comes — and it will take a few minutes, though it is well worth the wait. The guacamole was so fresh and sweet it could have been dessert. But the big winner is the chicken tortilla soup—I swear it might be the best around. As for the al pastor at Al Pastor, we had to take it home for we hadn't gastrically planned properly. I think it was pretty good when we wolfed it down at 4am. But honestly, all I can think about is the soup.

- Allison Walsh

INSIDERS TIP: Late at night hit Al Pastor's taco cart in front of the restaurant — a must if heading home from the bar.

We fell for Maria's Taco Xpress when it was just a roadside camper van. The potato, egg, and cheese tacos are perfect for a hangover. The place is great for a cohesive vibe, to chill out and listen to live music."

- Ryan Carter
Musician, Dewato

ALONZO'S TACOS II

907 Montopolis Dr. 78741
Phone: (512) 389-3338
Mon-Sat 6:30am-2pm
Closed Sunday
Breakfast 6am-11:30am
Cash only

Please see review on page 128

Other Locations: Far South, North

mexican food in austin

ARANDINAS TAQUERIA

2110 E Riverside Dr.
Phone: (512) 326-1182
Sun-Thu 6am-12am
Fri-Sat 6am-1am
Breakfast all day
Credit Cards

I counted five Mexican restaurants all located on the four blocks that make up this busy corner of East Riverside. They are all walking distance from each other, some only a few steps away. If you are having trouble deciding which one to choose, a sure bet to satisfy your hunger on a tight budget is Arandinas Taqueria, located next to Fast Freddy's Haircuts and Wild West Western Wear. It's open seven days a week from 7:00am to past midnight. You can't miss the white building with bright red trim and the huge 3-D red lettered sign on its roof. The interior is clean and simple, painted in mismatched colors, glossy pastel tangerine walls, industrial gray trim, mossy green ceramic tile floor, white low drop ceiling with long florescent tubes for lighting. The dining area is large enough to fit fifteen tables with four chairs comfortably. There is additional seating on the outdoor covered patio, great for watching all the people and action. The requisite jukebox plays Norteño music at just the right volume, good for conversation. The red, white and green menu with cute color illustrations, offers a huge selection of food, beer and soft drinks. There is a variety of seafood, beef, chicken and pork dishes. Of course there are enchiladas, tacos, tortas, flautas, etc. Try the caldo de camaron or the chicken mole. I had a hearty breakfast of Huevos a la Mexicana served with beans, potatoes, and four corn tortillas, all for $3.50, including coffee.

- Tomas Salas

Other Locations: East, North

"I have been going to El Gallo with my family for 25 years. I always see a relative there unexpectedly on Sundays, and they're form Kyle, Buda and Round Rock. I'll usually get the Special Dinner with a frozen margarita with no salt. They have great queso and great hambugers and fries. Mariachis play on Sundays, but they are tame and not annoying like others."

- Armando Garcia,
Personal Banker

BABY ACAPULCO RESTAURANT Y CANTINA

1705 A S. Lakeshore Dr. 78741
Phone: (512) 447-1339
Sun-Thu 11am until Midnight
Fri-Sat 11am-1am
Breakfast all day
Credit Cards

Please see review on page 99

Other Locations: South, North, Far North

EL JACALITO RESTAURANT

2030 E Oltorf St. Ste. 110 78741
Phone: (512) 445-4109
Mon-Sat 8am-8pm
Sun 8am-2pm
Breakfast all day
Credit Cards

Imagine a bright and cheery 50's diner decked out with all of the Mexican panoply and you've arrived at El Jacalito. The walls, adorned with old Mexican photographs (some of which I recognize from Güero's) and brightly painted plates coupled with the peppy mariachi music make you want to swill a few margaritas even if it had not been your intention. The menu selection is tremendous. Though they might not specialize in anything, they certainly offer something for everyone. This is a great spot for out-of-town guests who are not completely sold on the whole Mexican food concept and want less ethnic choices. Burgers, chicken fried chicken, and an entire fried seafood selection promise to please your deranged relatives. Warning: the huge portions, somewhat *de rigueur*, seem especially huge here. The large guacamole salad was enough for ten jacalitos.

- Allison Walsh

mexican food in austin

El Meson Taqueria

5808 Burleson Rd. 78744
Phone: (512) 416-0744
Mon-Thu 6am-8pm
Fri-Sat 6am-9pm
Sun 7am-3pm
Breakfast until 11am
Credit Cards

Don't let the middle-of-nowhere roadhouse location fool you. This pleasant diversion from your everyday Tex-Mex is first rate. Chef Mariela Godinez, has melded traditional interior Mexican flavors into some of the most blessedly delicious concoctions anywhere. Period. El Meson is counter service only with self-serve sodas, chips and wonderfully spicy salsa. I believe they are still working on their margarita recipe. Located in what looks to be an old Taco Bell, the décor is sparse with lovely tile tables so that you may concentrate on the food without distraction. Though you'll be hard pressed to find anything over six dollars, the portions are large and served on vividly colored hand-painted plates. Such home-style dishes include a pumpkin seed-based chicken mole and an achiote-marinated pork tenderloin. They offer vegetarian items as well such as fresh calabacitas and enchiladas verdes. Everything was cooked to perfection and unlike anything you'll find in town. Flavorful and sumptuous I think pride must be an ingredient in each recipe. No wonder previous reviews of this gem have appeared alongside Austin's finest eating establishments.

- Allison Walsh

southeast

oto by Derek Hatley

El Regio

1928 East Riverside Drive 78741
Phone: (512) 326-1888
Mon-Thurs 10am-10pm
Fri-Sat 10am-11pm
Closed Sundays
Credit Cards

You have two choices from the menu at El Regio: one half chicken or one whole chicken. Along with this comes grilled onions, a pile of tortillas, rice and avocado salsa so good you will think it's made from crack rock. Many people have to go to Harvard to learn the golden rule of business: "Do one thing and do it well." El Regio has given new meaning to this adage with their incredible chicken, barbequed in red chili and piping hot when served. There are a few tables outside, but most people get theirs from the drive thru. The line moves quickly because, hey, there's 50/50 chance they know what you will order.

- Chris Nelson

Other Locations: East, Far South

El Sumbido Grill

404 Bastrop Highway
Phone: (512) 385-2440
Hours: See Review

This tiny café was difficult to review because their hours of operation were as random as the name "el sumbido". After a couple of attempts we almost gave up, but alas, found them open around 4pm on a Tuesday. I recommend calling first. They advertise a buffet seven days a week for $6.95 a person, but who knows? Everything was pretty good even though they were out of our first few choices. The place was as quiet as a church and only a couple of cabbies came in to get their orders to go. Despite the very inviting, well-painted exterior, El Sumbido has a very, very couldn't-care-less, almost abandoned feeling. I have a feeling they have their regulars who know what's up. And that's all that matters.

-Allison Walsh

dlp essay

MUSHROOM AND CHEESE EMPANADAS WITH CILANTRO CREAM

by John Buchanan

Empanada Filling:

3/4 lb.	wild mushrooms (porcini, shitake, cremini, chantrelle mushrooms or whatever looks freshest at the market)
1 tsp.	salt
3/4 lb.	Idiazabal cheese, grated (a wonderful, smoky sheep's milk cheese from Spain)
1	medium white onion, diced
3	garlic cloves, minced
1/2 tsp.	ground cumin
1 tsp.	dried oregano
	kosher salt and fresh ground pepper to taste

Sauté mushrooms in 1 Tbs. olive oil over medium heat until tender. Drain liquid. Heat a large skillet over medium flame. Add onion and garlic; season with cumin, oregano, salt and pepper. Cook and stir for 5 minuets, until the mixture is soft. Fold mushrooms into the pan. Season with salt and pepper to taste. Allow filling to cool. When cool mix in the Idiazabal.

Empanada Dough:

1 1/2 cups	all-purpose flour
1 cup	masa harina
1 tsp.	baking powder
1 tsp.	salt
1/2 cup	(1 stick) unsalted butter, melted and cooled
1	large egg with 1 Tbs. water, for egg wash
	butter for greasing pans

dlp essay

In a large bowl, sift together flour, masa harina, baking powder and salt. Stir in melted butter. Gradually add 1/2 cup to 3/4 cup water, working it in with your hands to incorporate. The dough should be easy to handle and not sticky. Roll the dough into a ball, wrap it in plastic and chill for 30 minuets. Lightly flour your rolling pin and counter. Divide the dough in half so it will be easier to work with and roll it out into 1/8 inch thickness. Using a 4 inch biscuit cutter, cut into 10 circles of dough; repeat with the other half.

Spoon two heaping Tbs. of filling into the center of each pastry circle, leaving 1/2 inch border. Brush the edges with egg wash and fold the dough over in half to enclose the filling and form a semi-circle. Tightly seal the edges by crimping with the tines of a fork. Chill at least 30 minutes before baking.

Preheat oven to 375 degrees. Place the empanadas on a buttered baking sheet and brush the tops with additional egg wash. Using a knife, cut three small slits in the top of the empanadas for steam to escape. Bake for 30 minuets, until the pastry is golden brown.

Makes about 20 empanadas.

Cilantro Cream:

1 cup	sour cream
1/4 cup	finely chopped fresh cilantro leaves
1/2 cup	lime juice
	kosher or sea salt and fresh ground pepper

In a small mixing bowl, combine sour cream, cilantro and lime juice together. Mix thoroughly and season with salt and pepper. Serve with empanadas.

Hacienda

2408 S Hwy. 183 78744
Phone: (512) 389-3959
Daily 7am-2am
Breakfast all day
Credit Cards

"El Sabor de Texas," this friendly little café has combined our love of Mexican with our love of ribs. A little outside of town, this place has captured the feel of a real Mexican patio with lovely tables and nice traditional woven chairs. Our food was simple but delicious — a quick roadside meal with a lot of charm. After a brief conversation with the owner we learned that the adjacent building that reads "Herbivore" used to be their banquet facility until a drunk driver ran his car right inside through the cement blocks. The owner of the car was never charged and their business is suffering until they can rebuild. So if you're out that way please stop in and lend them your support. And tell us how the ribs are.

- Allison Walsh

Happy Taco

4606 Burleson Rd. # B 78744
Phone: (512) 447-2992
Mon-Fri 5:30am-2:30pm
Breakfast until close
Credit Cards

Happy Taco is open on weekdays for breakfast and lunch. The folks at Happy Taco have been in business for twenty-two years and have been in the same location for seventeen. The location is not glamorous and the décor is sparse at best. The food is typical Austin Tex-Mex and very tasty. They have an extensive taco offering as well as enchiladas and tender carne guisada. In case someone in your party would like a hamburger, they came highly recommended as well. If you're lucky, you might also receive a bit of friendly and nosy questions from the ladies who work there, but only if they don't know you. It's all in good fun.

- Shazza Calcote

dlp

Janitzio Restaurant

1422 Town Creek Dr. 78741
Phone: (512) 442-6275
Mon-Thu 7am-12pm
Fri-Sun 7am-3am
Breakfast all week 7am-11am
Credit Cards

There are so many good things to say about Janitzio, where does one start? The margaritas are strong. That's the quickest way to my heart. The next way is through food — and they hit me there, too. Seafood is the specialty of the house but their land food is also tasty. Or, have the surf and turf, Mar y Tierra, a spicy dish of grilled shrimp and chicken served with rice and French fries. They don't hold back here and that's admirable as well as delicious. One dish, which I did not eat (and didn't need to, thank you very much), was called The Viagra, a collection of 16 shrimp in various sauces grilled, boiled, etc. It's probably not the best thing to order The Viagra on a first date, although your intentions will be made crystal clear.

- Chris Nelson

"I have a ritual of visiting the Tex-Mex restaurant at the Econo Lodge called Los Jalisciences. We call it "the flower" due to the atomic-age architecture of the building, a circular dome with points of a crown sticking up. The best dish is the Jalisco plate, with cactus and marinated skirt steak, and their spicy avocado-based salsa. They also have seafood dishes like mojo de ajo — oysters on the half shell — and plenty of beer. Plus the prices are very low, so you can try everything on the menu."

- Jason Schell,
DJ, www.jasonschell.com

La Casuelita

6002 Burleson Rd. 78744
Phone: (512) 479-7911
Daily 7am-2am

What a delightful surprise here in deep Southeast Austin. She doesn't look like much: a simple wood building painted reddish brown that you'll miss if you blink. Six tables inside with a couple more just outside the front door. This place obviously caters to the brisk workweek lunch crowd, but my lunch companion and I strolled in mid-afternoon on Saturday. Except for a father and daughter at one table, the place was empty. We were seated promptly and given a delicious salsa to go with perfectly fresh chips. So far, so good. I ordered fajitas and my pal ordered the beef chile relleño. Food took a while but was it ever worth the wait: fresh and delicious and just the right spice to pep you up — not the spicy hot that sinks into your tongue all wet and creeping and lingering, but the quick-strike dry fire that burns pleasantly for a few seconds and then slips away without a peep. C'mon, you know what I mean: just enough fire to get your hungover Saturday afternoon hopping. Oh, and the portions were *huge* with all the fresh fajita fixings you could possibly desire. And … all entrees were between five and seven bucks. I suggest you go hunting for this hidden gem.

- *Stephen LeVay*

La Regiomontana

1928 E Riverside Dr. 78741
Phone: (512) 326-1888
Sun-Thu 8am-10pm
Fri-Sat 8am-11pm
Credit Cards

Located in what I call the *cul de mex* of Riverside, La Regiomontana shares some prime Mexi-real estate with hidden gems such as Janitzio and drive-thru primo, El Regio. All the seating is outside with rows of benches both covered and uncovered. With the oom-pah-heavy Tejano playing through the speakers, La Regiomontana could pass for a Munich beer garden if it weren't for the oversized shredded chicken tostadas and tacos al pastor. The third item on this menu, as brief as it is tasty, is the Regiomontana hamburger which many people seemed to be enjoying when I visited. So, add this place to list of hamburger-serving German beer garden-like Mexican food restaurants in the Austin area.

- *Chris Nelson*

dlp

La Tapatia

2506 Ben White Blvd. 78741
Phone: (512) 693-8843
Mon-Sat 6:30am-12am
Sun 7am-12pm
Breakfast all day
Cash only

Please see review on page 116

Other Locations: South

La Terazza

1605 E Oltorf 78741
Phone: (512) 444-0018
Mon-Fri 10:30am-11pm
Sat-Sun 7am-12pm
Mariachis Sat @ 8pm
Credit Cards

In the olden days of motel dining, you could count on finding a half-drunk, narcoleptic cook in the kitchen, a pit-bull named Geof on a stool and canned pineapple in every single Chinese dish on the menu. But now that Patti Reagan has put her clothes on and HBO is available in all the rooms, things have changed. Motel eatin' is now *faaaaaaaancy*! La Terazza proves that you can eat for the same price as your room and still come out cheap. And, it won't make you puke. *Oh contraire!* La Terazza sets the bar high for motel eateries. Straight-up, down-home and armed with a liquor license, La Terazza will ease your road warrior stomach with a little carne asada, grilled cactus, chicken enchiladas and the only dish guaranteed to shut those children up — chile con queso. So be brave on those American roads and fear not the scratch of dry-aged sheets, for the motel food you receive here shall put you into a warm, peaceful slumber.

- Chris Nelson

Marisco's Seafood Restaurant

1504 Town Creek Dr. 78741
Phone: (512) 462-9119
Sun-Thu 11am-10pm
Fri-Sat 11am-11pm
Credit Cards

Marisco's is a seafood lover's paradise. The restaurant is completely split into two octagons (perhaps one for the bar and more rowdy diners and one for families) separated by palm trees and an outdoor deck. The theme is Gilligan's island beach bar with every bit of nautical kitsch you can think of.   Red Lobster with Mexican overtones: menu offerings, translations, staff and patronage. The portions are enormous so they have kindly offered a half size for almost everything on the menu. We could fill a soup bowl with our side order of guacamole which was only a whoppin' $3.00! Everything was fresh and well spiced including the shrimp a la Diablo. Be prepared to be offered white rice and steamed vegetables with your dinner instead of refried beans. The pick of the night was the ceviche with thinly sliced peppers adding the perfect amount of zing.

- Allison Walsh

Porfirios Restaurant Dos

3100 S HW 183 78744
Phone: No listing
Hours of Operation: Random

Please see review on page 75

Other Locations: East

dlp essay

CRACKERS

by Juliana Hoffpauir

Approximately 1974. Then, it was only El Rancho. I was a baby in the highchair placed next to my lifetime compadre, Bradley. Our parents were friends. She had a brown curly afro and advanced human intelligence while I had straight blonde hair and chubby cheeks. Too young for Bob Armstrong and cheese enchiladas with verde sauce, our mothers handed us saltine crackers. Hand-to-mouth, hand-to-mouth, hand-to-mouth. We shoved crackers in our faces as fast as we could. Stale dough flakes flew everywhere. The flying crumbs stuck to our eyelashes and crept up our noses. At the end of the meal, our parents generously tipped the waiters to help ease their embarrassment with the crumbs that covered the floor underneath our table.

2004. Today it's Maudie's or Güero's. I go to Maudie's with my family and in front of me are always chips and salsa, a frozen margarita and usually cheese enchiladas with verde sauce. Some days are better than others when it comes to the control I have over the chips and salsa and margaritas, and I really shouldn't be ordering all those cheese enchiladas, but they're better than crackers. I meet my friends at Güero's for frozen margaritas. The Sunday afternoon before Memorial Day, I had four frozen mango margaritas with Bradley. And we both had a couple of cigarettes. Hand-to-mouth. Hand-to-mouth. Hand-to-mouth.

Taco Cabana

2507 E Riverside Dr. 78741
Phone: (512) 462-2236
Beer & Margaritas
Breakfast weekly until 11am
Weekends until 2pm
Credit Cards

See review on page 30

Other Locations: All over the damn place

Vallarta Jalisco Taqueria

1644 E Riverside Dr. 78741
Phone: (512) 444-9484
Mon-Thu 6:30am-12am
Fri-Sun 6:30am-4am
Breakfast until 12pm
Sometimes Mariachis
Credit Cards

Taquería Vallarta has many things going for it: 1) excellent prices — you can slip out sated for under six dollars. 2) a drive-thru window — there's no excuse for going to Taco Bell now. 3) horchata — on any given day 70% of the people eating will be drinking a tall glass of this sweetened rice milk. Translation: theirs is some of the best in town. 4) busy lunch crowd — it's no secret that this is a great place for a quick mid-afternoon refueling of tacos, gorditas, carnitas y más.

- Chris Nelson

Other Locations: Far South

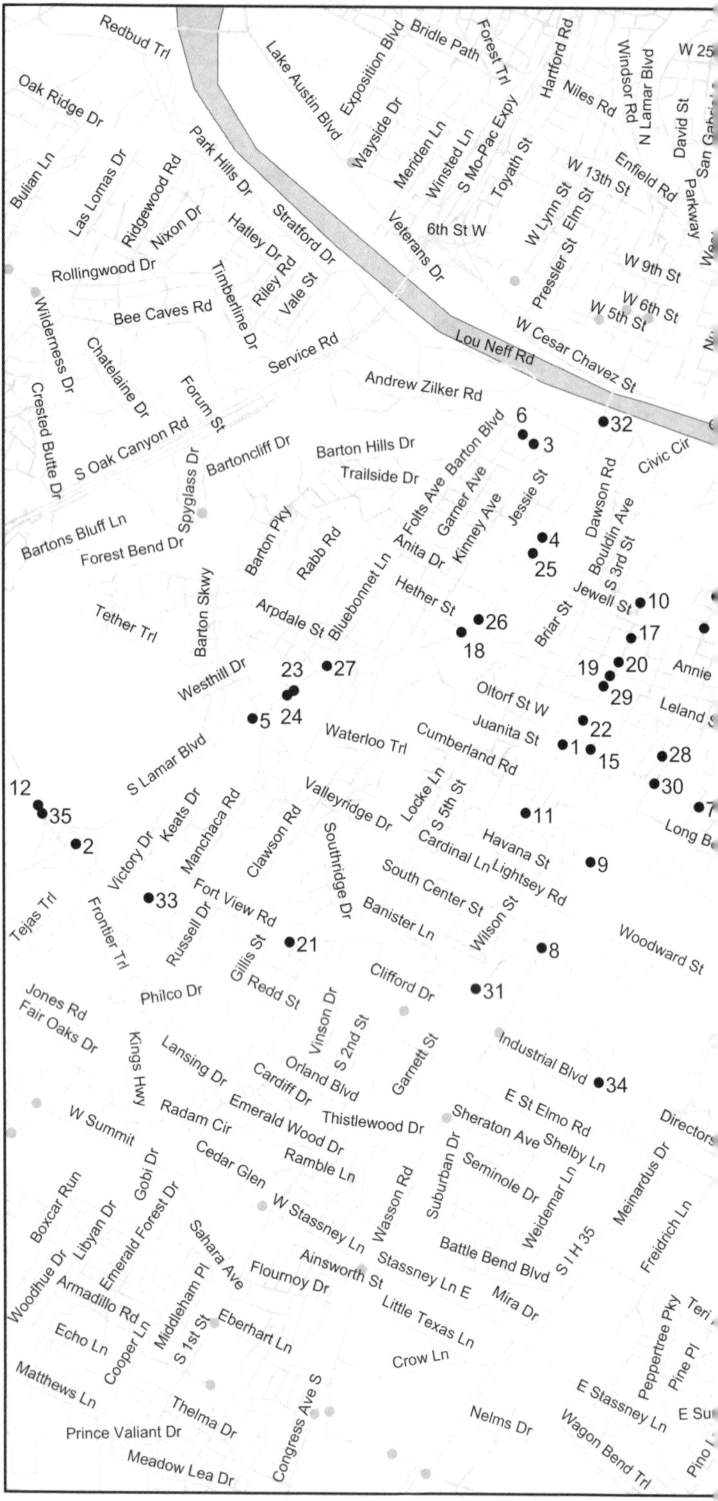
Redbud Trl
Oak Ridge Dr
Lake Austin Blvd
Exposition Blvd
Bridle Path
Forest Trl
Hartford Rd
Windsor Rd
N Lamar Blvd
David St
W 25
Niles Rd
Wayside Dr
Meriden Ln
Winsted Ln
S Mo-Pac Expy
Toyath St
Enfield Rd
Parkway
W 13th St
Bulian Ln
Las Lomas Dr
Ridgewood Rd
Park Hills Dr
Nixon Dr
Hatley Dr
Stratford Dr
Veterans Dr
6th St W
W Lynn St
Elm St
Pressler St
W 9th St
Rollingwood Dr
Riley Rd
Vale St
Timberline Dr
W 6th St
W 5th St
Bee Caves Rd
Wilderness Dr
Chatelaine Dr
Service Rd
Lou Neff Rd
W Cesar Chavez St
Andrew Zilker Rd
Crested Butte Dr
Forum St
S Oak Canyon Rd
Spyglass Dr
Bartoncliff Dr
Barton Hills Dr
Trailside Dr
Barton Blvd
Folts Ave
Garner Ave
Kinney Ave
Jessie St
6
3
32
Civic Cir
Dawson Rd
Bouldin Ave
S 3rd St
Bartons Bluff Ln
Forest Bend Dr
Barton Pky
Rabb Rd
Anita Dr
4
25
Tether Trl
Barton Skwy
Arpdale St
Bluebonnet Ln
Hether St
Jewell St
10
Briar St
17
26
18
Westhill Dr
23
27
24
5
19
20
29
Annie
Oltorf St W
Leland S
Juanita St
22
Waterloo Trl
Cumberland Rd
1
15
28
S Lamar Blvd
30
12
35
Valleyridge Dr
Locke Ln
S 5th St
11
7
Long B
2
Victory Dr
Keats Dr
Manchaca Rd
Clawson Rd
Southridge Dr
Cardinal Ln
Havana St
Lightsey Rd
9
Tejas Trl
Frontier Trl
33
Fort View Rd
Russell Dr
South Center St
Banister Ln
Wilson St
Woodward St
Gillis St
21
8
Clifford Dr
31
Jones Rd
Philco Dr
Redd St
Fair Oaks Dr
Vinson Dr
S 2nd St
Garnett St
Industrial Blvd
Kings Hwy
Lansing Dr
Orland Blvd
Cardiff Dr
34
Radam Cir
Emerald Wood Dr
Thistlewood Dr
E St Elmo Rd
Directors
W Summit
Sheraton Ave
Shelby Ln
Gobi Dr
Cedar Glen
Ramble Ln
Seminole Dr
Meinardus Dr
Boxcar Run
Emerald Forest Dr
W Stassney Ln
Wasson Rd
Suburban Dr
Weidemar Ln
Libyan Dr
Battle Bend Blvd
S I H 35
Friedrich Ln
Sahara Ave
Ainsworth St
Stassney Ln E
Woodhue Dr
Flournoy Dr
Mira Dr
Armadillo Rd
Middleham Pl
Little Texas Ln
Peppertree Pky
Teri
Echo Ln
Cooper Ln
S 1st St
Eberhart Ln
Crow Ln
Pine Pl
Matthews Ln
E Stassney Ln
E Su
Thelma Dr
Congress Ave S
Nelms Dr
Prince Valiant Dr
Wagon Bend Trl
Meadow Lea Dr
Pino

mexican food in austin

"**78704** It's not just a zip code, it's a way of life." This frequently seen bumper sticker elicits revile in some and pride in others. Nonetheless, it represents the fierce independence and community spirit found in the many of the neighborhoods "south of the river." It's here where you'll find the most vivid reminders of Austin's cosmic cowboy era and the old hippies who were there. Hip modernity mixes with the past on South Congress where hipsters, hippies, bikers, mommies and everyone else under the sun seem to get along just fine. The farther south you go, the more Mexican food you'll find along with liquor stores, new age centers and a strip club. The western part of this area is home to the natural playgrounds of Barton Springs, Zilker Park and the Greenbelt where you can hike, fly a kite or swim at a cool and unchanging 68 degrees. Down from there, South Lamar offers a long strip of independent stores, muffler repair shops and an unending array of diverse eating establishments.

1 Arandas #5
2 Azul Tequila
3 Baby Acapulco
4 Casa Garcia
5 Chango`s Taqueria
6 Chuy's
7 Curra's
8 El Flaco
9 El Gallo
10 El Mercado
11 El Nopalito
12 El Rey
13 El Sol Y La Luna
14 Güero's
15 Habanero
16 Jalisco's
17 Jovita's
18 La Feria
19 La Mexicana Bakery
20 La Reyna
21 La Tapatia
22 Little Mexixo
23 Maria's Taco Xpress
24 Matt's El Rancho
25 Maudie's Too
26 Mexico Lindo
27 Mr. Natural
28 Nueva Onda
29 Polvos
30 Rosie's Tamales
31 Serrano's
32 Taco Cabana
33 Taco Cabana
34 Taco Cabana
35 Trudy's South

Arandas Taqueria #5

2448 S 1st Street 78704
Phone: (512) 707-0887
Mon-Thu 7am-11pm
Fri-Sun 7am-1am
Daily breakfast 7am-11am
Credit Cards

Arandas #5 is fast becoming the hands-down favorite amongst enlightened, serious Tex-Mex aficionados. It is the holy grail of quick, cheap eats in South Austin and where to go when you're famished and only have a few bucks. Slowly becoming its own scene, be prepared to wait for a table on the weekends, making to go orders a viable and easy option. The tacos al pastor, the breakfast tacos and the tostadas are all fantastic and complimented by their super fresh salsa and corn tortillas.

- Allison Walsh

INDSIDERS TIP: The weekend menudo though smelling of a rodeo, will pile drive through any hangover—guaranteed.

Other Locations: East, Far South, North, Far North

Azul Tequila

4211 S Lamar Blvd., Suite A2 78704
Phone: (512) 416-9667
Sun-Thu 10am-10pm
Fri-Sat 10am-12pm
Breakfast all day – Sat & Sun until 2pm
Music Fridays & Thursdays Eve Mariachi
Credit Cards

It can be strange going to a Mexican food restaurant in a strip shopping center. You can imagine my surprise when I rolled up to Azul Tequila and found it next to an Erotic Pet Shop. I thought to myself, "What kind of strip shopping center puts a gourmet Mexican food restaurant and an Erotic Pet Shop together? Who is the mad genius behind this?" Upon further inspection I realized that it was in fact an Exotic Pet Store and not erotic at all. Why am I talking more about the Pet Store than the restau-

mexican food in austin

rant? It's because Azul Tequila is one of the best kept secrets in town and I want to keep it that way. Yes — gourmet food at everyday prices. Don't tell anybody!

- Chris Nelson

BABY ACAPULCO RESTAURANT Y CANTINA

1628 Barton Springs Road 78704
Phone: (512) 474-8774
Fax: (512) 476-5299
Mon-Thu 11am-12am
Fri-Sat 11am-1am
Sun 11am-11pm
Breakfast all day
Credit Cards

Need to get liquored up cheaply and quickly? Baby A's is the place, but don't expect the top shelf, baby. Their seemingly infinite margarita and cocktail concoctions come in as many bright colors as Joseph's coat and, if you're not careful, they too will come back up in Technicolor. While not exactly tasty, Baby A's cocktails are strong and cheap. In fact, some of the drinks have a limit of two. So if you need to catch a buzz before going out or simply need to catch up to friends who have been out, stop by Baby A's and throw back two purple margaritas to put you on your way.

- Chris Nelson

This is the kind of Happy Hour you would sneak into when you were in your teens and thought you had really arrived socially. It is full of college coeds on a budget who want to get their drink on early and dance the night away. A brilliant plan. At first I was little nervous about all of the "rules" concerning their libations, feeling as if I should certainly be allowed to show off my hollow leg. Alas, no. I was giggling like a teenager after one half of one of those purple things and had to retreat dumbfounded. The toasting, the laughter, and the overall din increases at a fast clip at this joint so be careful to get out before you're sitting in some student's lap making plans to meet at Element.

- Allison Walsh

Other Locations: Southeast, North, Far North

Casa Garcia Mexican Restaurant

1000 S Lamar Boulevard 78704
Phone: (512) 851-8684
Sun 7:30am-3pm
Mon 11am-9pm
Tue-Sat 7:30am-9pm
Fri 7:30am-10pm
Breakfast all day
Mariachis on Fridays
Credit Cards

Do you ever wonder what the first Hard Rock Café was like? Or the first Pappadeaux's? Or the first Cracker Barrel? Something tells me they were pretty much like the rest of them. Casa Garcia seems like it was created to be a franchise, even though they are currently only a franchise of two. Everything is glossy, from the bright yellow sign out front to the professional graphic design on the menus. This is a chain waiting and wanting to happen. As far as the food goes, the kids are doing alright. All the basic dishes are represented as well as good old-fashioned USA food like cheeseburgers and French fries. The patio has a nice eastward facing view of Lamar and the main room is stucco and expansive. I do have to say that the house mariachi band is bad ass. These boys cranked out one Mexi-barn burner after another and gave much respect to Guadalajara. Pretty soon when there's a Casa Garcia in Pyonyang, North Korea, you might say that you once ate at the original in Austin, Texas. It's a good story anyway.

- Chris Nelson

Other Locations: Far South

Chango's Taqueria

3005 S. Lamar Boulevard
Phone: (512) 416-1500
Daily 11am-10pm
Credit Cards

Please see review on page 4

Other Locations: Central

Chuy's Restaurant

1728 Barton Springs Rd. 78704
Phone: (512) 474-4452
Sun-Thu 11am-10:30pm
Fri-Sat 11am-11:30pm
Credit Cards

Wacky place with lots of Elvis kitsch and some waitresses with nice cans. Other than than that, Chuy's is pretty much standard Tex-Mex. The queso is pretty good, and the beer is cold. I'd recommend the enchiladas supreme. Decent food, good bar, nice cans.

- *Clay Langdon*

Chuy's is always busy. Even at 1:30 on a rather mundane and overcast Tuesday afternoon there is a wait for a table, but you can always pass the time at the bar. After one deliciously hand-shaken margarita, fodder for review starts to become effortless. A table for two becomes available and we are led past a velvet Elvis into a room of mirrors and reflective hubcaps with a birthday party of typical and fabulously Austin folk in full swing. The table is a mixture of greasers, tattoo enthusiasts and yuppies. The birthday boy is holding a slightly suggestive Push-Up pop topped whipped cream as the staff serenades. This "atmosphere de fiesta" prompts a second rita and now it's time to get down to business. Our waitress arrives with the second round of drinks and suggests the tortilla soup with a side of Hatch green chile sauce to start. If this is the way the staff has it, then it's the only way to have it. The flavors and heat are perfect when this sauce is mixed in and it's definitely the only way I'll ever have it again! This is followed by the Tuesday special of Hatch chicken enchiladas. The enchiladas are topped with a creamy queso blanco sauce and served with green chile rice and refried beans. My friend ordered the Elvis Presley Memorial Combo (a little bit of everything) and it was fabulous as well. I really didn't want to like Chuy's, but dammit, this food is good!

- *Leanne Heavener*

Other Locations: Far North

Curra's Grill

614 E Oltorf Street 78704
Phone (512) 444-0012
Fax: (512) 444-2542
http://www.currasgrill.citysearch.com
Sun-Thu 7am-10pm
Fri-Sat 7am-11pm
Sun 9am-9pm
Breakfast all day
Credit Cards

Curra's is one of my favorite Mexican restaurants in the US. I recommend sitting outside – the colorful patio really feels like Mexico. The charming atmosphere and delicious margaritas (the fresh lime juice is never bitter) make the erratic service irrelevant. Besides, the food is well worth any confusion or attitude displayed by the wait staff. Though I'm sure everything is good, I always order the tacos al pastor or the cochinita pibil. Good enchiladas verdes, etc… are a dime a dozen in Austin, and I like to take advantage of rarely available, properly prepared interior Mexican food when I have the chance. The tacos al pastor are the real thing, not the tough, chopped meat that is marinated and cooked any old way that one is so frequently disappointed by. The pork at Curra's is slow cooked on a rotisserie, and the delicate flavor of the tender, shaved meat is complemented perfectly with warm pineapple and onion. Even if you are a fan of cilantro, I would tell them to go easy on it as a little goes a long way. The cochinita pibil is superb, not only more tender and flavorful than you will find at Fonda San Miguel, but infinitely more affordable. I highly recommend this restaurant.

- Fay Wallace

Curra's and Güero's are my top two choices for Mexican restaurants. Whenever Güero's is packed with a wait and people spilling out of the door, you can always rest assured that you will have a short wait at Curra's Grill — even on a Saturday night. The atmosphere is not as festive as Güero's, and it is never as hectic as Güero's open kitchen dining, but the food is very good and reasonably priced. Curra's offers cuisine from the Yucatan peninsula. This type of Mexican food offers more fruits of the sea unlike most Tex-Mex joints. Fresh chips and salsa are served upon request and go beautifully with their margari-

mexican food in austin

tas. The frozen margaritas served at Curra's are large and refreshing and have the perfect mixture of sweet and sour. They are very smooth and their alcoholic effects tend to sneak up on me. Dishes not to miss are the ceviche, tacos al pastor on red corn tortillas and the stuffed jalapeño appetizer smothered in a pecan cream sauce. If you like enchiladas, try their avocado sauce. It is a spicy and delicious addition to any enchilada filling.

Please note that Curra's is not known for its speedy service. I have gone in several times with a toddler in tow and have had waitresses that are clueless to the fact that small children have a holding time of about 30 minutes —10 minutes without some sort of food in front of them. Curra's offers open patio dining, but the seating is limited. You must get there early on a cool night and those who do, tend to camp out. There is plenty of seating inside but it is not as relaxing as the patio so the turnover is rather quick despite the slow service. Expect to spend about $30 including tip for entrees and margaritas for two but don't expect to get in and out too quickly.

- Stacey Stoddard

INSIDER'S TIP: For breakfast try the Oaxacan coffee and later in the day, order an avocado margarita.

Other Locations: North

photo by Derek Hatley

EL FLACO CAFÉ

3632 S Congress Avenue 78704
Phone: (512) 444-2767
Breakfast all day
Closed for dinner
Closed Sundays

Down a little ways on South Congress, in the St. Edward's University neighborhood, is a great little Mexican diner, El Flaco. Seeing as I was the only gringa, I was a little excited that the clientele matched the ethnicity of the restaurant. Definitely a good sign. Here's a question: whatever happened to serving chips hot and crispy? Well despair no longer, this place has 'em. And our waitress was definitely one of the nicest and most attentive around. She seemed genuinely excited to see us, and apologetically pointed to a sign explaining that their food might take a little longer because everything is freshly made. Musica to my ears. If you're a chili relleño fan, you're in luck. Actually, you're in luck for a thousand reasons, only one of which is their all day breakfast menu. Another good sign: no one in El Flaco is flaco.

- Allison Walsh

EL GALLO RESTAURANT

2910 S Congress Avenue 78704
Phone: (512) 444-2205
Fax: (512) 444-7857
Tue-Thu 11am-10pm
Fri-Sat 8:30am-11pm
Sun 8:30am-9pm
Breakfast Fri-Sun until 1pm
Music Thu-Sat Trio
Credit Cards

A throwback to the 1960's paradigm for Tex-Mex restaurants, El Gallo will remind you of your childhood haunt with its chile con carne on everything, bullfighters on the wall and mariachis belting out songs from Guadalajara. The overall tone of the restaurant is a family one — granddaughter being taught the register by mom while old cousins make sure you have everything you need. You can tell that many of the patrons have been coming there for years and have grown up with El Gallo as their favorite comfort food. As I took a bite of the complimentary praline at the end of my Mexican dinner, memories of my own neighborhood place in Ft. Worth came rushing back — and great memories at that.

- Chris Nelson

EL MERCADO RESTAURANT

1302 S 1st Street 78704
Phone: (512) 447-7445
Mon-Fri 10:30am-10pm
Sat 9am-11pm
Sun 9am-10pm
Breakfast all day – weekends until 3pm
Brunch Sat-Sun 9am-3pm
Credit Cards

Please see review on page 8

Other Locations: Central, North

EL NOPALITO CAFÉ

2809 S 1st Street 78704
Phone: (512) 326-2026
Tue-Sat 8am-3pm
Sun 8am-2pm
Closed Mondays
Breakfast all day
Credit Cards

The nopalitos at El Nopalito are good, damn good. Not being a big fan of the edible cactus slice, I am a convert. This cute Tex-Mex diner at the end of the Tex-Mex mile on South 1st Street is straight-up sabroso. Definitely sample at least one of the nopalito offerings. I suggest the nopafajitas or the rojos with guagillo sauce. They have an extensive breakfast menu, which by the way, is served all day with every kind breakfast taco you can think of. Sit at the bar, sip on a horchata or tamarindo and read the paper while your fellow Austinites trickle in to kill their hangover with the weekend menudo. Everything is pleasant at El Nopalito: the smiling waitresses, the low mariachi music, and the comfortable South Austin ambiance. It's even fun to say El Nooopuhhhleeeeeetoe. The cook even came over to make sure I was happy....hmmmm did he know what I was up to? Naaah, just being nice.

- Allison Walsh

dlp essay

A REGIONAL OVERVIEW OF THE CUISINES OF MEXICO

by Stephen Malina

Brief History of Mexican Food and its Origins. The richness of Mexican cuisine, or any cuisine for that matter, stems from the strong emphasis placed on the overall sensory experience of eating. As a social affair eating offers more than simply the company of family and friends, it enriches the spirit and brings happiness to the heart and to the whole when everything is in place, the taste, the smell, the presentation and of course, the company too. As a result, the entire process of cooking and eating together is a valued celebratory tradition in Mexican culture, not thought of as the simple and necessary process of sustaining yourself with food in order to survive, but rather as a necessary process of enriching and sustaining the mind, body, and spirit together in harmony to promote wellness. To understand Mexican food it is necessary to understand a little bit about the origins of the cuisine, after all, as they say, "cuisine is culture."

During the pre-Columbian period, the Mexican diet consisted mostly of native agriculture which was limited at the time. The women were forced to use what was available to them, and on the top of the list was corn, the staple product of Mexican agriculture, which, when mashed and boiled, could be made into tortillas, tamales or flour, which was then used for a variety of purposes. Thus, supplemented with native vegetables, meats, and a myriad of herbs, spices, and chiles the roots of Mexican cuisine were born. But it was in the colonial period when Mexican cuisine experienced a dramatic transformation as a direct result of the culinary influences of the Spanish conquistadores, influences including Indian spices, rice, wines, olives, beef, garlic, capers and a variety of different fruits. Mexican cuisine was born out of this confluence of cultures, Spanish, Indian, and the established indigenous Mexican culture meshed and something wholly different formed.

dlp essay

From this period forward it was the nuns of the famous convents of Puebla, Michoacan and Oaxaca who mastered the culinary techniques of this Mexican food. The most noteworthy creation was the spicy mole poblano sauce. The sauce was the product of experimentation, derived from adding non-traditional seasonings like cinnamon, chocolate, peanuts and sesame to the mulli (a traditional sauce composed of a variety of chiles). The sauce was then used in a dinner prepared by the nuns of the Convento de Santa Rosa de Puebla to welcome and celebrate the arrival of a new archbishop. It was this willingness to experiment combined with an exceptional improvisational ability in the kitchen that led to the culmination of Mexican food.

Today, each region throughout Mexico boasts traditional dishes and mole sauces native to their particular geographic area, all based on local variables including proximity to the ocean and the availability of indigenous herbs, spices, fruits and vegetables with which to work. Much the same as it was in the beginning; the differences in cuisine exist partly as a result of the rugged topography of the Mexican landscape. Thus, when we talk about regions it becomes less about states and more about the geographically-defined regions within Mexico. To understand the differences in the regional Mexican cuisine is an important part of understanding the culture and the food that proudly represents a large part of that culture. A look at some selected states within the many regions of Mexico will lend a better understanding to the varied culinary culture of the country.

This is by no means meant a comprehensive overview of all of the cuisines of Mexico; we have only just scratched the surface of a culture with a deep culinary history. One could devote years to the exploration of Mexico's culinary roots and the traditional cuisines of the country's regions. Food is an integral part of celebration in Mexico, and Mexican culture is a celebratory culture, so it is easy to see why food is a very strong part of the culture, something which people can gather around to celebrate each other, life, and the things that matter the most. The culinary traditions and customs of Mexico are fascinating and deserve continued interest, if not simply to visit a wonderful country and experience a different culture, something that

dlp essay

oftentimes helps put things into perspective.

Northern Mexico

Heavily influenced by the European ranching culture and the beef imported with it, the cuisine of northern Mexico favors grilled meats, frijoles charros and the use of milder chiles. The terrain of northern Mexico is characterized by arid to semi-arid desert and, as a result, is fine grazing land for cattle, sheep, and goats, all of which are used in the regional cuisine of northern Mexico, the region encompassing the states of Tamaulipas, Nuevo Leon, Coahuila, Sonora, and Chihuahua. Not surprisingly the culinary tradition that resulted from the ranching lifestyle was dominated by the men. Kitchens were typically on the range, and cooking was done outdoors with grilling as the method of choice for most dishes. The similarities in the cuisine throughout much of the region leave few distinguishing culinary factors with which to characterize each state, so a brief overview of the region is a more appropriate way to address the northern region of Mexico.

Sonora is probably the most well known state for its beef. Here one might expect to find dishes such as filet mignon in chipotle-tomatillo sauce, a sauce that utilizes milder chiles like chipotle and Anaheim in order to preserve the subtle flavors of the grilled meats. The same holds true throughout most of the region; in Nuevo Leon, local favorites include arrachera, a marinated flank stake prepared on the grill.

Tamaulipas style fajitas, better known as fajitas al sombrero, a fajita dish containing onion and bell pepper sautéed in bacon fat and then tossed with the steak, topped with cheese and served with tortillas and salsa is a delectable norteno favorite in Tamaulipas.
But while the northern states are well known for their beef, they are equally as renowned for the dairy industry which is a byproduct of the ranching culture. Local cheese-making in Chihuahua is among the best in Mexico where queso fundido, a cheese fondue seasoned with chiles, chorizo, and mushrooms is a common local dish. Also known for their sweet jams and dried chiles, Chihuahua is one of the largest cultivators of fruits

continued on page 147

mexican food in austin

El Rey Mexican Restaurant

4109 S Capital of Tx Highway, Suite 100 78704
Phone: (512) 443-1911
Mon-Thu 11am-9:30pm
Fri 11am-10:30pm
Sat 9am-10:30pm
Sun 9am-9:30pm
Breakfast until 2pm
Music Evenings with Guitarists
Brunch – separate breakfast menu on the weekends
Credit Cards

Right out of the starting gate the host tried some of his ill-conceived standup routine. We were, at once, poised to be hateful; tongues sharpened, wits honed, and it just didn't happen. We all kinda enjoyed our Sonoran-style meals. Our sardonic wishful thinking fell away as we swapped forkfuls of pork stew, authentic style beef tacos, and Portobello spinach quesadillas. The only really big no-no was that the table flyer named their salsa an award-winning "best hottest." This seemed to be a blatant lie until I read this happened in Tucson. So when in doubt, assume the place is going to suck and then sit back and wait to be wrong. It's like trying to hiccup on the spot. Impossible. They have also caught on to the low-carb mania if anyone is interested.

- Allison Walsh

El Sol y La Luna

1224 S Congress Avenue 78704
Phone: (512) 444-7770
Fax: (512) 444-4554
www.elsolylaluna.citysearch.com
Sun-Tue 7am-3pm
Wed-Sat 7am-10pm
Breakfast all day
Music Thu-Sat
Credit Cards

Some years ago, a harmonica player broke up with me over breakfast at El Sol y La Luna at the little two top just inside the front door. He needed more personal space, as I recall. It was one of those moments when I would normally drop my fork, push my plate away and cross my arms in front of my chest. And while I do remember considering that very move, I had barely touched my

dlp

omlette del Eclipse. I was torn — could I still eat while getting dumped? It is my favorite omelette in town. An omelette so full of jack cheese, spinach, tomatoes, onions and mushrooms; one so good that I could never push it away, no matter the current emotional turmoil. I was determined to combine breakfast with a breakup, and thus enjoyed every bite, let him pay and that was that. I return often for weekday Caldo del Sol, Pozole on the weekends, wonderful salads (the beet and jicama a personal fave), enchiladas, smoked salmon, gorditas, breakfast tacos, tres leches, all-day breakfast entrees, live music, the covered patio, fresh sangria and lemonade and roomy booths to spread out the Sunday funnies. Perched at the entrance to the Austin Motel, this spot is the long-standing lass of 78704.

- Gracie Salem

GÜERO'S TACO BAR

1412 S Congress Avenue 78704
Phone: (512) 447-7688
Fax: (512) 447-6255
Mon-Fri 11am-11pm
Sat-Sun 8am-11pm
Music 1st Thurs
Fri & Sat 6:30pm-9:30pm;
Sun 3pm-6pm
Credit Cards

1. Güero's is a Tex-Mex institution in South Austin.
2. It is the definitive place to take people from out of town.
3. You will always run into someone you know or someone you recognize here.

Situated in a huge old feed store, the ambiance is old Austin charm with its exposed brick walls and wood floors. Everybody can find something they like at Güero's though people like to complain that it's too commercial and, perhaps, not as authentic as they'd like. But hell, Güero's means "whitey". Someone will always complain, but the nice thing about Austin is that we all get along. Everyone is welcome which makes the people watching here perfect. You never know what kind of person is going to come traipsing through the doors for their legendary tortilla soup or a "Don" margarita on the rocks made by my man Greg who has taken care of me for

mexican food in austin

more than ten years. So swing by and sit at the bar and soak up the Austin energy. By the way, the homemade corn tortillas are heavenly.

- Allison Walsh

Güero's is the most hotly debated Mexican restaurant in town. Some people hate it and others go nowhere else. The fact that people are passionate about it is an achievement in itself. So complex is the alchemy of Güero's that I will give my own two-sided debate.

Pros: 1. Hot women. Güero's is one of maybe two* Mexican food restaurants that is consistently frequented by babe-a-licious ladies. I could stop here. 2. Awesome margaritas. From well to top-shelf, frozen to rocks, it's all tasty and strong. The bartenders do an amazing job and take great pride in their craft. 3. It's loud. When the margaritas flow and you've got a fun group of friends together, there's definitely a great energy going around. 4. South Congress. There's always something to do when you finish eating. Also good for getting a little nourishment and a little loose before going to the Continental Club. 5. Tortilla soup, shrimp fajitas, and tacos al pastor — my favorite dishes there.

Cons: 1. Cheese-dick overload. It's not often, but sometimes the cheese-dick quotient is a little high. 2. Getting a table. If you just want to run in for a quick bite, Güero's is not the place. 3. The food is heavy. It's heavy not in a Tex-Mex way but some other uniquely Guerian way. Many of the plates are good going down but feel like a sack of buckshot once settled in your stomach. 4. Always the same. Not a whole lot changes at Güero's and its predictability can be positive or negative—just depends how you choose to look at it.

I like Güero's. I like drinking there. I like the people watching. I like that after four margaritas, screaming into some poor girl's ear seems like the best way to get her number. I like that often, it is. Such is the magic of Güero's, take it or leave it.

*Trudy's Texas Star is the other place. Whether it is a true Mexican food restaurant is debatable, the multitude of nubile beauties is not.

- Chris Nelson

dlp

HABANERO MEXICAN CAFÉ

501 W Oltorf Street 78704
Phone: (512) 416-0443
Tue- Sat 7am-5pm
Sun-Mon 7am-3pm
Breakfast all day
Credit Cards

Lent specials. That's what I had on my last visit. Habanero's food specials change according to the Christian religious calendar and this can be comforting to those who follow it as well. Even if you don't celebrate Palm Sunday (that means you, Dalai Lama), you can still enjoy Habanero's special horchata on Saturdays and Sundays and their specialty grilled items every day of the week. The chicken tacos are outstanding, but sadly there's no beer or tequila to wash it down. Don't fret, you can take your South Austin communion of Lone Star and popcorn a block away at the G&S Lounge and get in a game of foosball while you're at it.

- Chris Nelson

JALISCO RESTAURANT AND BAR

414 Barton Springs Road 78704
Phone: (512) 476-4838

CLOSED

Smack dab in the middle of town, next door to popular Hooter's is this chain restaurant. It's an enormous place that seems to do well with large lunch office parties. It is immense: the second floor balcony is a huge bar complete with several TVs and lots of video games. The décor is Mexican hacienda with orange and purple painted adobe. That is all I want to say. Well, except that Hooter's has great wings.

- Allison Walsh

mexican food in austin

JOVITA'S

1619 S 1st Street 78704
Phone: (512) 447-7825
Closed Mondays
Tue-Fri 10:30am-2pm & 5pm-10pm
Sat-Sun 5pm-10pm
Music as scheduled
Credit Cards

This is a bittersweet review to write. Jovita's is one of those places where I just feel at home. I've seen more Don Walser and Gourds shows there than I can remember and the beer is as cold as the environment is warm. The food — and it pains me write anything negative about the place — is another story. It's just not that good. I remember one occasion when my date dug her fork into her chicken taco salad and attached to the end of her fork was an entire chicken skin. Needless to say forks immediately hit the table as we dropped them in unison. Other experiences with enchiladas and tacos have been average at best. Now, as a music venue Jovita's is as fantastic as its food is bad. And when Austin's best live band, The Gourds, declare it their favorite place to play in town — well then you realize there is something to the place. There are few better intimate settings for live music than Jovita's. While it does get tricky to navigate to the bathrooms and bars when it gets crowded, you always feel at home when the music begins. Go to Jovita's to see some local music and drink a few beers, just make sure you eat before the show.

- *Chad Hamilton*

south

"After skateboarding and all sweaty with my best friend Johnny Walker, I'll hit Arandas #5 'cause I can eat super cheap for $3 with tip. I usually get the tostada al pastor. I go to Guero's with my sweet lady mainly for margaritas because they are not too sweet. I get frozen with salt and the tacos al pastor. Curra's food is excellent and I used to be a fan. Sometimes I'd go three times a day when there was a nice friendly older staff, but all of a sudden the waitstaff became passive, inattentive, pierced and tattooed with too much attitude. And, unfortunately, at Maria's Tacos X-press, it's too hard to park and the lines are too long."

- *Mandon Maloney*
Musician, Lil' Cap'n Travis, Adam Bork Slide Show

dlp

"I'm a sucker for the breakfast tacos from Porfirio's on Holly Street. Perfect. As far as salsa goes, it's the hot green sauce that they keep under the counter at Maudie's. You have to ask for it."

*- Julie Speed,
Artist*

LA FERIA RESTAURANT

2010 S Lamar Boulevard 78704
Phone: (512) 326-8301
Fax: (512) 326-9456
http://www.laferiaaustin.com
Sun 9am-10pm
Mon-Wed 11am-10pm
Thu-Fri 11am-11pm
Sat 9am-11pm
Breakfast all day – weekends until 11am
Music Mariachi on Thursdays 7pm until close
Credit Cards

Viva el patio! In a town where residents can spend damn near the entire year dining outside, there's a serious dearth of al fresco options. In fact, if Austin is the self-proclaimed-live-music capital of the world, then I say it should be the one-place-where-every-restaurant-should-have-a-patio-but-it-doesn't capital of the world. But La Feria is bucking this trend with a charming, spacious patio that's lit in that kind of industrial-Mexican-cool kind of way. As for the food — my dish was fine standard combo plate — and my date's was quite good — shrimp, cheese something. But the real reason to come here is for the Carta Blanca (properly served with Mexican authenticity of an ice cold, salted mug and lime) and the traditional yet post-modernist zocalo feel of the patio. So get off your butt and go eat outside! By the way, the patio would be a great space to rent out for a party. I know of a good band.

- Jeff Fraley

LA MEXICANA BAKERY

1924 S 1st St. 78704
Phone: (512) 443-6369
Daily 4am-8:30pm
Breakfast all day
Credit Cards

mexican food in austin

You want 24-hour Mexican cookies and tacos? You got it! La Mexicana Bakery never closes, but they don't need a round, bald, Yankee to advertise it. They rely on hungry folks leaving the bars and coming home down South 1st to see that the lights are on and tacos are cooking. The food comes in standard flavors, but the baked goods—whoa, you need a separate guide just for that. Everything under the sun is available from their expansive cases. And when they start baking late night, get ready to get your bread on because nobody can resist those sweet, sweet smells. You might never need quincinera cookies at 3am, but if you ever did…

- Chris Nelson

LA REYNA MEXICAN RESTAURANT

1816 S 1st Street 78704
Phone: (512) 447-1280
Fax: (512) 447-1536
http://lareyna.citysearch.com
Mon-Thu 7am-10pm
Fri-Sat 7am-11pm
Sun 8am-10pm
Breakfast until 2pm
Credit Cards

Upon entering La Reyna, I had flashbacks from my youth in North Texas and the wonderful Tex-Mex memories of that time. From the red pleather booths to the butter served with the chips, La Reyna preserves the tradition of Tex-Mex and serves it up proud. Situated next to Polvos, La Mexicana, Jovitas and El Mercado, possibly one of the highest concentrations of quality Mexican food in Austin, La Reyna serves its own signature food which complements the diversity in this holy strip of culinary delight. I have to say that the beef gorditas taste smoky and rich. The frozen margarita there defies gravity. It's soft, almost creamy, and is the way frozen alcohol should taste. La Reyna is not just some place before you get to Polvos (and if Polvos hadn't have recovered their liquor license, *they* would have been the place just past La Reyna).

- Chris Nelson

dlp

LA TAPATIA

1333 W Ben White Boulevard 78704
Phone: (512) 693-8843
Mon-Sat 6:30am-12am
Sun 7am-12am
Breakfast all day
Credit Cards

Oh the justice of three breakfast tacos paired with kick-your-butt salsa for only $1.99. But get there before 11:00 AM or the tacos become $1.35 each ... sorry. The most expensive plate they've got going is their T-bone for $6.75. And even though the interior makes you think you're at Whataburger, still feel free to order a beer or margarita. La Tapatia has all the usual suspects — made to order and unbelievably good. Don't worry about your inability to speak Spanish for they have kindly translated their menu (in green ink). This is a great place to take a huge appetite for a quick stop. If only this chain was as ubiquitous as 7-Eleven or Starbucks.

- Allison Walsh

Other Locations: Southeast

LITTLE MEXICO

2304 S 1st Street 78704
Phone: (512) 462-2188
Mon-Sat 7am-10pm
Sun 7am-9pm
Breakfast until 3pm
Music Mariachi
Thursdays 7pm-9pm
Fridays 7:30pm-9:30pm
Credit Cards

I dated a girl one time who loved Little Mexico. She introduced me to the creamy cheese enchiladas like a naïve country boy being introduced to city drugs. There was surprise at first. Then, abuse. Next, respect. And finally, moderation. The power of the enchilada must not be underestimated. Little Mexico's red, white and green color scheme mirrors those of the Mexican flag and runs throughout the interior. This strategy works only because it's Little Mexico. If it were called Little Sweden, I don't think it would work as well. It has grown steadily since 1963 from one small house to two houses and a deck

Mexican food in austin

with a busy atmosphere. The customers come from all ethnicities and walks of life, which is a good indicator that Little Mexico pleases the most demanding palettes. The chips and salsa are spicier than most while the beer tastes colder in Little Mexico.

- Chris Nelson

Maria's Taco Xpress

2529 S Lamar Boulevard 78704
Phone: (512) 444-0261
Mon 7am-3pm
Tue-Fri 7am-9pm
Sat 8am-9pm
Sun 9am-2pm
Breakfast all day
Music Tue-Sat 7pm-9pm
Sun 10am-2pm
Cash only

Longtime cornerstone of South Austin, Maria's is not just a taco store, it's a way of life. Over the years Maria's has grown to include an outdoor patio with a stage where musicians perform on special occasions. As with many other places in "'04" like Threadgill's, Horseshoe Lounge, and Saxon Pub, you'll find old hippies waxing poetic about the old Armadillo and the time they had sex with Blaze Foley where the WalMart now stands. Luckily, Maria's clientele includes the whole spectrum of Austin residents who flock to this place for affordable, well-proportioned and delicious tacos. Out-of-towners will get a wonderful dose of the city on Saturday and Sunday mornings when the crowds show up to cure their hangovers with greasy breakfast tacos piled high with Maria's special lovin'.

- Chris Nelson

Thousands of research efforts have tried to find a cure for hangovers but the only real cure I've found is Taco Express. The worst part is everyone in Austin knows this as well, and battling long lines from 9:30 a.m. to 1:00 p.m. on the weekends is really hell. My personal favorite, and their specialty is the Migas Taco (or try the migas plate). Scrambled eggs, cheese, potatoes, onions, chips and peppers all crammed in a taco—what genius stoner invented this one!! I also highly recommend the chorizo, egg and cheese taco—yum.

If you have just moved to Austin and want to catch glimpse of rock and roll in person, get to Taco Express early and camp out at an indoor table. This eatery has a line out to the door waiting for tacos and spotting rock royalty is commonplace. If you want to come for dinner, they also have an outdoor dining area with live music, and a new liquor license. The salsa here is epic and the crispy tacos are some of my favorite in town. Also, try the queso, but the pieces de resistance are the soft tacos—these tacos rock. Maria works hard for the restaurant and her staff has been their from the get-go, showing that they believe in the place and make an excellent product.

Taco Express is a great place to cure your hangover, take a first casual date or hang out after a day at the lake or at Barton Springs. This establishment needs support as Maria has fought to keep South Austin unique, despite development efforts of mundane condominiums. Everything on the menu is great, but you must try the tacos and keep Austin weird!

- Catherine Bower

Matt's El Rancho

2613 S Lamar Blvd 78704
Phone: (512) 462-9333
Sun-Thu 10am-10pm
Fri-Sat 10am-11pm
Closed Tuesdays
Breakfast all day
Music as scheduled
Credit Cards

I have assigned but a handful of restaurants a speed dial number on my cell phone, and Matt's El Rancho was the first. I resisted the enormous outpost on South Lamar for an upsettingly long time, until a friend shook her head in disappointment at my inexplicable abstinence. That's a shame, she told me. And right she was. In many ways, the restaurant is perfect: meaning it is exactly what it claims to be. It is a family place, begun by the Martinez family over fifty years ago and it is still run by those same hands today. As the story goes, Matt Martinez sold tamales from his father's cart on Congress when he was just six years old.

It is simple Tex-Mex fare, without silly food combinations or overt flare. The tone matches the space and the food

mexican food in austin

matches the tone and that's why I always feel comfortable when I go. Menu favorites include the Crenshaw steak, which is a fat ribeye topped with a spicy mixture of green bell peppers, tomatoes, onions and jalapeños and the smoked brisket tacos, which are stuffed with pecan-smoked meat and served with frijoles a la charra. Here the flautas are grilled, not fried, the margaritas are wonderful and generous and the chicken mole is out of this world. You can even get frog legs, grilled or fried, with a cheese chalupa on the side.

On Thanksgiving day 2003, the restaurant lost Matt Martinez, former prizefighter and founder of his famous El Rancho, whose black-and-white boxing pictures don the placemats. Despite the great loss, the restaurant feels the same on the inside, warm and bustling like always. As the sign says, this is the King of Mexican Food. And in case there's any question, the sign also lets us know that it's Always Good.

- Gracie Salem

As a child, I remember heading to the original Matt's #1 every week for our family dinner out. I made a game of counting the Firebirds on the way through the parking lot. Venturing into the door, Matt would greet us in his bow tie. Same booth, same waiter, same meal: the Regular dinner – for years. The restaurant grew into two restaurants: Matt's #1 and the new El Rancho. Then, the Four Seasons came along and turned the property into a parking lot. So, Matt's moved to a much larger location on Lamar. Super-popular with the locals, no one is lukewarm about Matt's: you either love it or hate it. I love it.

Matt's is 100% Tex-Mex comfort food that agrees with all tastes. I put it into my "Mexican cafeteria food" category. Perfect for children, out-of-towners and those who can't handle super-spicy stuff. Matt's covers all of the basics.

Even if you aren't a regular, you can order like one. Start with the Bob Armstrong dip, a combination of queso, guacamole, and ground beef, and a margarita. Next I recommend the Deluxe Dinner or the No. 1 Dinner, depending on your appetite. Finish with one of their yummy homemade pralines. Easy on those margaritas! One will leave you spinning.

Matt's also offers delicious lighter fare: Fish a la Mexicana is grilled catfish topped with Ranchero sauce, onions and peppers; or try the light chicken fajita plate with borracho beans and guacamole salad (a new personal favorite).

Super hungry? Gorge on the Cowboy Style Chicken Fried Steak smothered in chile con carne, onions and cheese. Yum yum.

More queso, please….

- Cile Montgomery

Maudie's Too

1212 S Lamar 78704
Phone: (512) 470-8088
www.maudies.com
Sun 9am-9:30pm
Mon-Thu 9am-10pm
Sat 9am-10:30pm
Breakfast until 4pm
Credit Cards

Please see review on page 151

Other Locations: Far South, West, Far North

Mexico Lindo

1816 S Lamar 78704
Phone: (512) 326-4395
Sun 7am-3pm
Mon-Thu 7am-9pm
Fri 7am-10pm
Music as scheduled
Credit Cards

Situated on a busy intersection of South Lamar, this full service restaurant and bar has a great outdoor deck from which to while away the afternoon and watch the cars go by. The interior decor has taken the no frills concept to new heights: white stucco walls, a bar with a few stools, a juke box and a TV. Most of the time it seems quiet enough to bring your homework or read a book. A great place to hide out on a lazy day and enjoy the fish soup with lots of lime or, even better, their killer cheese chile relleño.

- Allison Walsh

Mr. Natural

2414 S Lamar Boulevard 78704
Phone: (512) 916-9223
http://www.mrnatural-austin.com
Mon-Sat 9am-9pm
Music as scheduled
Credit Cards

I just can't understand how Mr. Natural passed under my radar during my eleven years of vegetarianism. Well, I knew of it ... tried to find it a couple of times, but just never had the calling. Maybe it was the name, or maybe it is so easy to eat vegetarian at other restaurants I didn't feel the need. Who knows...but I have the feeling now and I am going to make up for lost time. As I entered the very clean health food store/café I wasn't sure exactly what I was supposed to do...and where is the Mexican food? After a couple of seconds, the nicest lady asked me if this was my first time. She held my hand all the way down the buffet line carefully describing each dish and how to combine the savories into their very reasonable lunch special. I had a green salad with an avocado yogurt dressing, tofu a la mexicana, homemade tamales and tortas. Everything was fresh and spiced to perfection — not the normal tasteless crap meat lovers think that vegetarians live for. To round off an already incredible fare you have your choice of fresh juices sweetened with honey or rice horchata. All of their baked goods are made with either spelt or whole wheat and some without sugar and dairy. I was in heaven and even though I couldn't resist a raisin scone on my way out I could tell that Mr. Natural and I would be pals for a long time. Finally, a way to kill the craving, yet keep my jeans fastened and not rush home for a nap.

- Allison Walsh

Other Locations: East

dlp essay

¡¡MEXICAN SUICIDE!!

by Todd Erickson

2 oz.	*Don Julio Anejo*
Splash	*Dry vermouth*
1/2 oz.	*Grand Marnier*
3/4 oz.	*Sour mix*
Splash	*Lime juice*
Splash	*Olive juice*
Pinch	*Sugar*
2	*Olives for garnish*

If this doesn't perfectly suit your palette on the first go around, drink it anyway and make your own adjustments — or keep drinking until it doesn't matter.

Nueva Onda

2218 College Avenue 78704
Phone: (512) 447-5063
Sun 8am-3pm
Mon-Thu 7:30am-3pm
Fri 7:30am-9pm
Sat 8am-9pm
Breakfast until 3pm
Credit Cards

Nueva Onda is a small piece of Mexico down off South Congress. The brightly colored walls make the interior fresh and light. Outside, there is a covered patio as well as tables in a courtyard that features a small fountain. The vibe at Nueva Onda is cool and calm and the people who work there are extremely nice and welcoming. I couldn't help but think I was on the beach in Oaxaca when I lounged there one Sunday morning. Perhaps it was the lingering intoxication that usually accompanies a Sunday morning in Mexico or the straightforward huevos a la mexicana that I inhaled. After I washed down a handful of aspirin with a horchata, I was well on my way to transcending both my physical and mental states. The protocol is a casual, order-at-counter, brought-to-the-table service that works well in this locale. There really is something magical about the ambiance at Nueva Onda that sets it apart as one of Austin's best places to lazily munch al fresco.

- Chris Nelson

Polvos Mexicanos

2004 S 1st Street 78704
Phone: (512) 441-5446
Sun-Fri 7am-10pm
Sat 7am-11pm
Breakfast all day
Credit Cards

Polvo's is a favorite of many a South Austinite and with good reason. From the laid back patio to the plain goodness of the food, it exudes the ethos and taste of this eclectic part of town. Though it is Interior Mexican food, the seafood is the star of menu. The ceviche is always fresh, packed with cilantro and served in large portions. The fish a la plancha is pan-seared at 500 degrees, served on a bed of rice and awash in Polvo's secret sauce. I suspect that part of the secret involves a ton of garlic. Do not get their house margaritas unless you prefer rot-gut booze, otherwise you'll go home feeling like a frat boy slipped you a rohypnol. The service at Polvo's is awful but it always has been and that's part of the fun. Whether it's a long lunch of fajita enchiladas or a long dinner of camarrones, bring some good friends, good conversation and the desire to relax in one of Austin's best restaurants.

- Chris Nelson

NOTE: The service is getting much better. Thank you, Polvos.

ROSIE'S TAMALES

102 E Oltorf Street 78704
Phone: (512) 440-7727
Mon-Sat 11am-10pm
Closed Sundays
Credit Cards

According to a plaque in the lobby of Rosie's Tamale House, they have been in business since 1973. That just goes to show that they must be doing something right. Rosie's longevity is probably due to the excellent service they provide because it certainly isn't the food. The salsa was obviously made with canned tomatoes and my taste buds couldn't decipher between the tamales or the chile con carne gravy they were drowned in. My companion ordered Willie's Plate which consisted of a beef taco, a cheese enchilada, queso and a little bit of guacamole salad, all of which were completely devoid of flavor. On a more positive note, staff was friendly and the margarita was decent.

- Lucrecia Gutierrez

Other Locations: West

SERRANO'S CAFÉ Y CANTINA

321 West Ben White Boulevard 78704
Phone: (512) 447-3999
Mon-Thu 11am-9pm
Fri 11am-10pm
Sat 12am-9pm
Sun 12am-8pm

mexican food in austin

Breakfast all day
Credit Cards

Please see review on page 29

Other Locations: Central, North, Far North

TACO CABANA

211 S Lamar Blvd 78704
Phone: (512) 472-8098
Open 24hrs – 7 days
Credit Cards

2117 W. Ben White Boulevard 78704
Phone: (512) 462-2242
Open 24hrs – 7 days
Credit Cards

711 E Ben White Blvd 78704
Phone: (512) 462-0714
Sun-Thu 6am-11pm
Fri-Sat 6am-12am
Drive-thru only otherwise
Credit Cards

Please see review on page 30

Other Locations: All over the damn place

TRUDY'S SOUTH

4141 S Capital of Tx Highway 78704
Phone: (512) 326-9899
Fax: (512) 326-5695
www.trudys.com
Sun-Thu 11am-12am
Fri-Sat 11am-2am
Bar open daily until 2am
Breakfast all day – weekends until 3pm (Brunch)
Credit Cards

Please see review on page 33

Other Locations: Central, Far North

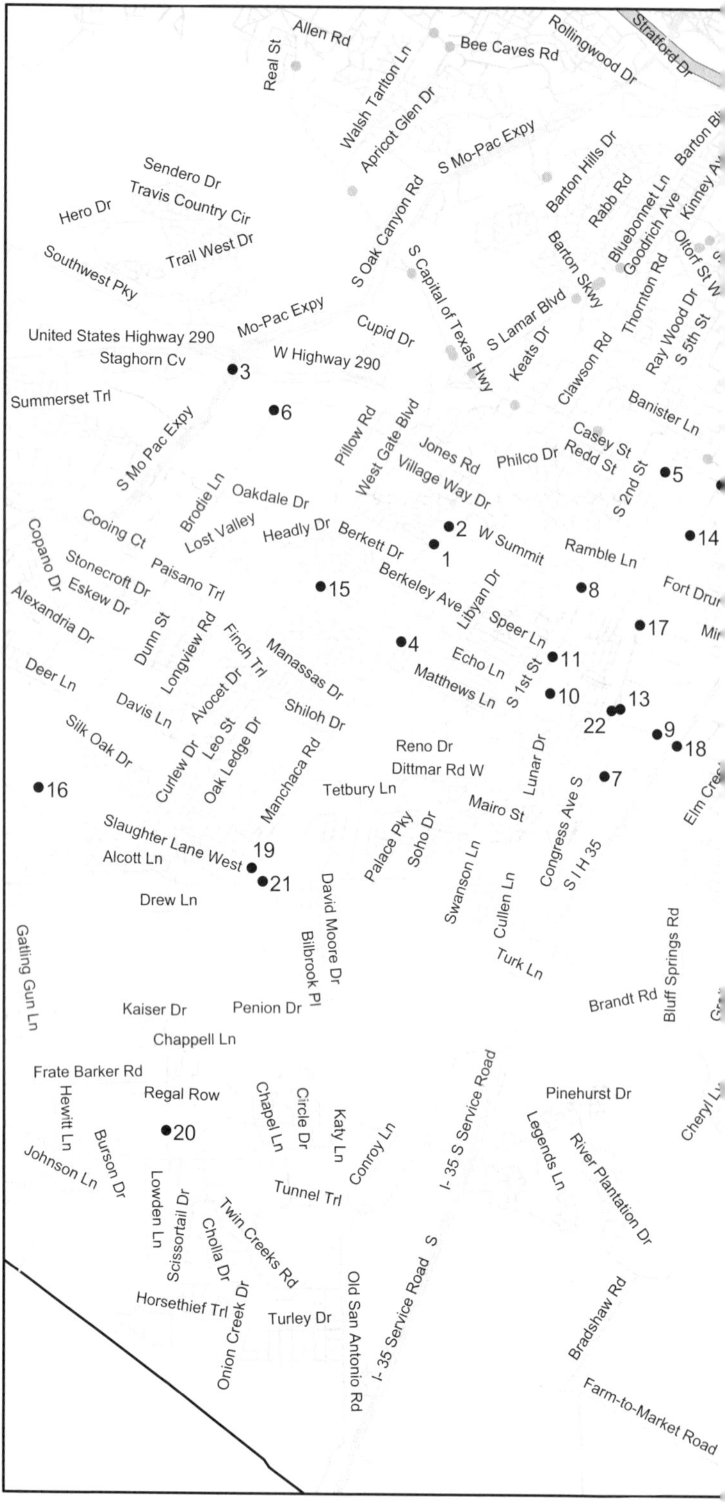
Allen Rd
Real St
Bee Caves Rd
Rollingwood Dr
Stratford Dr
Walsh Tarlton Ln
Apricot Glen Dr
S Mo-Pac Expy
Barton Hills Dr
Barton Bl
Sendero Dr
Travis Country Cir
Hero Dr
Trail West Dr
Southwest Pky
S Oak Canyon Rd
S Capital of Texas Hwy
Rabb Rd
Bluebonnet Ln
Goodrich Ave
Kinney Av
Oltorf St W
Barton Skwy
Thornton Rd
S Lamar Blvd
Keats Dr
Ray Wood Dr
S 5th St
Clawson Rd
Mo-Pac Expy
Cupid Dr
United States Highway 290
Staghorn Cv
W Highway 290
3
Summerset Trl
6
S Mo Pac Expy
Pillow Rd
West Gate Blvd
Jones Rd
Philco Dr
Banister Ln
Casey St
Redd St
S 2nd St
5
Village Way Dr
Brodie Ln
Oakdale Dr
Lost Valley
Headly Dr
Berkett Dr
2
1
W Summit
Ramble Ln
14
Cooing Ct
Copano Dr
Stonecroft Dr
Eskew Dr
Paisano Trl
15
Berkeley Ave
Libyan Dr
8
Fort Drum
Speer Ln
17
Alexandria Dr
Dunn St
Longview Rd
Finch Trl
Manassas Dr
4
Echo Ln
11
Deer Ln
Davis Ln
Avocet Dr
Matthews Ln
S 1st St
10
13
22
Shiloh Dr
Silk Oak Dr
Leo St
Oak Ledge Dr
Curlew Dr
Manchaca Rd
Reno Dr
Dittmar Rd W
Lunar Dr
9
18
7
16
Tetbury Ln
Mairo St
Congress Ave S
Elm Cree
Slaughter Lane West
19
Alcott Ln
21
Palace Pky
Soho Dr
Swanson Ln
S I H 35
Drew Ln
David Moore Dr
Cullen Ln
Bilbrook Pl
Gatling Gun Ln
Turk Ln
Bluff Springs Rd
Brandt Rd
Kaiser Dr
Penion Dr
Chappell Ln
Frate Barker Rd
Regal Row
Chapel Ln
Circle Dr
Katy Ln
I- 35 S Service Road
Pinehurst Dr
Cheryl Ln
Hewitt Ln
Burson Dr
20
Johnson Ln
Conroy Ln
Legends Ln
River Plantation Dr
Lowden Ln
Tunnel Trl
Scissortail Dr
Twin Creeks Rd
Cholla Dr
S
Horsethief Trl
Onion Creek Dr
Turley Dr
Old San Antonio Rd
I- 35 Service Road
Bradshaw Rd
Farm-to-Market Road

mexican food in austin

Far South Austin is a mix of leafy, hidden neighborhoods and typical suburban sprawl ranch-style houses, much like what you would find in other Sunbelt cities that experienced a building boom in the 80's. Big box shopping centers and older strip shopping malls dominate the landscape though a few independent outposts still survive and prosper.

1 Alonzo's III

2 Arandas #2

3 Baja Fresh

4 Casa Garcia

5 Casa Maria

6 Chipotle

7 Chumikal's

8 Dina's

9 El Regio

10 El Sol

11 Evita's Botanitas

12 Garibaldi's

13 La Fuentes

14 La Playa

15 La Posada

16 Maudie's Hacienda

17 San Juanita

18 Taco Cabana

19 Taco Cabana

20 Texican Café

21 Tres Amigos

22 Vallarta Jalisco

Alonzo's Tacos III

5700 Manchaca Rd. 78745
Phone: (512) 441-6838
Mon-Thu 5:30pm-2:30am
Fri 5:30pm-9pm
Sat 5:30pm-2:30am
Closed Sundays
Cash only

With three locations in Austin and growing, Alonzo's has maintained a down-home fast food allure. Choose from all of the requisite tacos or one of the gringo offerings such as a burger and fries. My bet is on the Frito pie. And if you're feeling a little melancholy, the lady at the window at this location called me sweetheart seventeen times.

- Allison Walsh

Other Locations: Southeast, North

Arandas Taqueria #2

2038 W Stassney Ln. 78745
Phone: (512) 448-4771
Mon-Sun 7am-12am
Breakfast all day
Credit Cards

Please see review on page 38, 98

Other Locations: East, South, North, Far North

Baja Fresh

5300 S MOPAC 78749
Phone: (512) 899-1009
Mon-Fri 11am-9:30pm
Fri & Sat 11am-10pm
Sun 11am-9pm
Credit Cards

Please see review on page 3

Other Locations: Central

Casa Garcia Mexican Restaurant

1901 W William Cannon Dr. Ste. 159 78745
Phone: (512) 441-9504
Tue-Thu 7am-9pm
Fri-Sat 7:30am-10pm
Sun 7:30am-3pm
Music Fri 7pm-10pm Mariachi
Breakfast all day
Credit Cards

Please see review on page 100

Other Locations: South

Casa Maria Restaurant and Bakery

4327 S 1st St. Ste. 102 78745
Phone: (512) 444-8861
Mon-Thu 7am-9pm
Fri 6am-10pm
Sat-Sun 6am-11pm
Breakfast all day
Bands Fri-Sat 11am-9pm Mariachi
Credit Cards

Casa Maria comes highly recommended by friends in the kitchen of one of Austin's finer eateries. Shockingly bright, lime and neon green walls with matching art and curios make for a festive "Is it time for a drink?" atmosphere. Happy Hour is from 4-7 — complete with a list of homemade concoctions including the Vampira, a mixture of Hornitos, grapefruit juice and sangria. Breakfast is served all day from an extremely friendly, all-smiles wait staff. It is packed at lunch with a wide range of Mexican expats, from vatos to abuelos to trabajadores and las familias. This place has obviously loyal customers who count on the large servings and the prompt service. They have now opened an adjoining bakery with all of your favorites and a nice selection of coffees.

- Allison Walsh

dlp

CHIPOTLE MEXICAN GRILL

5400 Brodie Ln. 78745
Phone: (512) 892-4222
Mon-Sun 11am-11pm
Credit Cards

Please see review on page 6

Other Locations: Central, West, Far North

CHUMIKAL'S

7211 S Circle Rd 78745
Phone: (512) 440-2179
Mon-Fri 5am- around 1:30pm
Closed weekends

The award for best hamburger basket served at a Mexican restaurant in Austin goes to Chumikal's. If your eating party unfortunately possesses a Mexican food hating Yankee or some feeble-minded child who refuses to eat tacos, then a trip to Chumikal's might defuse the situation and give everybody something they'll like. The lunch crowd is a nice mix of businessmen, cops, blue collar Joe's and prison work crews along with their handlers. In addition to great food, it's easy to leave on a full stomach for less than $5.

- Chris Nelson

photo by Derek Hatley

dlp essay

IN SEARCH OF...
CARNE GUISADA

by Jesse Proctor

First of all, let's start with the basics. The phrase carne guisada literally means beef stew. In Mexico, the type of stew you will be served depends on where you are. Near Mexico City, you might receive a carne guisada that is made of chunks of pork in either a red cascavel pepper sauce or a green sauce. In the north of Mexico, you get something more akin to a dark beef stew swimming in garlic and cumin. Carne guisada, as I know and love it here in Central Texas, is a stew made of cubes of tender beef, onions and bell peppers seasoned with cumin, garlic and jalapeño. Simple, yet elegant and able to please the most refined of tastes, here is a baseline recipe:

1/2 tbsp	*Shortening. Add a little bacon grease for more flavor.*
1 1/2 lb	*Cubed stew meat; the better the meat, the better the guisada. Rump roast works great!*
1	*Large onion, chopped*
1	*Large green bell pepper, chopped*
1	*Large can stewed tomatoes*
1	*Large fresh jalapeno, diced (and seeded if you're a wuss)*
2	*Chopped tomatoes*
1/2 tsp	*Ground cumin; best found at your local Mexi-market*
1	*Large clove garlic, chopped*

Take the shortening and bacon grease and melt over high heat. Add meat and brown on all sides. Add the onions and bell peppers. Sauté until vegetables are tender. Then add the rest of the ingredients and add

dlp essay

salt/pepper to taste. Reduce heat and simmer covered for an hour or longer (longer is always better). A crock pot works well. During this time make sure that the mixture doesn't get too dry. Add water as needed. If it is too wet, just add a little corn starch mixed in water to thicken it up.

So now that that's out of the way, let's look at some of my favorite carne guisada hangouts. First you have to give props to the old school. When I was a kid growing up here in Austin, Matt's El Rancho was Austin's main purveyor of Tex-Mex food. Before the Four Season's Hotel, there was Matt's El Rancho on 1st Street, now called E. Cesar Chavez St. They served up a good plate of carne guisada from the early 70's on through to the present. God bless Matt Martinez. Then the torch was passed to Güero's Taco Bar, first located on Oltorf, later moving to its present location in the old feed store on South Congress. Güero's has the most consistently solid carne guisada in town. You'll find that consistency in preparation is hard to find in some restaurants, but at Güero's you can always look forward to a great carne guisada taco. Make sure to order them on flour tortillas and add white cheese if you're into dairy. Also, in that same vein is Curra's. Located on Oltorf (in the original Güero's building) and on North Burnet, you can find a good carne guisada taco there as well. If you're really ready for a nap, then try the carne guisada enchiladas.

Now on to some of the smaller spots here in town. Mi Madres, situated east of I-35 on Manor Road, is a little spot that serves breakfast and lunch and boy, do they have their carne guisada down pat. A little on the spicy side, it's the best there is in town, hands down. Order the Ricky's Special on the breakfast menu and you'll get a plate of huevos rancheros with beans, potatoes and carne guisada. Now that's a way to start off the day. Also, don't miss their carne guisada enchiladas.....zzzzzz. Next, we're off to Nueva

dlp essay

Onda. Right off South Congress, south of Live Oak, you'll find Nueva Onda nestled back off the road with a nice outdoor patio. It's my new favorite spot for breakfast tacos and carne guisada. Mmmm goood. For you Northside people, try the carne guisada over at El Caribe on North Lamar, just south of 2222. It has a slight twist, they add a little red ancho chile to their guisada giving it a twang that works very well. Don't sleep on the rest of their menu either, the steak ranchero plate rocks! And finally, in a category of its own, I have to mention Porfirio's tacos. Often found in an Igloo cooler in the back of a small pick up truck in some downtown alley, their carne guisada y papas tacos are excellent. I fantasize sometimes about their origin, the smell coming from some delightful Mexican woman's kitchen with birds chirping in the windows and all. Oh the love. . .

"My girlfriend and I base our choice of Mexican restaurants solely on the margarita; favorites include the house margarita at Nuevo Leon, Curra's, Güero's and the Paloma at Vivo."

- *Chris St. Leger*
Painter, christopherstleger.com

DINA'S

730 W Stassney Ln. Ste. 130 78745
Phone: (512) 428-9425
Fax: (512) 416-3617
Mon-Thu & Sun 7am-9pm
Fri-Sat 7am-10pm
Breakfast Mon-Sun 7am-11am
Credit Cards

Formulas. Equations. Uniformity. Over a hundred Mexican meals and my brain is jelly. A weathered veteran of the houses of enchilada, I don't see the Mexican blankets anymore, nor do I hear the Tejano jukebox. I can hardly taste the lime in the margarita and chips are just paste in my mouth. I'm spent. Like a comatose patient being shaken after a mind-glazed slumber, I awoke at Dina's where I ate their brisket with Ranchero sauce. Suddenly there were choices, glorious choices. The space around me faded into whiteness with only myself and the brisket, staring back at each other and reflecting on each other's existence. "You are not a taco!" I yelled at the brisket. It looked back at me, smirking delicately, and forced its way into my mouth. No, this is not a taco.

- *Chris Nelson*

EL REGIO

700 E. William Cannon Dr. 78745
Phone: (512) 326-1888
Mon-Thurs 10am-10pm
Fri-Sat 10am-11pm
Closed Sundays
Credit Cards

Please see review on page 86

Other Locations: East, Southeast

mexican food in austin

El Sol Panaderia y Restaurant

500 W William Cannon Dr. Ste. 402 78745
Phone: (512) 443-7374
24 hours sometimes

All I can say is that 24-hour Mexican food is genius — well at least 24 hours Friday and Saturday, especially if there isn't a Taco Cabana in sight. What's interesting is that we went for lunch and it still felt like 3 am: the deafening drone of the refrigerators, unbussed tables, empty display cases and one disinterested waitress. They offer a complete menu with a lot of all day breakfast specials, so I'm wondering if you're a panadería if you can make a better pancake? Everything we ordered was perfectly good, but I can't help thinking how much more I would have appreciated El Sol if it had been the middle of the night.

- Allison Walsh

Evita's Botanitas Mexican Restaurant

6400 S 1st St. 78745
Phone: (512) 441-2424
Fax: (512) 441-3669
Mon, Wed & Thu 9am-9:30pm
Closed on Tuesdays
Sat 9:30am-10pm
Sun 9:30am-8:30pm
Breakfast all week until 11am
Credit Cards

This restaurant is one of those rare jewels that you hardly want to expose. It saddens me to write this review knowing that throngs of people might discover what is truly one of my favorites. Hopefully, its extreme south Austin location will deter at least some. Evita's has won all sorts of awards for its various hot sauces presented on its famous salsa wheel. Six mixtures in all with a hot basket of chips sitting on a pedestal — ahhh, utopia. The first thing you might notice is their use of the pepper system — usually a completely invalid method of gauging spiciness until Evita's. What you ask for is what you get — what you can handle is up to you, not to your know-it-all server summing you up by your milky white skin. Very spicy is, get this, very spicy. And, EVERYTHING is out of this world. Order the especial botanitas platter and a margarita to get started. If you're not afraid, try the chipotle "Extra Hot Rico, Rico" enchiladas.

- Allison Walsh

GARIBALDI'S

4201 S Congress Ave. 78745
Cross street: Industrial Boulevard
Phone: (512) 326-9788
Mon-Thu 8am-9pm
Fri-Sat 8am-10pm
Breakfast all day
Music Fri 7pm-9pm
Credit Cards

Never judge a book by its cover. Though Garibaldi's sits in an all American strip shopping center, their food is 100% Mexican. The menu is expansive with many interior Mexican specialties as well as standard Mexican fare. The specialties of the house are the seafood dishes. Perhaps the most interesting are the tuna flautas—Starkist wrapped in a deep fried tortilla—just like mom used to make. If you are passing through Austin via HWY 71 or 290 and have little time venture into town, Garibaldi's is the perfect place to exit quickly, have a satisfying, authentic meal and get back on the road. Happy hour specials make it a good snack place after work.

- Chris Nelson

LA FUENTES MEXICAN FOOD RESTAURANT

6507 S Circle Rd. 78745
Phone: (512) 442-9925
Mon-Thu 11am-9pm
Fri 11am-10pm
Sat 8am-10pm
Sun 8am-3pm
Breakfast Sat 8am-12pm & Sun 8am-3pm
Credit Cards

Sometimes you can tell the food is going to be great just by walking in the door. La Fuentes had me salivating as soon as my eyes adjusted from the overbearing summer sun; the right smell, the right permanent Christmas decorations, the right dim lighting, the right energy and the right amount of attention from the waitstaff. They've been around for more than 30 years for a reason. My enchiladas were greasy and satisfying as were my beans which often times these days aren't worth touching. The migas were first rate and worth going back for alone. It was nice to be in the company of other Austinites enjoying serious Tex- Mex and a couple of cold ones during lunch.

- Allison Walsh

La Playa Mariscos y Taqueria

4619 S Congress Ave. 78745
Phone: (512) 440-0205
Mon-Thu 7am-10pm
Fri-Sat 7am-11pm
Breakfast 7am-11am
Credit Cards

I find it odd that this restaurant is touting their seafood when as far as I can see they don't offer any more or less than any other joint in town. And, most of their fish and shrimp are fried — does that even count? However, the Camarones Diablo appetizer worked and the various tacos we ordered were exactly what we expected. Nothing thrilling, but certainly palatable. Their signature dish is their fried seafood platter with catfish, shrimp, oysters and slaw. If that's what you're in the mood for, but still want get your chips and salsa on, forgo Long John Silver's and head here.

- Allison Walsh

"I'll go to Maudie's Lake Austin for the three cheese enchilada with verde sauce, unless I need some protein, in which case I'll get the chile con carne sauce. I will have that with two frozen margaritas with salt and a straw. The drinks and the food are always well-timed."

- Juliana Hoffpauir
Wedding Videographer/Photographer
Marketing Director, The Garden Room Boutique

La Posada Mexican Restaurant

6800 Westgate Blvd. Ste. 143 78745
Phone: (512) 444-2631
Mon-Wed 7am-9pm
Thu-Sat 7am-10pm
Sun 8am-9pm
Breakfast Mon-Fri 7am-12pm
Sat-Sun 7am-1pm
Credit Cards

La Posada was, at least, an interesting experience. Could it have been the Middle Eastern music? I'm not really sure. The cracked pleather booths patched with duct tape patch were charming and reminiscent of my childhood. They proudly feature a full bar with a three beer and two drink limit, and they sell beach towels in the display case. All I can say about the food is that I thought it would be fun to write my name in guacamole from a cake icing bag.

- Allison Walsh

Maudie's Hacienda

9911 Brodie 78748
Phone: (512) 280-8700
http://www.maudies.com
Sun-Thu 8am-9:30pm
Fri & Sat 8am-10pm
Breakfast all day
Credit Cards

Please see review on page 151

Other Locations: South, West, Far North

San Juanita Tacos

5607 S Congress Ave. 78745
Phone: (512) 443-9308
Mon-Sat 6am-2pm
Closed Sundays
Breakfast 6am-2pm
Credit Cards

San Juanita's is a charming little café strategically located just south of the Department of Public Safety on South Congress. I highly recommend grabbing a number at the DPS and heading down for a quick snack to go. I appreciated the fact they don't offer chips and salsa only because I've never been able to eat chips in moderation. Counter service, styrofoam plates, grade school lunch trays, all day breakfast and the food was really delicious. Our breakfast tacos hit the spot, but the real highlight was the homemade salsa — so good we bought a pint to take home.

- Allison Walsh

Taco Cabana

6430 S I H 35 78745
Phone: (512) 462-3082
Sun-Thu 6am-1am
Fri-Sat 6am-2am
Drive-thru otherwise
Credit Cards

9705 Manchaca Rd. 78748
Phone: (512) 280-5626
Sun-Thu 6am-1am
Fri-Sat 6am-2am
Drive-thru otherwise
Credit Cards

Please see review on page 30

Other Locations: All over the damn place

TEXICAN CAFÉ

11940 Manchaca Rd. 78748
Phone: (512) 282-9094
Mon-Thu 11am-9:30pm
Fri 11am-10pm
Sat 9am-10pm
Sun 9am-9:30pm
Credit Cards

We drove so far south on Manchaca, it felt like we'd left town all together when we came upon the Texican Café — an enormous warehouse of an establishment with a bright friendly billboard just up the road, telling you to keep on coming a little farther. Inside small rooms have been created with clever walls and neon beer signs. El Paso has the most influence on this spot, using chile peppers indigenous to the West Texas town. I tried goat for the first time — as it was noted as Award-Winning on the menu — and the cabrito was tender as could be and simply served with raw slices of white onion, tomato and bell pepper with a side of charro beans. Enchiladas were hot and bubbly, and the rest of the huge menu was charming with no real surprises. Super friendly service — perfect in every way. If you find yourself way down south (or way up north at the Cedar Park locale), the Texican Café won't disappoint.

- Gracie Salem

TRES AMIGOS

1807 Slaughter Ln. W 78748
Cross Street: Manchaca Road
Phone: (512) 292-1001
Fax: (512) 441-0218
Mon-Thu 11am-10pm
Fri-Sat 11am-11pm
Sun 11am-9pm
Breakfast all day weekends 11am-3pm
Credit Cards

Please see review on page 154

Other Locations: East, West

mexican food in austin

Vallarta Jalisco Taqueria

6628 S Congress Ave. 78745
Phone: (512) 462-2515
Sun-Thu 7am-12am
Fri-Sat 7am-1am
Beer only
Credit Cards

Please see review on page 95

Other Locations: Southeast

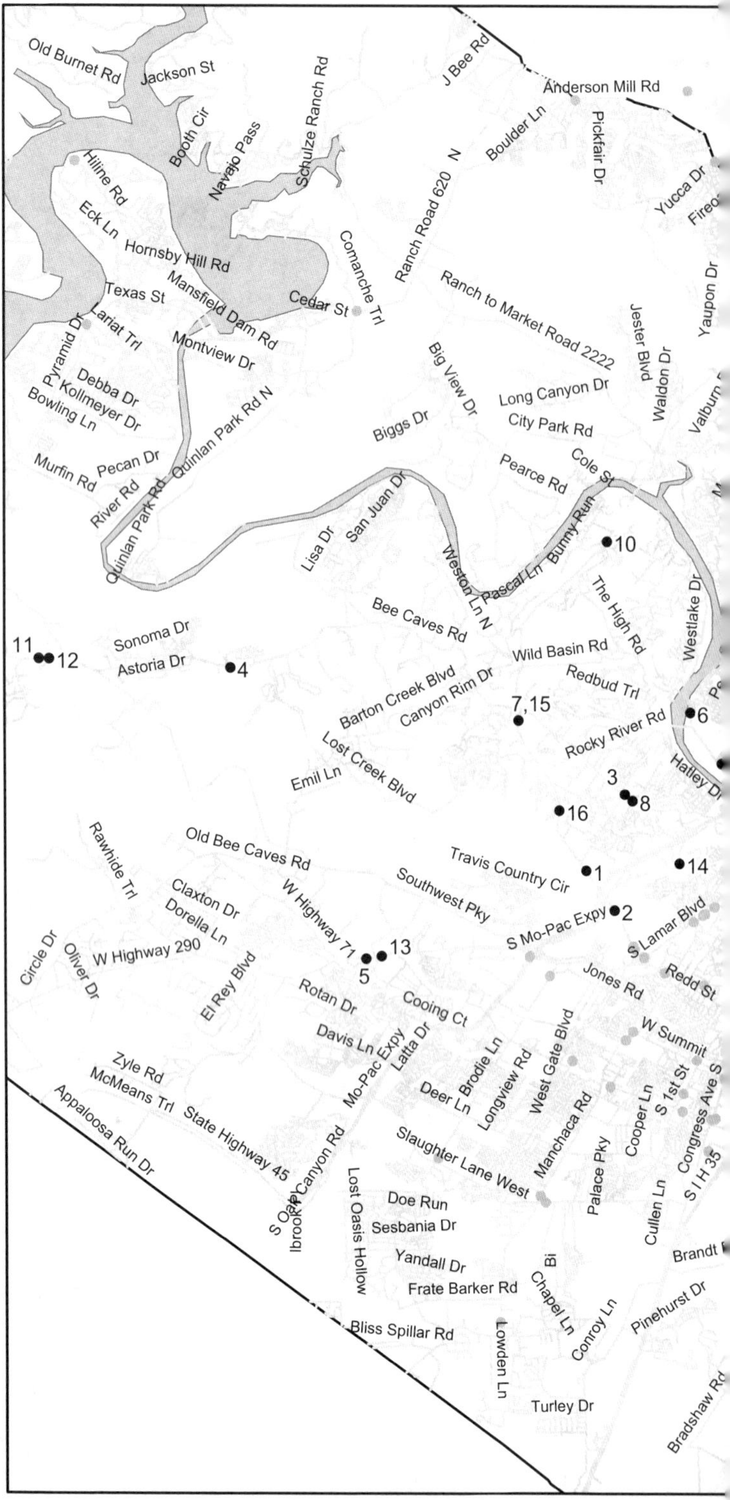
Old Burnet Rd
Jackson St
Booth Cir
Navajo Pass
Schulze Ranch Rd
J Bee Rd
Anderson Mill Rd
Boulder Ln
Pickfair Dr
Ranch Road 620 N
Yucca Dr
Hiline Rd
Eck Ln
Hornsby Hill Rd
Comanche Trl
Texas St
Mansfield Dam Rd
Cedar St
Ranch to Market Road 2222
Jester Blvd
Yaupon Dr
Pyramid Dr
Lariat Trl
Montview Dr
Big View Dr
Waldon Dr
Debba Dr
Kollmeyer Dr
Bowling Ln
Quinlan Park Rd N
Long Canyon Dr
City Park Rd
Biggs Dr
Murfin Rd
Pecan Dr
River Rd
Quinlan Park Rd
Pearce Rd
Cole St
San Juan Dr
Lisa Dr
Bunny Run
10
Weston Ln N
Pascal Ln
The High Rd
Westlake Dr
Bee Caves Rd
Wild Basin Rd
11
12
Sonoma Dr
Astoria Dr
4
Redbud Trl
Barton Creek Blvd
Canyon Rim Dr
7,15
6
Rocky River Rd
Lost Creek Blvd
Emil Ln
Halley Dr
3
8
16
Rawhide Trl
Old Bee Caves Rd
Travis Country Cir
1
14
Southwest Pky
Claxton Dr
Dorella Ln
W Highway 71
S Mo-Pac Expy
2
S Lamar Blvd
Circle Dr
Oliver Dr
W Highway 290
El Rey Blvd
5
13
Jones Rd
Redd St
Rotan Dr
Cooing Ct
W Summit
Davis Ln
Latta Dr
Mo-Pac Expy
Brodie Ln
Longview Rd
West Gate Blvd
Zyle Rd
McMeans Trl
Deer Ln
Manchaca Rd
Cooper Ln
S 1st St
Congress Ave S
Appaloosa Run Dr
State Highway 45
Slaughter Lane West
Palace Pky
S I H 35
Doe Run
Sesbania Dr
Cullen Ln
Lost Oasis Hollow
Yandall Dr
Brandt
Frate Barker Rd
Chapel Ln
Pinehurst Dr
Bliss Spillar Rd
Lowden Ln
Conroy Ln
Turley Dr
Bradshaw Rd

mexican food in austin

West Austin begins as you cross MOPAC (also Loop 1 — everything has two names in Austin) and enter into the large residential neighborhoods like Tarrytown and Westlake. Many houses around these parts have beautiful hillside views of the city or are in close proximity to Town Lake. Parks, museums, and a municipal golf course maintain the vibrant greenery. Going farther west are testaments to the wealth the tech boom generated with large office buildings out 360 and smatterings of expensive developments. The scenery, however, is quite beautiful with the rolling hills that mark the beginning of perhaps the most lovely part of Texas, the Hill Country.

1 Abuelo's

2 Berryhill Baja Grill

3 Chipotle

4 El Arroyo

5 Flores

6 Hula Hut

7 La Salsa

8 Las Palomas

9 Maudie's

10 Maudie's Milagro

11 Rosie's Tamale

12 Rosie's Tamale

13 Serrano's

14 Tacodeli

15 Tia's Tex Mex

16 Tres Amigos

dlp

ABUELO'S MEXICAN FOOD EMBASSY

2901 S Capitol of Tx Hwy. 78746
Phone: (512) 306-0857
Sun-Thu 11am-10pm
Fri-Sat 11am-11pm
Breakfast all day
Credit Cards

What was once a hollow, for-rent movie theater that got passed over for the bigger, better theater inside the mall, has in the last year had a makeover and now houses a chain restaurant. The self-proclaimed Embassy of Mexican Food. Such an odd name. Especially since what we found within the walls of the embassy about as far from Mexico as one can find in Austin. If the people that run the Outback Steakhouse decided to try a Mexican concept, this is close to what would happen. Really pretty on the inside, the menu is as bland and silly as it could be. Seared tuna with a honey lime vinaigrette? I tried the coctel de camarones, a little shrimp cocktail with salad and avocado. Zero spice, anywhere. House specialties include surf and turf combo plates with mashed potatoes as a side and grilled salmon with vegetables. If I ever were to return, I would try one of the most expensive margaritas they offer and order the traditional nachos. Oh, they do let you add fried eggs to enchiladas, a gesture I truly adore. Lunchtime, the place is packed.

- Gracie Salem

BERRYHILL BAJA GRILL

3600 S Capital of Tx Hwy. Ste A -110 78746
Phone: (512) 327-9033
www.berryhillbajagrill.com
Mon-Thu 11am-10pm
Fri-Sat 11am-11pm
Sun 11am-9pm
Breakfast all day
Fast food Mon-Fri until 4pm
Credit Cards

A sure bet to satisfy everyone, Berryhill has so many appealing things about it that even the most fickle Mexican food lover will like it. Located in a shopping center in West Austin (the land of soccer moms and tech

mexican food in austin

execs), the odds are immediately stacked against it, but upon entering you notice the beautiful view from the back patio overlooking the rolling green hills of Austin. The margaritas make this a great place to enjoy weekend afternoons or evening sunsets and their food make it a great to visit anytime of day. Most everything I've tasted here is surprisingly good, with the chicken flautas and bacon-wrapped shrimp being my favorites. Lunchtime is counter service only while dinner and weekends have a full-service wait staff. Berryhill is a small chain and not very authentic with its ambiance — things that usually turn me off. But none of that seemed to matter as I ate, drank and soaked in the excellence of this enigmatic gem (prices are also very reasonable).

- *Chris Nelson*

CHIPOTLE MEXICAN GRILL

3300 Bee Caves Rd. 78746
Phone: (512) 329-8600
Mon-Sun 11am-11pm
Credit Cards

Please see review on page 6

Other Locations: Central, Far South, Far North

EL ARROYO

12432 Bee Cave Rd. 78638
Phone: (512) 402- 0007
http://www.ditch.com
Mon-Fri 11am-10pm
Fri 11am-11pm
Sat 10am-11pm
Sun 10am-10pm
Breakfast all day weekends 10am-3pm
Music Thu-Sun
Credit Cards

Please see review on page 8

Other Locations: Central, North

```
dlp
```

FLORES RESTAURANT

6705 W Hwy. 290 78735
Phone: (512) 892-4845
Mon-Fri 11am-10pm
Sat-Sun 9am-10pm
Breakfast all day weekends 9am-3pm
Credit Cards

Please see reviews on pages 168, 206

Other Locations: North, Lake Travis

HULA HUT

3825 Lake Austin Blvd.
Phone: (512) 476-4852
Sun-Thu 11am-10pm
Fri-Sat 11am-11pm
Credit Cards

I remember tropical drinks out on a deck by the water. A beautiful afternoon, sorority types, tourists, ringing cell phones, boats and lots of relaxation. We lunched out back on the deck after being told of an hour wait inside, and the deck is what I would recommend anyway. The view of Lake Austin alone is worth the trip. It is very casual with good service and friendly servers. They offer traditional Tex-Mex as well as a Tex-Mex-Polynesian influenced hybrid. The queso was not really spicy enough for me, but the enchiladas were more than enough to satisfy. Long after the food however our table lingered on in margarita bliss and talked for another hour digging the sights as lakegoers, families, business lunchers and attractive hipsters mingled into one. It gets busy on the weekends, so a reservation might be a good idea.

- Cory Plump

"I love Maria's Taco X-Press and her potato, egg and cheese taco."

- Nina Singh
Drummer, Kitty Gordon

dlp essay

MEXICAN CUISINE *continued from page 108*
and vegetables which are often times dried for preservation.

Beans and dried meats like machaca, a salted and dried meat often served with eggs to create a typical ranch-style breakfast, are other staples in the arid climate of northern Mexico, where anything that could be kept without refrigeration became an important part of the nortenos diet. And for that reason beans throughout the region are prepared not as refried, but rather as whole bean dishes that resemble hearty soups and usually accompany most meals throughout the states of northern Mexico. Frijoles charros, frijoles borrachos, and frijoles maneados are all northern-style bean dishes prepared with bacon and multiple spices and seasonings, or, in the case of frijoles borrachos, with beer. The beans make perfect mid-afternoon or pre-lunch snacks, and you can expect to find beans served with almost every meal in any of the northern states of Mexico.

Pacific Coast

The pacific coastal states of Mexico utilize the abundance of fresh seafood available in the region in combination with a myriad of locally grown herbs, spices and chiles, and a strong tropical culinary influence to create the signature dishes that are the trademark of this regions cuisine. Sinaloa, Nayarit, Jalisco and Colima all serve up culinary delights for the seafood lover. However, there is some degree of variety as the topography and terrain change as one moves further inland from the coast.

Sinaloa

Along the coast of Sinaloa seafood is the cuisine of choice, prepared in a number of ways from fresh fish, shrimp, squid, or octopus cocktails to poached fish fillets served with shrimp and oysters, better known as pescado Dona Margarita, a local favorite. The cuisine changes with the terrain as one moves inland, where the restaurants offer more traditional meat dishes like grilled pork served with chorizo, vegetables and olives. A staple of Sinaloan cuisine, Caldo, a hearty beef or chicken broth made by simmering the meat for tacos, gorditas, and other late night dishes is used by locals in many of the homemade recipes of the region.

dlp essay

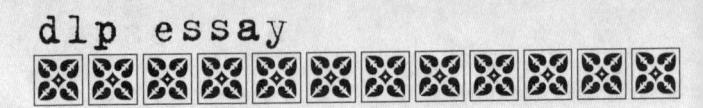

Nayarit

The geographical make up of the terrain in Nayarit lends to a healthy agricultural yield of tropical fruits and vegetable due to the tropical forests and fertile soil of the regions lowlands. Here too, seafood is a mainstay. Regional specialties include pescado zarandeado, fish marinated in fresh lime juice, soy sauce and chile, then smoked over a wood fire with the help of woven rack known as a zaranda, or albondigas de camaron, shrimp balls in a fish and tomato broth. Other local favorites are pescado tatemado (grilled mullet), crab fajitas, chicharron de pescado, and ceviche tostadas, oftentimes accompanied with a tropical fruit drink and/or a sweet fruit jam, both of which are typical of the regional flavor that defines the states cuisine.

Jalisco

A renowned state, Jalisco, home to mariachis and tequila, offers some delectable seafood dishes along its border with the Pacific Coast. As with the rest of the states along the Pacific Coast, seafood is at the center of most of the cuisine, including, but not limited to by any means, fresh lobster, shrimp, oysters, octopus, and huachinango or red snapper. Inland, however, is another story and as the terrain begins to change so, too, do the culinary influences. Inland of Jalisco is the birthplace of pozole, a Mexican pork and hominy stew, and birria, goat meat or mutton seasoned in adobo sauce and served in a tomato and meat broth with sides of fresh chopped onions, cilantro, and, of course, hot sauce. Local favorites include tortas ahogadas, traditionally a roasted pork sandwich topped with a spicy red sauce but also available with shrimp instead of pork, and pollo valentine, chile and chorizo sauce with chicken.

Colima

In Colima, one can enjoy both the abundance of seafood dishes as well as the more traditional ranch style dishes of the northwest. Largely a rural state, Colima has a wealth of agriculture at their disposal with fields of coffee, avocados, limes, and tropical fruits. Favorites of the region include tatemado, pork mari-

dlp essay

nated in coconut vinegar then stewed, chilayo, a pork and vegetable stew, as well as the Jaliscan favorites of birria and pozole. Other local dishes of choice are smoked fish ceviche and the sopitios, small tortillas with shredded meat and topped with local cheeses. The utilization of the many local ingredients here is a testament to the improvisational ability of the Mexican cook.

Southern Mexico

The region of southern Mexico enjoys a confluence of culinary influences. The area bordering the Pacific Coast, not surprisingly, serves the traditional coastal cuisine of fish and shellfish while the inland areas are more heavily influenced by native indian cultures. Here dried peppers and local herbs are used to prepare hearty stews and rich sauces, providing an intense flavor base. The region is known for its sauces, and many of the dishes in the southern region utilize sweeter spices and bolder chiles in their dishes than most other regions in Mexico. Their heavy dependence upon the native wild game of the area adds another unique and distinguishing characteristic to the flavorful southern Mexican cuisine. Coffee, fruits and vegetables are cultivated for culinary usages while corn continues to be a staple product used in a multitude of ways.

Guerrero

Cultural roots run deep in Guerrero; the ancient Mexican culinary influences are still present throughout the region. Most of the dishes here will consist of wild game such as pigeon, rabbit, or iguana, usually stewed using local herbs, including purslane and chepil, a native spinach-like herb, and then flavored with green chile salsa which you will find accompanying dishes throughout the region. As one moves towards the coastal area of Guerrero the more traditional coastal cuisines of grilled or smoked fish and seafood cocktails become more prevalent. However there is some differentiation as the chefs' improvisational abilities yield unique, regional dishes of mixed origin such as shrimp and bacon, sea snails served with nopales (cactus), tuna steak and nopales, and red snapper served with garlic and chiles. Local favorites in Guerrero, chalupas and ayamole,

continued on page 176

La Salsa

701 S Capital of Tx Hwy Ste. 550 78746
Phone: (512) 306-9003
Daily 11am-9pm
Credit Cards

Please see review on page 172

Other Locations: North

Las Palomas Restaurant

3201 Bee Caves Rd. Ste 122 78746
Phone: (512) 327-9889
http://www.laspalomasrestaurant.com
Tue-Thu 11am-2pm
5pm-9pm
Fri & Sat open till 10pm
Closed Sun & Mon
Music as scheduled
Credit Cards

Nestled in the Southwest corner of the Bee Caves & Old Walsh Tarlton strip mall sits this Westlake favorite. Touting their CitySearch vote of best margaritas on the outdoor chalkboard, this restaurant has even more to offer including many rich fish and shrimp dishes. We had the corn mini quesadillas with pico and guacamole, which was perfect for a light meal or to share. The rajas, a yummy mixture of melted cheese, poblano peppers, onions, and sour cream, are ideal for a hangover. The Tres Marías enchiladas are great for the indecisive allowing you to sample their verde, ranchero and mole sauces. The soothing mauve walls and dim lighting makes this restaurant a little more suitable for a romantic date than most Mexican places. But… lunch is a viable option if you're wanting to gawk at the handsome young Westlake businessmen.

-Allison Walsh

Maudie's

2608 West 7th Street, Austin, TX 78703
Phone: (512) 474-7271
Daily 9am-10pm
Credit Cards

3801 N Capital of TX Hwy. 78746
Phone: (512) 306-8080
Daily 9am-10pm
Tues Mariachi
Breakfast all day
Credit Cards

Fans of Maudie's include sorority girls, Westside breeders and Luke Wilson — and all for good reason. Located at the foot of Tarrytown, it's close for young mothers to take the whole crew and not have to trek across town, or better yet, call in an order and swoop down in the Suburban for a little take-out. Sorority girls love Maudie's for two reasons — it's next door to a laundry mat and their famous queso. So, while their party t-shirts tumble dry, they can sit and throw back a few margaritas. And the queso? Maudie's addictive queso is like Ranch Dressing to sorority girls. They should serve it by the shot. As for Luke Wilson, you'll have to ask him yourself. Maybe sorority girls are like Ranch Dressing to Luke.

- Chris Nelson

Other Locations: South, Far South, Far North,

Rosie's Tamales #1

13436 W Hwy. 71 78738
Phone: (512) 263-5245
Mon 11am-9:30pm
Tue 5pm-10pm
Wed-Thu 11am-9:30pm
Fri-Sat 11am-10pm
Breakfast all day weekends 7am-10:30pm
Cash Only

Please see review on pages 124, 152

Other Locations: South

ROSIE'S TAMALES & BREAKFAST TACOS

13303 W Hwy. 71 78738
Phone: (512) 263-5164
Closed Tuesdays
Open all other days 6am-9:30pm
Breakfast until 11am
Fri-Sun until 2pm
Cash only

Rosie's has two outfits out on HWY 71 past the 620 turn off. Though of the same name, the smaller of the venues on the south side of the road is a completely different affair than their north side counterpart which offers a similar menu to that of their Oltorf and Congress location. Confusing, yes, but worth making the distinction due their excellent breakfast tacos and the friendliness of the man responsible for them. Also, remarkably different in that there is no usage of the bright yellow government cheese preferred at the other locations. The breakfast taco expertise exhibited here is unrivalled for twenty miles in any direction. Great tortillas, fluffy, fluffy never burned eggs, great salsa and always an interesting story while you wait—what more can you ask for? Oh I know—how about free doughnuts on weekdays.

- Allison Walsh

SERRANO'S CAFÉ Y CANTINA

6510 W Hwy. 290 78735
Phone: (512) 891-0000
Sun-Thu 11am-10pm
Fri-Sat 11am-1am
Breakfast all day
Credit Cards

Please see review on page 29

Other Locations: Central, South, North, Far North

mexican food in austin

TACODELI

1500 Spyglass 78746
Phone: (512) 732-0303
Fax (512) 306-8770
www.tacodeli.com
Mon-Fri 7am-3pm
Sat 8:30am-2:30pm
Credit Cards

Once upon a time, many men decided to develop pristine suburban living just outside the heart of downtown Austin. At one point, somebody looked around and saw that there was no taquería. The gods smiled and Tacodeli was delivered unto them. Not only did they receive an abundance of taco choices but a house specialty called the Frontera Fundido Taco which melted in their mouths like sweet Mexican nectar. The Frontera Fundido has marinated chicken or sirloin, poblano pepper, onion and a light Monterey Jack sauce all grilled to perfection and wrapped in a warm flour tortilla. If you're not in the neighborhood, this taco is worth the trek out there. Tacodeli sits near a hiking trail going through the Greenbelt up from Zilker Park and is a perfect stop after a morning hike. Breakfast and lunch are the busiest times where you will see a quick moving line of Westlake kids, soccer moms and office techies waiting to order. The chips are thick, deep-fried wedges of tortilla and their best salsa is the Doña, a blended jalapeño sauce as creamy as it is spicy. Without a doubt, Tacodeli has some of the best gourmet tacos in town.

- Chris Nelson

INSIDERS TIP: Try the scallop tacos available only on Thursdays.

"My hands-down favorite is El Azteca, but I also hit Polvo's for the homemade corn tortillas, their fish tacos, poblano enchiladas and the chicken mole enchiladas. I'll go to Guero's for mole on the weekends. Maria's Taco X-press on South Lamar has an efficient call-in system where by you can move to front of the line. I've got that number memorized. Get your own chimichurri and pico de gallo for their potato, egg and chorizo taco with chimichurri sauce. Try Mexico Lindo for the secret green salsa, pork with poblanos, which are meticulously prepared to order. And I like La Mexicana for the tortas carnitas."

- Stephen Doster
Songwriter, Guitarist, Producer

Tia's Tex-Mex

701 S Capital of TX Hwy. 78746
Phone: (512) 732-0500
www.TiasTexMex.com
Sun-Thu 11am-10pm
Fri-Sat 11am-11pm
Credit Cards

Tia's, located in the Beecaves/360 shopplex, is the TGI Friday's of all Mexican restaurants. This is a family-friendly franchise with all the standard fare along with an entire array of mesquite grilled meats, shrimp, and salmon. Prepare yourself for the oversized portions, enthusiastic, almost hyper staff and housemade tortillas. The interior is formulaic: neon coupled with a Mexican seaside village stage set. The service was fast and the food savory. The shrimp were large and cooked perfectly. The low-fat enchiladas were delicious and satisfying. Really, however, I wished I'd saved room for one of their chocolate desserts. A definite for a happy hour margarita if you're stuck in traffic on 360, a family of ten or even a child's birthday party.

- Allison Walsh

Tres Amigos

1801 S Capital Of Texas Hwy 78746
Phone: (512) 327-1776
Fax: (512) 327-1643
Mon-Thu 11am-10pm
Fri-Sat 11am-11pm
Sun 11am-9pm
Breakfast Sat & Sun 11am-2pm
Credit Cards

There is category of Mexican food which I refer to as "Mexican cafeteria food." Perfect for children, out-of-towners, and those recovering from the stomach flu, it follows Tex-Mex to a T without delivering too much spice. Tres Amigos (Westlake location) falls into this category but falls short compared to the other popular family restaurants (see: Maudies or Matt's El Rancho).

Dinner at Tres Amigos started with fairly good queso and

some not-so-good margaritas, pungent with synthetic lime flavoring. This was followed by a sampler including a guacamole salad, beef puffy taco, beef enchilada, rice and beans. The guacamole salad was creamy and cold but lacking any spice. The ground beef in the taco and enchilada was bland and the cheese covering my enchilada was cooked to a rubbery state. Not good, in a nutshell.

One deviation from an otherwise abysmal review – the paper-thin Mexican Lace cookies flavored with oatmeal and Mexican vanilla are outstanding and inexpensive. If you are throwing a party and need a delicious dessert, you can give them a call and order dozens in advance.

See you at Maudie's or Matt's.

-Cile Montgomery

Other Locations: East, Far South

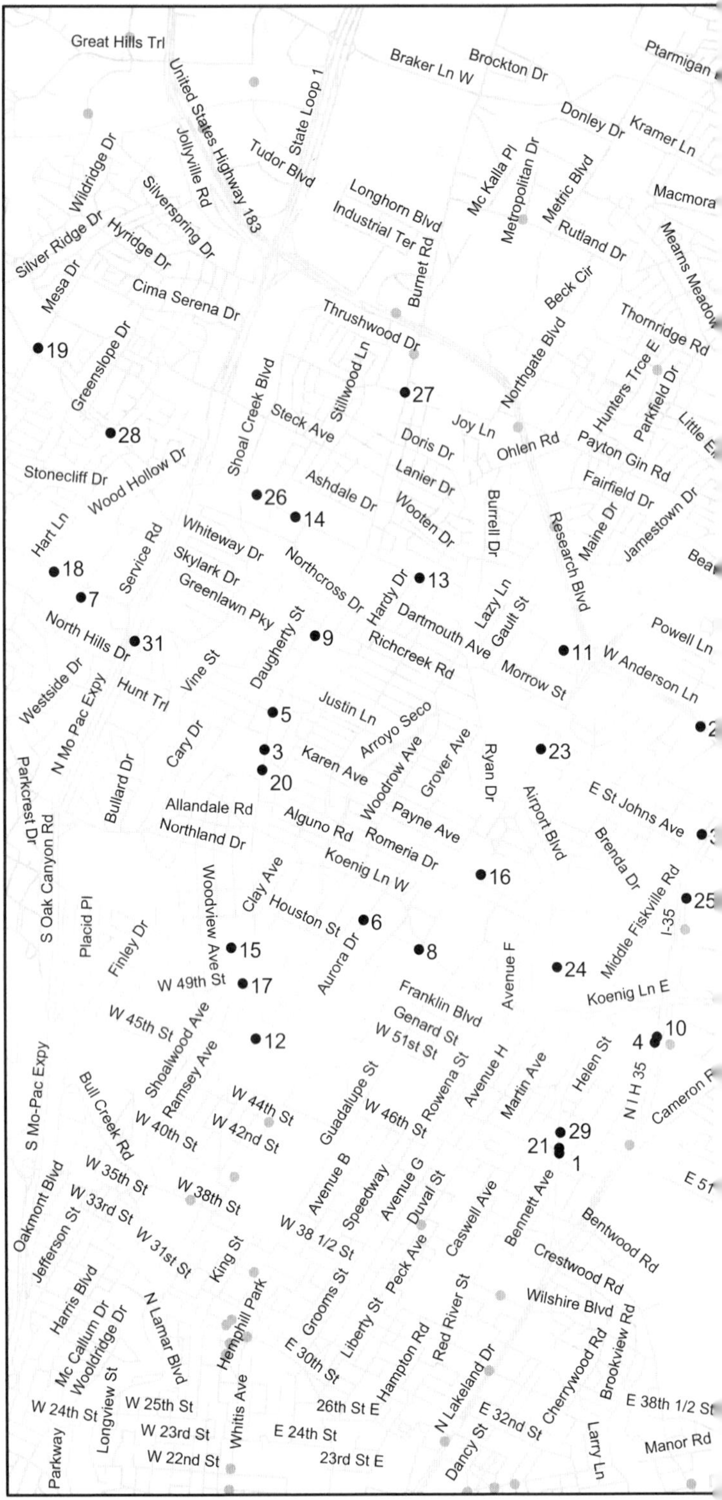

Great Hills Trl
United States Highway 183
State Loop 1
Braker Ln W
Brockton Dr
Ptarmigan
Donley Dr
Kramer Ln
Jollyville Rd
Tudor Blvd
Wildridge Dr
Silverspring Dr
Longhorn Blvd
Mc Kalla Pl
Metropolitan Dr
Metric Blvd
Macmora
Industrial Ter
Burnet Rd
Rutland Dr
Silver Ridge Dr
Hyridge Dr
Mearns Meadow
Mesa Dr
Cima Serena Dr
Beck Cir
Thrushwood Dr
Thornridge Rd
19
Greenslope Dr
Stillwood Ln
Northgate Blvd
Hunters Trce E
Parkfield Dr
27
Shoal Creek Blvd
Steck Ave
Joy Ln
Little E
28
Doris Dr
Ohlen Rd
Payton Gin Rd
Stonecliff Dr
Wood Hollow Dr
Lanier Dr
Fairfield Dr
Ashdale Dr
26
14
Wooten Dr
Burrell Dr
Research Blvd
Maine Dr
Jamestown Dr
Hart Ln
Whiteway Dr
Service Rd
Bea
18
Skylark Dr
Northcross Dr
Hardy Dr
13
7
Greenlawn Pky
Lazy Ln
Gault St
Daugherty St
Dartmouth Ave
Powell Ln
North Hills Dr
31
9
Richcreek Rd
11
W Anderson Ln
Westside Dr
Vine St
Morrow St
Hunt Trl
N Mo Pac Expy
Justin Ln
5
Arroyo Seco
2
Cary Dr
3
Karen Ave
Woodrow Ave
Grover Ave
Ryan Dr
23
Parkcrest Dr
20
Bullard Dr
Airport Blvd
E St Johns Ave
Allandale Rd
Payne Ave
3
Northland Dr
Alguno Rd
Romeria Dr
S Oak Canyon Rd
Brenda Dr
Koenig Ln W
16
Clay Ave
Middle Fiskville Rd
25
Woodview Ave
Placid Pl
Houston St
6
I-35
Finley Dr
15
8
Aurora Dr
Avenue F
24
W 49th St
17
Franklin Blvd
Koenig Ln E
W 45th St
Genard St
Shoalwood Ave
12
W 51st St
10
4
Ramsey Ave
Avenue H
Helen St
S Mo-Pac Expy
Bull Creek Rd
Rowena St
Martin Ave
N I H 35
Cameron R
W 44th St
Guadalupe St
W 40th St
W 46th St
W 42nd St
29
21
1
W 35th St
Avenue B
Avenue G
Speedway
W 38th St
Duval St
Caswell Ave
Bennett Ave
E 51
Oakmont Blvd
W 33rd St
W 38 1/2 St
Bentwood Rd
Jefferson St
W 31st St
King St
Peck Ave
Crestwood Rd
Red River St
Harris Blvd
Hemphill Park
Grooms St
Wilshire Blvd
Mc Callum Dr
N Lamar Blvd
Liberty St
Brookview Rd
Wooldridge Dr
E 30th St
Hampton Rd
Cherrywood Rd
Longview St
N Lakeland Dr
W 24th St
W 25th St
Whitis Ave
26th St E
E 32nd St
E 38th 1/2 St
W 23rd St
E 24th St
Dancy St
Larry Ln
Manor Rd
Parkway
W 22nd St
23rd St E

mexican food in austin

North Austin is an interesting mish mash of culture and influence. North Lamar after 45th Street combines the funky with the light-industrial, becoming more recently developed as you move north. Amid the Targets and car dealerships are restaurants and shops seemingly plain from the outside, but teeming with activity on the inside. A large Asian and Indian community give some flavor and pride to an otherwise pedestrian landscape. It's the Mississippi Delta of sorts in Austin--where all the freeways converge and mix many things Austin into a strangely beautiful masala.

1 Alonzo's II	**17** Jorge's
2 Antonio's	**18** La Salsa
3 Arandas #3	**19** Las Colinas
4 Baby Acapulco	**20** Marisco Grill
5 Curra's North	**21** Mary's Bar
6 Dart Bowl	**22** Ninfa's
7 El Arroyo	**23** Sabor a Mexico Tipico
8 El Caribe	**24** Santiago's
9 El Mercado	**25** Serrano's
10 El Paraiso	**26** Serrano's
11 El Rancho Grande	**27** Taco Cabana
12 Elsi's	**28** Taco Shack
13 Enchiladas Y Mas	**29** Tamale House
14 Flores	**30** Tierra Caliente
15 Fonda San Miguel	**31** Zuzu
16 Jefes	

Alonzo's Tacos II

4905 Airport Blvd. 78751
Phone: (512) 451-3326
Mon-Sat 6am-2pm
Breakfast until 11:30am
Cash Only

See review on page 128

Other Locations: Southeast, Far South

Antonio's Mexican Restaurant

7522 N IH 35 78752
Phone: (512) 419-7070
Sun-Tue 11am-9pm
Wed 11am-10pm
Thu-Sat 11am-11pm
Breakfast all day
Bar open Fri-Sat until 2am
Credit Cards

I couldn't help noticing that everyone inside this faux adobe eatery was at least twenty pounds overweight, including me and including the wait staff. I figured this was a good omen and that I was in good company. Antonio's has been around for over thirty years and though their competition is the neighboring Applebee's and Bennigan's what they lack in originality they make up for in taste. Outwardly, the place seems like just another boxy, huge chain restaurant sitting on the highway attracting hungry, indiscriminate motorists. But there is something to be said for these corporate-type places. I was well taken care of by several waiters who seemed intelligent and actually somewhat happy. And though I didn't expect much from the food because my chips were stale, the salsa was right on the mark. (I don't know why those two can't ever seem to get it together.) My chicken enchiladas were actually fantastic; stewed white meat with actual flavor and just enough kick to make me pay more attention. I didn't know these types of places were allowed to use any sort of spice lest they be sued. Regardless, I was more than satisfied with my lunch right down to the stewed black beans and rice. This joint isn't really my cup of tea, but if I had to go I wouldn't complain.

- Allison Walsh

mexican food in austin

Other Locations: Far North

ARANDAS TAQUERIA #3

6534 Burnet Rd. 78757
Phone: (512) 452-9886
Daily 7am-12am
Mon-Thu 7am-12:30am
Breakfast all day
Credit Cards

Please see review on pages 39, 98

Other Locations: Far North, East, South, Far South

BABY ACAPULCO

5610 N I-35 78751
Phone: (512) 302-1366
Fri-Sat 11am-1am
Sun-Thu 11am-12pm
Breakfast all day
Credit Cards

Please see review on page 99

Other Locations: Southeast, South, Far North

CURRA'S GRILL NORTH

6801 Burnet Rd. 78757
Phone (512) 451-2560
http://www.currasgrill.citysearch.com
Mon-Thu 11am-10pm
Fri 10am-11pm
Sat-Sun 9am-11pm
Breakfast all day
Credit Cards

Please see review on page 102

Other Locations: South

dlp essay

STAR CROSSED
TAQUERIA LOVERS

by Chris Nelson

For awhile I was living in close proximity to a wonderful taquería where I would eat most of my lunches. At some point a new addition to the kitchen staff came — a girl. She was young, beautiful and innocent (I think). She breathed new life into the taquería and excited me each time I came to eat.

Like a princess protected by a castle, she too, was surrounded by a wall of a portly Mexican woman, feverishly working to fill orders while keeping an eye on the new arrival. And at the counter was the gatekeeper, the only person who took orders and spoke to the customers. As a first line of defense, he was formidable.

The only way to communicate with my taquería girl was with my eyes. I would gaze at her, not looking away when she turned and saw me. She would blush and look back at her tacos. It was our routine, our courtship. After a few months she was allowed to bring customers their to-go orders — a big step in the chain of command. I was proud of her promotion, but we were still under the watchful guard of the gatekeeper.

She made the first move. I had ordered a tostada and a taco (my usual) and she walked my food slowly over to me. Our eyes briefly met, and with the transfer of my food, her hand touched over mine. Light enough not to arouse suspicion but long enough to be deliberate, her touch was expressive, supple and sexy. I

dlp essay

punctuated the moment with a smile and "gracias."

These touches continued as our courtship turned more serious. The glances became longer and the smiles less guarded. I thought about asking her out, but we both knew this was impossible. I was not only a gringo but a good-timing, broke one at that. By the way the ladies in the kitchen looked at her, I knew that her virginity was being guarded for good marital prospects and the chance for a better life. By the way she looked at me, I knew that if given the chance, she would have handed me her virginity with same ease and sweetness she handed me my tacos. But there was no future with me and she knew this.

Soon she began to physically change. The cute, darkened peach fuzz on her upper lip became more like a moustache. Her waistline ballooned and her breasts dropped from their happy perch. She no longer contrasted the chubby ladies in the kitchen and grew more rotund with each passing day. I knew this could only mean one thing—she had found a husband.
I can't say that I was devastated. Confused and disappointed—yes, but not devastated. What hurt the most was what I had to do after that. Her sweet gazes did not stop with her transformation. They continued on but seemed to acquire of tinge of longing and desperation. Was it an unhappy marriage? A bad match? Was it a union of convenience and not passion? Perhaps.

The flower of her youth had wilted. Her physical maturation mirrored what had happened in her heart. She was different. It was over between us. I could not deceive her and continue answering her gazes with my smiles, for they would be hollow and do more damage than good. So I looked away. To the floor, to the gatekeeper, to the banks of salsa — anywhere but her eyes.

dlp essay

I could feel her heart drop and eyes well up briefly with tears. Though I didn't see it, I know those tears were quickly put down. She knew we would never last. She was now a woman who lived in a world of realities and pragmatic solutions. Her last dalliance with romantic notions had passed and she was no longer a dreamer. Everything had changed.

But in the end, our wordless, unrequited love will last longer than any real relationship and burn bright in our minds with daydreams of what could or would have been. In her heart I am a better man than in reality, just as she will always be the shy, beautiful, young girl that I once saw at the taquería.

mexican food in austin

Dart Bowl Steak House

5700 Grover Ave. 78756
Phone: (512) 452-2518
Mon-Thu 8am-11pm
Fri-Sat 8am-2am
Sun 8am-11pm
Breakfast until 11am
Credit Cards

I know, I know, what is a bowling alley doing included in a book about Tex-Mex? And then I'm sure you'll say this lovely establishment across from McCallum High School doesn't qualify because they only serve one Tex-Mex item — cheese enchiladas. Well, now that you've got two gutter balls against you why don't you just sit down in one of the lovely pastel booths and get ready for a 300 game to hit your mouth. The cheese enchiladas, the staple of any self respecting Tex-Mex establishment, are as close to perfection as you can get—I've gone there on more than one occasion to just eat and didn't touch a bowling ball. These cheese-filled tortillas topped with onions, peppers and chile con carne are the old school variety — the kind I ate on Wednesday Enchilada Night in any town across Texas as a youth. These enchiladas aren't gourmet, they're not good for you and they aren't served with rice and beans. Instead they include the perfect amount of grease and are accompanied by delicious, toasted bread that is made fresh daily. If you find yourself with an inkling to bowl a few frames and craving some greasy goodness Dart Bowl is your one-stop shop.

- Chad Hamilton

photo by Derek Hatley

north

El Arroyo Restaurant

7023 Wood Hollow Dr. 78731
Phone: (512) 345-8226
http://www.ditch.com
Mon-Wed 11am-10pm
Thu 11am-11pm
Fri 11am-12am
Sat 10am-11pm
Sun 10am-10pm
Open on weekends until 3pm
Breakfast all day weekends until 3pm
Credit Cards

Please see review on page 8

Other Locations: Central, West

El Caribe

5610 N Lamar 78751
Phone: (512) 452-6207
Mon-Thu 11am-9pm
Fri-Sat 11am-10pm
Breakfast all day
Weekends 10am-2pm
Credit Cards

Don't let the façade fool you, El Caribe is the real deal. Situated in the culinary DMZ that is central Austin, El Caribe is just south of Koenig on North Lamar and most have driven by it numerous times without ever noticing it. This unassuming family-run restaurant (Senora Lopez in the kitchen y su hija Denia in the front) shares a parking lot with a Korean grocer that makes the number of parking spots available fewer than the number of fresh homemade sauces kept chilled and awaiting your self-service. As can be gathered by the name, El Caribe has a well above average seafood presence on the menu which is a result of the family's origins in Veracruz. El Caribe offers enough variety on the menu to keep you coming back dozens of times before you could get through all the choices that are not available on any standard Combo #1 platter. Despite the myriad fish and shrimp dishes available, on my initial foray I could not resist ordering Pollito Relleño, a piece of chicken breast pounded and spread thin enough to qualify as one half of a short stack, rolled around a ball of chorizo and mushrooms, breaded and deep fried into a smallish meteorite, then carefully glazed with a special sauce and finally blessed with a spoonful of queso blanco. Who are you to resist? A compatriot's whole baked fish stuffed with garlic cloves distracted the table and is another dish that Taco Bell will not soon be commoditizing. Standard Tex-Mex fare will surely not disappoint as tacos, burritos, enchiladas and the rest keep on par with the more exotic fare. House rocks margaritas live up to their name and weekends bring the requisite menudo but additionally pork pozole, a pork and hominy soup complete with onion, jalapeños, cilantro, lime and fresh Mexican oregano.

-Jordan Actkinson

EL MERCADO RESTAURANT

7414 Burnet Rd. 78757
Phone: (512) 454-2500
Mon 10:30am-10pm
Tue -Thu 10:30am-10:30pm
Fri 10:30am-11pm
Sat 9am-11pm
Sun 9am-10pm
Credit Cards

Please see review on page 8

Other Locations: Central, South

EL PARAISO RESTAURANT

5656 N IH 35 78751
Phone: (512) 451-7777
Mon-Thu 7am-11pm
Fri 7am-12am
Sat 8am-12am
Sun 8am-11pm
Fri 8pm Mariachi
Sat-Sun Karaoke Eng & Esp.
Breakfast Mon-Fri 7am-11am
Sat-Sun 8am-11am
Credit Cards

El Paraiso is an uninteresting restaurant on the feeder road of I-35. In fact, the front door opens onto the highway. They offer standard Mexican fare, which is unfortunately rather insipid. The rice and beans are bland, as was the carne guisada, pastor, and nopalitos. There is little to no excuse for flavorless and boring Mexican food. So, as for El Parasio, we would just keep driving past it.

- Shazza Calcote

El Rancho Grande

911 W Anderson Ln. 78757
Phone: (512) 458-5454
Daily 7am-10pm
Credit Cards

The architectural blandness where Taquería El Rancho Grande is located betrays the cultural diversity and rich ethnic influences that abound here. Beyond the drab facades of the numerous strip shopping centers are Indian, Korean, Chinese and Mexican food restaurants whose originality is understood through the tongue instead of the eye. El Rancho Grande's crowd is distinctly local, speaking Spanish and ordering up Caldo des Rey and the tastiest fajitas within 100 feet of 183. Definitely get some grilled cactus, scallions and jalapeños along with your meal.

- Chris Nelson

Elsi's Restaurant

4708 Burnet Rd. 78756
Cross Street: W 47th St
Phone: (512) 454-0747
Sun-Tue 7am-3pm
Wed-Sat 7am-9pm
Credit Cards

Elsi's is perfect for a late breakfast and a beer in your pajamas and sunglasses. It is quiet, ridiculously modest in décor and wonderfully tasty. This combination restaurant offers all of usual Mexican fare with a smattering of Salvadoran specials. The biggest difference is the white rice and black beans sides. The daily specials menu highlight the Salvadoran items, two of which I have sampled and so far think merit a stray from one's normal favorites. A Friday option is the pescado chipotle, a filet of fresh tilapia with a nice smoky sauce, that hits the spot. Thursday's winner was the chayote plate, a version of a chili relleño where the chili is substituted with a chayote squash. My over all impression was that this cuisine tended to be on the healthier side of Central America, but equally as delicious and a very welcome change of pace for someone who eats Mexican food all the time.

- Allison Walsh

Enchiladas y Mas Restaurant

1911 W Anderson Ln. 78757
Phone: (512) 467-7100
Fax: (512) 385-8992
http://enchiladasymas.citysearch.com
Sun 7am-2pm
Tue-Sat 7am-10pm
Closed Mondays
Breakfast all day only weekends
Credit Cards

Although I have dined at Enchiladas y Más more times than I could possibly count, I really couldn't tell you much about their enchiladas. But if the quality of the migas is any kind of indication on how good the enchiladas might be, then I can personally guarantee that they are pretty damn good.

I've heard that people from El Paso when in Austin will only eat migas at Enchiladas y Más. I don't know if that is true, but simply gazing upon the plate of food causes me to believe the veracity of this El Pasonian wisdom. When it is delivered (always quickly, I might add) it is a vision of bright bubbling goodness. This plate of grub is truly an oasis in the hangover desert and it tickled me pink and rendered me speechless as I shoved it all into my hungry mouth. Just like always.

As far as true negatives go, I would have to say there are two. The first being that it is a pay-up-front-on-your-way-out type of gig so once the check is dropped, no more service. The second drawback is that the hours of operation are so convoluted, you need a palm pilot to keep track of them. But if you happen to catch Enchiladas y Más at just the right time on just the right day, you can go home after your meal and lie on the couch for the rest of the day and still feel fulfilled.

- Fleetwood Wilson

Flores Restaurant

2700 W Anderson Ln. Ste. 200 78757
Phone: (512) 302-5470
Mon-Fri 11am-10:30pm
Sat 9am-10pm
Sun 9am-5pm
Breakfast Sat-Sun until 3pm
Credit Cards

Flores is a large family-friendly local chain restaurant. We visited the Flores on W. Anderson where the spinach enchiladas were very fresh but a bit uninspired. The salsa was a little too heavy on the ground black pepper, which may not be typical. The crispy hot tortilla chips are made on the premises and excellent. Their rice and beans are standard and slightly weak. Flores would be fine if you work close by and need a quick Mexican food fix. Otherwise, there are many other more authentic and interesting choices in Austin.

- *Shazza Calcote*

Other Locations: West, Lake Travis

Fonda San Miguel

2330 W North Loop Blvd. 78756
Phone: (512) 459-4121
Mon-Thu 5pm-9:30pm
Fri-Sat 5pm-10:30pm
Sun 11am-2pm
Credit Cards

The lush landscaping of this large well-appointed grand hacienda has an elegance and a sophistication that stirred up memories of lazy, long lunches in San Miguel de Allende. The interior Mexican cuisine was delicate and smart and the margaritas flowed too, too perfectly. The white fish ceviche was our table's favorite only to be followed by the most tender cochinita pibil in town. Our waiter was smart and on the ball and kept our fun-loving table of eight quite happy. Though the brunch buffet served on Sundays seems to be their claim to fame, I'll take dinner at Fonda with my friends anytime, for whatever reason.

- *Allison Walsh*

mexican food in austin

Smoothness. I live in smoothness. These will be your thoughts as you step inside the lush wonderland of Fonda San Miguel. From the large, carved wooden door, you are ushered into a sky-lighted bar with towering plants and fountains and immediately offered a beverage. Have a margarita. Get the top-shelf. If you're already at Fonda San Miguel, you should be ashamed to go halfway on anything. The last time we were there in typical Dirty Lowdown Press fashion, we ordered everything. There was white fish and tuna tartar ceviche, cactus confections, three types of chile relleño, carne asada, filet of snapper and a mixed grill with every animal on the Texas Parks and Wildlife hunting license. That was just dinner. Dessert was awash in caramel crepes, flan, tres leches cake and bottles of champagne. Toasts abounded and the DLP crew became the loudest, most smiling party at the restaurant. Some tables looked over disapprovingly, but the waitstaff was having a great time with us. To truly enjoy Fonda San Miguel you must not treat it as one would a summer fling or first date. In this relationship, you must put out. It's only then that the ecstasy will follow.

- Chris Nelson

Fonda San Miguel is a classy Mexico City restaurant without Montezuma's Revenge. Fonda with the Friday night crew is the right recipe for any gastronome that enjoys a great time. At Fonda you get by far the best interior Mexican food in Austin, margaritas that compete with Matt's El Rancho and an ambiance that makes you feel like you're in Old Mexico.

- Kevin Burns

north

photo by Derek Hatley

JEFES TAQUERIA

720 N Lamar Blvd. 78752
Phone: (512) 459-0034
Tue-Thu 7am-10pm
Fri 7am-12am
Sat 8am-12am
Sun 8am-10pm
Credit Cards

Where else can you enjoy enchiladas suizas while watching *The Mummy* on a big-screen TV in surround sound? This little taquería on North Lamar has many small things like a mini-theater and spicy salsas that add up to a largly enjoyable experience. The menu is standard Tex-Mex fare with the regular trappings like pastoral Mexican paintings on the wall and Tejano jukebox. Jefe's specialties are their tacos suados, al pastor and chicharrones. It is their salsa roja that enjoys the spotlight with its creamy texture and latent kick. Lunch is affordable with specials running throughout the week and a mariachi band plays on Sundays. Breakfast is served everyday until 11am. Mexican Coke in a bottle — need I say more?

- Chris Nelson

JORGE'S RESTAURANT

2203 Hancock Dr. 78756
Phone: (512) 454-1980
Fax: (512) 323-6690
Mon-Tue 10am-9pm
Wed-Sat 10am-10pm
Credit Cards

T. G. Jorge's, né Casa Jorge's, is a little different than most old schoolers will recall due to new management. And anybody who lived in Austin in the 1970's and 80's will bend your ear with Jorge stories. Casa Jorge's used to be famous for their margaritas, so lethal there was a two-drink maximum. I was told this while traveling in Brazil on a speck of an island out in middle of nowhere in the Atlantic when I happened to hear a rowdy bunch of Texans talking about Austin. This is where I met Jimmy who explained to me that he had once sent the famous margarita off to a lab to be analyzed. Yes, there was Everclear and yes, there were almost 1,000 calories per drink. Wow! I couldn't believe my ignorance, and upon my return rushed to the restaurant to find out that all the tomfoolery had ceased. Oh well, the restaurant still has a similar menu and a seedy smoky little cantina attached to get away from the kids playing video games. The Mitsy Special is a unique item worth trying and the asado de puerco melts in your mouth. Meat lovers should stick with the beer-simmered brisket tacos.

- Allison Walsh

LAS COLINAS MEXICAN RESTAURANT

8127 Mesa Dr. 78759
Phone: (512) 794-8128
Mon-Fri Lunch 11am-2pm
Dinner 5:30pm-9pm
Closed Sat & Sun
Credit Cards

First, it was the scent. Then, the curious taste. I couldn't really make it out. I began to salivate as red savina habeneros awoke my tongue and sweat began to grow on my brow. There was a marriage of mental and physical stimulation. Then the hostess sat me. The joint is a rather small place, comfortable, and well attended. This is good news for North-siders because there isn't another place anywhere close by. Chips and salsa right away. Lighter, thinner chips (which I like) but the salsa was a little bland and uninteresting. I ordered the #4 chicken enchilada combo with verde sauce and sour cream. My date ordered the chicken chipotle (Oh, and by the way, she was smokin') The #4 had beans and rice with good presentation and flavorful for a great price (it's all about bucks, baby). Thumbs up on the chicken-chipotle as well, with fresh avacado wedges and good presentation. We were both happy with our meals and the service. Overall, we were pleased and would go again.

- James Moody

dlp

LA SALSA

3637 Far West Blvd. 78731
Phone: (512) 342-1010
Mon-Sun 8am-9pm
Breakfast Mon-Sun 8am-10:30pm
Credit Cards

La Salsa is the Michael Bolton of taquerías. No, you won't find curly locks with their cheese, but you will find food that hits every note perfectly—except that it's still a white man trying to be soulful and funky. La Salsa has two locations, one north and one west, both in a purgatory of office park and suburban sprawls. The restaurant décor has hints of TCBY, accents of Jack in the Box and just a dash of Taco Cabana. The food is fresh, light and tasty and great for a weekday lunch. The fish tacos come out fast, laden with crisp cabbage and guaranteed not to anchor you down for the next two hours. On the other hand, lard = flavor. You do the math. Speaking of numbers, three tacos, queso and a drink will run you close to $15! After eating it on a Styrofoam plate, off a fast food table, and bussing it myself, I was left with a very strange feeling—like I had digested something seemingly good and inoffensive, but was much poorer in pocket book and soul. Hmmm, sounds like a Michael Bolton concert.

- Chris Nelson

Other Locations: Far South

MARISCO GRILL

6444 Burnet Rd. 78757
Phone: (512) 474-7372
Mon-Thu 9am-10pm
Fri-Sat 9am-12am
Sun 10am-10pm
Credit Cards

Please see review on page 25

Other Locations: Central

Mary's Bar

4917 Airport Blvd 78751
Phone: (512) 451-9248
Daily 4pm-11pm

Mary's has flavor. The food is home cooking for a home crowd. Not much English goes on here and the good times definitely roll. Awhile back I was living off Airport and a big sign announcing Mary's new liquor license was draped across the building. For my buddy, The Boutros and me, a restaurant getting a liquor license is like a bar-mitzvah to a Jew — a day of celebration when a boy becomes a man. We decided to help Mary's celebrate by drinking some margaritas and eating some enchiladas. The chow was fantastic. As the evening wore on, more people flowed into the bar, the jukebox got louder and pool games got serious. The weekend crowd is definitely hard-working immigrant, cleaned-up-for-Friday-night-with-shined-buckles-and-fancy-boots type of crowd. Most of these guys' families, girlfriends and wives are back in Mexico, so there aren't too many women around, except for a few freelancers here and there. It didn't seem too rough when we were there, but a roomful of dateless dudes, drinking tequila all night can breed some frustration and might cause a man to blow off some steam.

Especially interesting were the two middle-aged Mexican women in spandex who made bedroom eyes and cat-called The Boutros and myself. I don't know if they were hookers, but their gold-toothed smiles suggested so. I smiled back and tried to think how to politely tell them they weren't my type ("My type" simply not being old and for sale). It was fitting end to a fine meal at Mary's Bar.

- Chris Nelson

INSIDERS TIP: Due to the lack of parking, Mary's patrons tend to park behind each other, blocking many cars in the process. If you get blocked, good luck finding the person behind you.

Mama Ninfa's Restaurant

214 E Anderson Ln. 78752
Phone: (512) 832-1833
www.mamaninfas.com
Sun-Thu 11am-9pm
Fri-Sat 11am-10:30pm
Breakfast all day
Credit Cards

Chain restaurants — we love to hate them. McDonald's, Starbuck's, Hooters. The list goes on and on. (Hold on, I don't hate Hooters). One thing about chains that is difficult to accept — there are so many of them because they *do* do some things very well. I hate to say it, but Starbucks coffee is pretty damn good. Now, walking into a Starbucks might make me want to punch myself in the groin and wear Che Guevara t-shirt on my head, but the fact remains that the coffee is better than the stuff that the philosophy grad student brews up across the street. Mama Ninfa's, though only in major Texas markets, has many locations serving the exact same food. The décor is a paint-by-numbers Mexican food restaurant job, but forget that for a second. Concentrate on the food. Can you taste that? That's good. That's damn good because Mama Ninfa's delivers big and does not disappoint. So, don't get all WTO-protester on Mama Ninfa's. Give her a chance. You won't regret it.

- Chris Nelson

Sabor a Mexico Tipico

7301 N Lamar 78752
Phone: (512) 323-2310
Daily 7am-10pm
Credit Cards

Mexican restaurants come and go with the frequency of a rock-n-roll drummer, but I sincerely hope newcomer Sabor a Mexico manages to stay in it for the long haul. (Or at least the second album). The Tacos Especiales are gourmet, if you prefer that term, with fresh al pastor and chorizo grilled with sautéed onions and cactus. Their seafood is also a star on the menu. I had a small order of the shrimp and octopus ceviche whose size and flavor thoroughly rocked. The lovely matron and the sweetness she delivered with my order made the whole experience entirely pleasureable.

- Chris Nelson

Santiago's

6001 Airport Blvd. 78752
Phone: (512) 451-5968
Daily 10am-9pm

If there is any reason in the world to ever, ever have to go to Highland Mall, (and there isn't), and you find yourself shamefully sneaking towards the food court for some of the wretchedness, opt for Chinese or a smoothie or a pretzel, anything but the Mexican food. Actually, there really is no reason to have to suffer through the poorly conceived, ill-prepared victuals offered at the disgraceful food court. In fact, the inaccessibility of the food court to the outside world is a prophylactic measure ensuring that only those buying sexual gag gifts at Spencer's or penny loafers at Dillard's are subject to the noxious gruel. There is too much good Mexican out there…don't do it.

- Allison Walsh

Serrano's Lincoln Village

6406 N I H 35 78752
Phone: (512) 323-2555
Sun-Thu 11am-10pm
Fri-Sat 11am-11pm
Breakfast all day
Credit Cards

3010 W. Anderson 78759
Phone: (512) 454-7333
Sun-Thu 11am-10pm
Fri-Sat 11am-11pm
Breakfast all day
Credit Cards

Please see review on page 29

Other Locations: Central, South, Far North, Central

dlp essay

MEXICAN CUISINE *continued from page 149*

a sauce consisting of pumpkin seeds and epazote, are served in many of the villages throughout the area, as well as Guerrero's own style of pozole, the traditional pork and hominy stew.

Oaxaca

Also known as the "Land of Seven Moles", Oaxaca enjoys a wealth of indigenous resources from the vegetables of the central valley, and the seafood of the southern coast, all the way to the endless supply of tropical fruit along its border with Vera Cruz. The state is subdivided into many small regions, each with their own culture within Oaxaca as the Sierra Mountain ranges criss-cross the state. The cuisine here is diverse as a result of the divisions, and the many local herbs throughout the region are vital ingredients in making the many moles of Oaxaca, most notably, the herb mole known as verde which utilizes hoja santa herb that is found in parts of Chiapas as well. One of the most characteristic ingredients here is the pasilla oaxaquena chile, a hot, smoky chile often used to flavor the typical frijoles negros of the region. Other chiles of the area include chilhuacles, chilcostles, and costenos. Here too, corn is a staple agricultural product used in a variety of ways, among them, entomatadas, empanadas de mole amarillo, and tamales. Expect to find flavorful pork, chicken or seafood dishes seasoned with a myriad of indigenous herbs and chiles and served with one of their many mole sauces. And for the sweet tooth, Oaxaca has the best chocolate in Mexico featuring ground cacao, combined with cinnamon, and almonds to yield a delectable treat.

Chiapas

As the southernmost state, Chiapas is relatively isolated from the rest of Mexico. Geographically it is a combination of mountains, plains, and seacoast and as a result enjoys a wealth of indigenous fruits and vegetables, cattle, and an abundance of seafood. There is a large Oaxacan influence here as much of the terrain of Chiapas is shared with Oaxaca and thus, so too are the resources such as huge avocados and anchiote pastes which were originally used in the cuisine of the Mayan people who once inhabited Chiapas. In fact, many of the dishes in the region use the same herbs that the Mayan people used, herbs like chipilin, a fragrant, thin-leaved plant, and hoja santa, an anise-scented herb that is sometimes combined with the corn dough of the renowned Chiapas tamales and is characteristic of the region's cuisine. Many dishes are prepared with wild game or, when not available, beef, pork, or chicken cooked with any one of a variety of sauces. The pumpkin seed sauce is well known throughout the region as the seed is a common ingredient. Some regional dishes include ninguijute, a seed-based pork mole, cochito horneado, young roasted pig basted with an adobo sauce of ground seeds and herbs, and pictes, sweet corn tamales. Throughout Chiapas, one might encounter an array of fried plantains, often filled with black beans, the frijole of choice here, and local cheeses. Regional desserts include coconut candies, flans, compotes, and crystallized fruits served with locally grown coffee.

Central Mexico

Dried chiles, a variety of herbs and spices, and traditional preparation methods characterize the cuisine of central Mexico. The flavors of this region are the result of both Spanish as well as native indian influences in concert with the agricultural products including squash and corn, and the ranch raised beef of the area. Among the most historic of Mexico's regions, central Mexican cuisine was born out of an experimental and improvisational spirit perfected by the nuns of the many conventos in the area. It is the native ingredients characteristic of the central states, prepared using traditional methods, that yield the quintessential central Mexican fare.

Tlaxcala

The smallest state in Mexico, Tlaxcala is nonetheless steeped in Mexican culinary tradition. The very meaning of the word Tlaxcala in Spanish is "place of bread made with corn," and so it is no wonder that they take great pride in the cuisine of their culture. The preparation of a masa, or corn dough, is a testament to the traditional methods used in the region. It is said one must feel the corn kernels at every step of preparation along the way, cooking, soaking and grinding, so that the prop-

dlp essay

er texture is achieved. As the corn varies with each crop, so too, accordingly, does the preparation. Indigenous produce of the area include maguey, nopales, corn, amaranth, and setas, a wild mushroom that is now cultivated in the fields of Tlaxcala. Additionally, a wealth of greens can be found throughout the region, known as quelites, these greens are used for nutrition and flavor in a number of the pork dishes and stews of the area. Regional favorites, pollo tizatlan and codillo aquiahuac, both derive their name from the villages in Tlaxcala where the characteristic ingredients are found. In pollo tizatlan, the most palatably notable ingredient is the native amaranth that is used in moles and homemade candy of the region. Codillo aquiahuac is a pork dish traditionally prepared by cutting the lower portion of the pork leg crosswise into rounds, then cooking it with purslane for flavor. It is usually served with nopales or verdolagas, two common indigenous plants of central Mexico.

Puebla

The cuisine of Puebla is a balance of the traditional and the new, where one can find a mix of dishes that incorporate both the indigenous ingredients of the area as well as the Spanish influence that migrated to the area so long ago. Here, in the conventos of Puebla, were born the traditional favorites like mole poblano, and chiles en nogada. Puebla is often called the cradle of corn for historical reasons (the oldest kernel specimens were uncovered in the area), and the State's dependence on corn is evident as it is used in almost every meal. An in depth sampling of the regions cuisine includes Molotes, a dish of chorizo, squash blossoms and new potatoes seasoned with the epazote herb all folded into a thin corn dough then fried; pipian blanco, a stew made with peanuts and cilantro seeds, ground and added to a turkey stock and allowed to simmer; chiles en nogada, ground meat seasoned and mixed with raisins, pine nuts and local fruits such as apples, peaches and/or pears stuffed into a poblano pepper that is then dipped, fried and served with a creamy sauce, garnished with pomegranates. The traditional mole poblano is a turkey stew mixed with ground chiles, various seeds, nuts and chocolate, a dish characteristic to this part of Mexico in particular. Other sea-

continued on page 209

mexican food in austin

Taco Cabana

8620 Burnet Rd. 78757
Phone: (512) 458-2211
Open 24 hrs – 7 days a week
Breakfast 11pm-11am
Credit Cards

Please see review page 30

Other Locations: All over the damn place

Taco Shack

3901C Spicewood Springs Rd 78759
Phone: (512) 416-8900
Mon-Fri 6:30am- 2:30pm
Sat- 7am-1Ppm

Please see review on page. 32

Other Locations: Central, Far North

Tamale House

5003 Airport Blvd 78751
Phone: (512) 453-9842
Mon-Fri 6:30am-3pm
Sat 7am-3pm
Closed Sunday
Breakfast until close
Cash Only

When I say Tamale House is cheap, I mean *cheap*. Tacos start at 85 cents and the most expensive item on the menu is $4.25. Don't let the price fool you. Tamale House serves up some of the best breakfast tacos around and in record time. There are a few tables outside the small storefront on Airport Blvd but most people call in their orders to pick up. The most popular item is their migas with cheese, which cures about 75% of North Austin's hangovers on Saturday morning. Their chalupas have generous helpings of guacamole and fresh tomato and frito pies can fuel you for the whole day. Many young, broke Austin musicians are walking proof that you can live on Tamale House alone.

- Chris Nelson

TIERRA CALIENTE

7300 N IH 35 78752
Phone: (512) 459-1415
Mon-Thurs 2pm-1am
Fri-Sat 2pm-2am
Sun 2pm-1am
Cash only

This cantina/restaurant/pool hall/motel/church combo, located adjacent to the American Inn lobby, is quite an experience. Move past two rooms filled with pool tables, prostitutes and beer swillin' vatos to find your way back to the more demure, if you will, dining room. The back windows afford a view of a seventies motel at its best with turquoise doors surrounding a well landscaped arena featuring the pool, complete with rock garden, strolling bridge and waterfall. A total trip. And the prices can't be beat: 29 bucks a night or 159 a week. Though initially a bit frightened, feeling as though I was way out of my element, I'm now thinking this would be a great little vacation spot. Our food was delicious. I went for the camarones tierra caliente and finished my plate. Mexican food, a cheap motel and pool tables…I'm in.

- Allison Walsh

INSIDERS TIP: Don't try to play the jukebox on Sundays during church lest you reap the Catholic wind that your Tejano may sow.

Zuzu

5770 N Mo Pac Expy. 78731
Phone: (512) 467-9295
Sun-Thu 8am-9pm
Fri-Sat 8am-10pm
Breakfast Mon-Sat 8am-11:30am
Sun 8am-2pm
Credit Cards

Despite its mission statement and kindergarten decor, Zuzu has a lot going for it. The food is fresh, handmade without lard, flavorful and healthy. Their menu has all the favorites, including a chipotle burrito and red mole enchiladas. But what makes Zuzu stand out is that you get to choose two sides with each entrée: corn salsa, black beans, rice, roasted potatoes or salad and then hit their amazing salsa bar. They have three salsas: two red and a tomatillo avocado, fresh diced jalapeños and red onions, pico de gallo, and sour cream! Free refills! Another plus for Zuzu is their variety of fresh salads made with leaf lettuce with a light dressing to which you can add either chicken, steak or mahi mahi. And who doesn't love a restaurant that has regular *and* spicy queso? They offer beer, a frozen lemon-limeade, and have several desserts on the menu. Zuzu is the perfect cure for the same old Tex-Mex.

- Jennifer Braflaadt

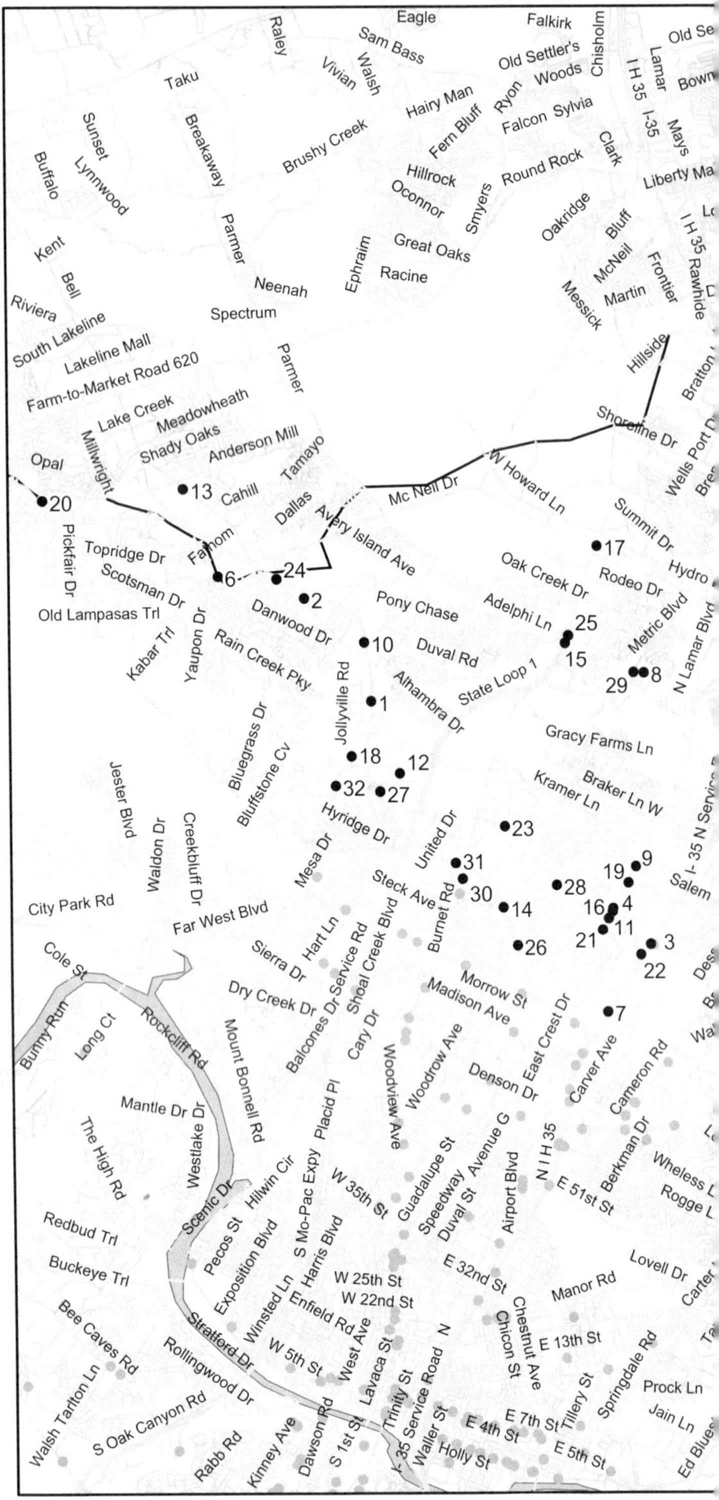

Eagle
Falkirk
Raley
Sam Bass
Old Settler's
Chisholm
Lamar
Vivian
Walsh
Woods
I H 35
Taku
Hairy Man
Ryon
Falcon
Sylvia
I-35
Sunset
Breakaway
Brushy Creek
Fern Bluff
Mays
Buffalo
Lynnwood
Hillrock
Round Rock
Clark
Oconnor
Smyers
Oakridge
Parmer
Great Oaks
Bluff
I H 35 Rawhide
Kent
Ephraim
McNeil
Frontier
Bell
Neenah
Racine
Messick
Martin
Riviera
Spectrum
South Lakeline
Lakeline Mall
Parmer
Hillside
Farm-to-Market Road 620
Lake Creek
Meadowheath
Shoreline Dr
Millwright
Shady Oaks
Anderson Mill
Tamayo
Opal
13
Cahill
Mc Neil Dr
W Howard Ln
20
Dallas
Avery Island Ave
Summit Dr
Pickfair Dr
Topridge Dr
Fathom
17
Scotsman Dr
6
24
Oak Creek Dr
Rodeo Dr
Hydro
2
Old Lampasas Trl
Danwood Dr
Pony Chase
Adelphi Ln
25
Metric Blvd
Yaupon Dr
Kabar Trl
Rain Creek Pky
10
Duval Rd
15
N Lamar Blvd
29
8
Jollyville Rd
1
Alhambra Dr
State Loop 1
Gracy Farms Ln
Bluegrass Dr
18
12
Braker Ln W
Kramer Ln
Jester Blvd
Bluffstone Cv
32
27
Waldon Dr
Creekbluff Dr
Hyridge Dr
23
United Dr
Mesa Dr
31
9
19
Steck Ave
30
Burnet Rd
28
Salem
City Park Rd
16
4
Far West Blvd
14
11
21
Hart Ln
Shoal Creek Blvd
3
Sierra Dr
26
22
Cole St
Service Rd
Dry Creek Dr
Morrow St
Madison Ave
7
Bunny Run
Long Ct
Rockcliff Rd
Balcones Dr
Cary Dr
East Crest Dr
Mount Bonnell Rd
Woodrow Ave
Carver Ave
Cameron Rd
Woodview Ave
Denson Dr
Mantle Dr
Westlake Dr
Placid Pl
The High Rd
Guadalupe St
Avenue G
N I H 35
Berkman Dr
Airport Blvd
S Mo-Pac Expy
Hilwin Cir
W 35th St
Speedway
Duval St
E 51st St
Scenic Dr
Redbud Trl
Pecos St
Exposition Blvd
Harris Blvd
Buckeye Trl
W 25th St
E 32nd St
Lovell Dr
W 22nd St
Manor Rd
Winsted Ln
Enfield Rd
Bee Caves Rd
Chestnut Ave
N
Chicon St
E 13th St
Stratford Dr
W 5th St
West Ave
Lavaca St
Springdale Rd
Rollingwood Dr
Trinity St
Service Road
Tillery St
Prock Ln
Walsh Tarlton Ln
S Oak Canyon Rd
Dawson Rd
S 1st St
I- 35
Waller St
E 7th St
Jain Ln
Kinney Ave
E 4th St
Rabb Rd
Holly St
E 5th St

mexican food in austin

Far North. This is technology country. The tech boom of the 90's is responsible for the explosive growth outwards into this area as can be seen by the glass office buildings with modern logos and the well-appointed suburbs surrounding them. The Arboretum offers upscale shopping with a slew of high-end national chains. Many Austin institutions like Whole Foods, Manuel's, Chuy's, Amy's, Waterloo and Alamo Draft House have outposts here, but the original charm of these places cannot be reproduced in such a planned environment.

1 A la Carrera
2 Antonio's
3 Arandas #4
4 Arandinas
5 Baby Acapulco
6 Camino Real
7 Cancun
8 Chipotle
9 Chuy's
10 Chuy's
11 El Tacolote
12 Iron Cactus
13 Jardin Corona
14 Juarez
15 La Morada
16 La Parrilla
17 Los Portales
18 Manuel's
19 Maudie's North Lamar
20 Mesa Rosa
21 Mr. Pollo
22 Rincon Catracho
23 Rita's
24 Serrano's
25 Taco Cabana
26 Taco Cabana
27 Taco Cabana
28 Taco More
29 Taco Shack
30 Trudy's North Star
31 Vasquez Tacos
32 Z Tejas Grill

A LA CARRERA

11150 Research Blvd. Ste. 210 78759
Phone: (512) 345-1763
Daily 7am-10pm
Breakfast 7am-11am
Credit Cards

A la Carrera has proudly held its own over the years against the virus of chain restaurants that have infested North Research. I hear from those who grew up in that part of town that their secret is excellent food. Imagine that. Bustling with a strong lunchtime crowd this place serves up a mean plate of Tex-Mex — affordably and quickly. And if you're in the mood they can whip you up a great big Mexican breakfast any time of day. I recommend the Numero Uno combo: an old school combination plate with one of all the majors. A la Carrera is a happy place — lively waiters buzzing around in a color scheme reminiscent of the movie Easter Parade with Judy Garland. Don't worry though, huge glass partitions cleverly separate the boozers at the bar from the four year olds singing happy birthday. I know where Judy would sit.

- Allison Walsh

ANTONIO'S MEXICAN RESTAURANT

11835 Jollyville Road 78759
Phone: (512) 257-2144
Mon-Thu 11am-9:30pm
Fri 11am-10:30pm
Sat 10am-10:30pm
Sun 10am-9:30pm
Music Fridays – sometimes Saturdays
Credit Cards

Please see review on page 158

Other Locations: North

ARANDAS TAQUERIA #4

834 E Rundberg Ln. 78753
Phone: (512) 835-4369
Fri-Sat 7am-1:30pm
Breakfast until 11am
Credit Cards

Please see review on pages 39, 98

Other Locations: North, East, South, Far South

ARANDINAS TAQUERIA

9616 N Lamar Blvd. 78753
Phone: (512) 490-0091
Mon-Sun 7am-12am
Breakfast until 11am
Credit Cards

Please see review on page 83

Other Locations: East, Southeast

BABY ACAPULCO RESTAURANT Y CANTINA

13609 N I-35 78753
Phone: (512) 670-9111
Fax: (512) 302-1707
Fri-Sat 11am-1am
Sun-Thu 11am-12pm
Breakfast all day
Credit Cards

Please see review on page 99

Other Locations: North, Southeast, South

CAMINO REAL RESTAURANT

8660 Spicewood Springs Rd. 78759
Phone: (512) 335-5517
Mon 8am-3pm
Tue-Thu 7am-9pm
Fri-Sat 7am-10pm
Sun 8am-3pm
Breakfast Tues-Sat 7am-11am
Sundays 8am-12pm
Credit Cards

Though Camino Real has a bustling lunch scene, what I really want to check out is the adjacent cantina with pool tables and full bar which must get happenin' at night. But as for lunch we were more than satisfied. Large plates, enough for two really, and service from a lady you wish was your mom. We were very pleased with the tortilla soup and gobbled our Shrimp a la Diablo, with the big tasty shrimp not the disappointing brine one sometimes gets.

- Allison Walsh

"Because I live so far south, I often find myself at the Texican Café for their cheesy layered dip. Otherwise, it's the poblano pepper enchiladas with green tomatilla sauce at La Feria."

- Scarlett,
Manager, Uchi restaurant

CANCUN MEXICAN RESTAURANT

8210 N I-35
Phone: (512) 719-9000
Open 7 days a week
Mon-Sun 6am-11pm
Breakfast every day until 11 am
Credit Cards

Taquería Cancun is one of those places you would never notice unless it was pointed out to you but it's definitely worth looking for. Walking inside you get the strange sensation that you've been to all of the fast food places this used to be. Mismatched pieces of an A&W, maybe a Braums and a Taco Tico stapled and glued together and directly adjacent to a motel pool. Sit in the back and enjoy the I-35 motel people watching or in some cases, the latest episode of Cops. Order the coldest, cheapest beer in town and the Shrimp a la Mexicana. Perfectly sautéed spicy shrimp, onions, tomatoes, jalapeños, rice and beans, this dish is out-of-this-world good and only six bucks. But after you're done with your cold beer, wait to go home and pee 'cause unless you want to reassemble the toilet in the ladies room yourself, you'll be aiming for a hole in the floor. Thank God, though, that they remembered the abundant ambrosia-scented potpourri.

- Leeanne Heavener

CHIPOTLE MEXICAN GRILL

1700 W Parmer Ln. 78727
Phone: (512) 837-0114
Mon-Sun 11am-10pm
Credit Cards

Please see review on page 6

Other Locations: Central, West, Far South

CHUY'S RESTAURANT

10520 North Lamar 78753
Phone: (512) 836-3218
www.chuys.com
Sun-Thu 11am-10pm
Fri-Sat 11am-11pm
Credit Cards

11680 Research Blvd. 78759
(512) 342-0011
www.chuys.com
Mon-Thurs 11:00am-10:30pm
Fri-Sat 11am-11:30pm
Credit Cards

Please see review on page 101

Other Locations: South

dlp essay

MEXICAN FLAVORED ICE CREAM

By Michael Thomson

Michael Thomson's recipes are reprinted with the permission of The Chile Pepper Magazine.

For Mexican flavored ice creams, combine the following flavor recipes into one gallon of store bought vanilla ice cream. In a large bowl, fully blend the flavorings with the ice cream with a small electric mixer or by hand. Place the flavored ice cream back into the original ice cream container or clean bowl. Freeze until serving.

Chipotle Piña Colada Ice Cream

1/2 cup	Coco Lopez
8 oz.	Cream cheese, softened
1/2 cup	Pineapple, canned, well-drained
1 Tbls.	Chipotle in adobo, pureed
Pinch	Chipotle chile flakes
1 cup	Toasted coconut
1/2 cup	Pistachio nuts, roasted & salted, chopped

Combine all ingredients in a bowl. Mix together with a spoon until well blended.

Avocado Ice Cream

2 Tbls.	Butter
2 Tbls.	Fresh garlic, minced
8 oz.	Fresh spinach, cleaned & finely chopped
1 cup	Avocado, ripe, cubed
1 tsp.	Tabasco sauce
2 Tbls.	Fresh line juice
1/2 cup	Brandy, Presidente (from Mexico)
8 oz.	Cream cheese, softened
Pinch	Salt & fresh ground pepper

Melt butter in a sauté pan over medium heat. Add the garlic and sauté until very lightly browned. Add spinach, avocado, Tabasco and lime juice. Sautee for several minutes until spinach is wilted. On a gas stove, carefully tilt pan to ignite alcohol. (On an electric stove carefully ignite alcohol with a long match). When the flame goes out, add cream cheese and season with salt and pepper.

Corn Ice Cream

2 Tbls.	Fresh jalapeño, roasted, seeded & minced
1 cup	Cilantro, minced
3 pcs.	Fresh sweet corn, roasted and cut from the cob
8 oz.	Cream cheese, softened
Pinch	Salt & fresh ground pepper

Mix all ingredients in a bowl with a spoon until well blended.

EDITOR'S NOTE: Frozen corn would be even better.

Fresh Basil Ice Cream

1 cup	Fresh basil, chopped
1 cup	Milk

Puree basil and milk in a blender until smooth.

dlp

EL TACOLOTE RESTAURANT

9425 N Lamar Blvd. 78753
Phone: (512) 835-6948
Open 24 hours
Breakfast all day
Credit Cards

Open 24 hours. Full Bar. The sign says it all and that's the only thing you need to know. El Tacolote does not hit its stride before 9 p.m. and any visit prior to that will not show you the full regalia of El Tacolote. Continuing the long tradition of late night taquerías, El Tacolote is next door to Desperados, a cowboy dance club that provides more than enough drunk and hungry patrons after 2 am to turn the place into a taco-crazy pick-up fest. Bring your Spanish.

- Chris Nelson

"Once a week I get a pollo and avocado tostada and a side of the tacos al pastor with pineapple from Arandas No 5. If you ask for it to go they put an extra tortilla on top of the tostada making it into the perfect sandwich."
- James Stockbauer,
Proprietor, The Longbranch Inn

IRON CACTUS MEXICAN GRILL AND MARGARITA BAR

10001 N Stonelake Blvd. 78759
Phone: (512) 794-8778
Sun-Thu 11am-10:30pm
Fri 11am-11pm
Sat 12pm-11pm
Music Thursdays & Fridays
Brunch 10am-2pm
Credit Cards

Please see review on page 13

Other Locations: Central

mexican food in austin

Jardin Corona Mexican Foods

13233 Pond Springs Rd. Ste. 301 78729
Phone: (512) 250-1061
Fax: (512) 996-9349
Mon-Thu 7am-10pm
Fri 7am-11pm
Sat 7am-11pm
Sun 8am-4pm
Music Thursdays Mariachi
Breakfast Mon-Fri 7am-11am
Breakfast Sat 7am-12pm
Breakfast Sun 7am-1pm
Credit Cards

This is your best bet for Mexican food in this area though don't expect a garden. The unassuming strip mall restaurant seems quiet from the outside, but is brimming with the lunchtime work force who evidently aren't afraid to swill down a few margarita midday. The food is good and the portions immense. The menu is one of those laminated tri-folds with every possible combination offered every which way. The steak fajitas were particularly tender and well seasoned. Jardín Corona is a well oiled machine — not subject to the hit or miss whimseys of many other mom and pops. Maybe this is the first step to franchising?

- *Allison Walsh*

Juarez Mexican Food

8766 Research Blvd. 78758
Phone: (512) 467-1915
Mon-Sat 7am-9pm
Closed Sundays
Breakfast all day
Credit Cards

Previously the Fishbone Grill, this Korean, family-run operation has made a bold move by shifting focus from their Asian-influenced dishes to the Mexican share of the menu. Reworking their business plan to accommodate their Tex-Mex addicted customer base was genius and easily accomplished by adopting a more Hispanic name. Touting a Mexican, Korean, Japanese and BBQ menu, this joint is well on its way to rivaling Epcot. After adjusting to

far north

the very un-Hispanic looking Juarez family, it becomes clear that they have not forgotten the first rule in the restaurant business across the Pacific: the photograph. Placed high above the counter is a full range of mouth-watering color photos meant to lure you into their culinary web. These photos trick your brain in that you can't decide if it's beef yakitori or beef fajitas, chicken mole or chicken tomburi. I had never noticed that these culinary traditions use such similar ingredients. Is it as simple as the difference between Thai chiles and Serranos? Plain white rice or with cumin? Order at the counter, fill up on your self-serve chips and sodas, and very soon a surprisingly good plate of Tex-Mex arrives. We had the ancho shrimp and some breakfast tacos, and honestly, I had no complaints. Actually, it was the first time in a while that the shrimp were so spicy that it made me sweat a little, which I like. So maybe this Mexican/Asian marriage has its rewards.

- Allison Walsh

La Morada Mexican Restaurant

12407 N MoPac Expressway Ste. 525 78758
Phone: (512) 836-6611
Sun-Thu 11am-10pm
Fri-Sat 11am-11pm
Credit Cards

I visited La Morada with three of my friends on a busy Friday night. To give this restaurant a fair review, we decided that everyone should order something different and share.

We all started off with margaritas: house on the rocks, house frozen and two top shelf — one with Sauza Hornitos and the other with Tres Generations. The house ritas were good but the top shelves were the favorites. Next came the Queso de Lodo, translation "queso with the works", refried beans, guacamole, sour cream and pico de gallo. There wasn't a lot of conversation during this appetizer, which meant that everyone loved it. The entrees promptly arrived: vegeladas, beef fajitas, chicken chile relleno and chimichanga.

mexican food in austin

This was the first time anyone in the group had dined at La Morada and all of us thought it was fantastic. It is moderately priced with great service and food. The only downfall was the salsa which was a little bland and not very spicy. Their location is a little too north for me but if you're willing to drive that far, it's definitely worth it.

- *Shelley Lamont*

LA PARRILLA NO. 1

9515 N Lamar Blvd.
Ste. 102 78753
Phone: (512) 491-9414
Fax: (512) 491-9414
Mon-Sun 7am-12am
Fri-Sat Open 24hrs.
Breakfast all day
Credit Cards

La Parrilla is in the strip shopping center category of Mexican places that are so numerous in this town. With neon beer signs, ample glass and high, exposed ceilings, one would not think of this as a Mexican cantina, but once you experience the lunch crowd and the booze being consumed, your illusions are quickly shattered. I'm not talking about a bunch of white guys sipping a Sam Adams between conference calls; I'm talking Mexicanos drinking daylight margaritas and feeling no shame. The food is standard fare with a few twists, but if you're up north with an itch for a quickie and a shot, it's the place.

- *Chris Nelson*

to by Derek Hatley

LOS PORTALES MEXICAN RESTAURANT

13717 N MoPac Expressway Ste. 250 78727
Phone: (512) 244-7006
Mon-Fri 10am-2pm; 5pm-9pm
Sat 11am-9pm
Closed on Sundays
Breakfast every day 10am-11am
Credit Cards

They've got everything in this shopping center. There's a discount cinema, Le Fun Arcade, an Indian restaurant called High Tech Masala, and, of course, Los Portales. The food is standard fare. "Standard" used to mean 'high' standard instead of passable. Standard Toilets were once some of the best in the world. Other toilet companies aspired to their high 'standard' of engineering. So, I will rephrase my judgement, and say that if Los Portales works hard, they could have standard food one day. It's really pretty okay. It's just that when I think about the shopping center and all of its glory, Los Portales should be held to a higher standard. Le Fun and High Tech Masala raise the bar and Los Portales must step it up a notch if they want to complete. This ain't Russia and the USA ain't givin' no free rides today or any other day as long as patriotism and free market capitalism provide us, as consumers and citizens, with the best the world has to offer. Amen.

- Chris Nelson

MANUEL'S AT GREAT HILLS

10201 Jollyville Rd. 78759
Phone: (512) 345-1042
Mon-Thu 11am-10pm
Fri-Sat 11am-12am
Sun 10am-10pm
Music Sundays 11:30am-2pm
Credit Cards

Please see review on page 20

Other Locations: Central

mexican food in austin

MAUDIE'S NORTH LAMAR

10205 N Lamar 78753
Phone: (512) 832-0900
http://www.maudies.com
Sun-Thu 9am-9:30pm
Fri-Sat 9am-10pm
Breakfast all day
Credit Cards

Please see review on page 151

Other Locations: South, Far South, West

"We go to Amaya's for the best Tex-Mex: the very best old-fashioned tacos and the limey homemade tortillas. I hit Cisco's for the huevos rancheros with biscuits and a side of fajitas. Or get the "ultimate" taco at Juan in a Million.
- *Alan Lazarus*
Chef/co-owner, Vespaio

MESA ROSA

10700 Anderson Mill Road Suite 100
Phone: (512) 335-3335
Sun-Thurs 11am-9pm
Sat-11am-10pm

Some people are reluctant to go to east Austin Mexican food joints because of some (incorrectly) perceived notion that it's dangerous, but the neighborhoods that inspire the most fear in me are far north-west. The part of town where Mesa Rosa is located scared the shite out of me not because it looked dangerous, but for the seemingly endless line of churches, gated subdivisions, strip shopping centers and churches in strip shopping centers. Yes, Mesa Rosa is located next to a church in a strip shopping center (God likes lots of parking). The patrons and food at Mesa Rosa share a 1950's white-bread, canned-up wholesomeness that's eerie and bland and bears no resemblance to anything remotely Mexican. But hell, if you're from Dubuque Iowa, it's just like home.

- *Chris Nelson*

dlp essay

KENNETH'S PERFECT MARGARITA

by Kenneth Adkins

8oz.	*Fresh Lime Juice*
8oz.	*Fresh Lemon Juice*
2 cup	*Simple Syrup**
	Silver Tequilia "100% Blue Agave"
	Grand Marnier
	Kosher Salt
	Lime Wedges

Combine lemon juice, lime juice and simple syrup. Salt the rim of a 16 oz. glass. Fill with ice, add 2 oz. tequila, 3/4 oz. Grand Marnier, and top with lemon-lime mix. Finish with a lime wedge.

1 cup sugar, dissolved in 2 cups water

Yield: approx. 10 drinks

MR. POLLO

9207 N Lamar Blvd. 78753
Phone: (512) 275-0544
Mon-Sun 10am-10pm
Breakfast Mon-Sun 10am-11am
Credit Cards

Mr. Pollo needs to be "Queer Eyed for the Straight Guy". Like the show's makeover subjects, Mr. Pollo has, at its core, the noblest of intentions. The fajita chicken is tender and flavorful, the salsas are carefully handmade and the quesadillas are quite satisfying. Mr. Pollo's good intentions are compromised by its location in a dilapidated ex-fast food building, the misleading and fading pictures of strange food hanging on the walls and untrained staff whose organizational skills remind us that physical comedy is not yet dead. But, to be able to say that you've dined at a place called Mr. Pollo is reason enough to visit just once.

- Chris Nelson

RINCON CATRACHO

9120 N IH 35 78753
Phone: (512) 821-2595
Mon-Sun 11am-10pm
Breakfast all day
Music Mariachi on Fridays 8pm-10pm
Credit Cards

Eating here is much like eating in the Twilight Zone. As I sat and ate delicious, authentic Honduran steak, I watched a string of policemen exit from the motel across the street, place small plastic baggies in the Crime Scene Unit van, and help an old man put a bicycle in the trunk of a Ford Taurus. Apparently all the razor wire on top of the motel fence failed to keep trouble out, or maybe in. While all of this was transpiring, a CD of blaring Tejano music kept skipping and playing the same fifteen seconds over and over again. Nobody else in the restaurant seemed to notice or mind it. After ten minutes, I informed the waitress of this fact and she seemed surprised. Don't let the weirdness dissuade you. This is a hub for immigrant Hondurans and great one at that. When the Honduran national team plays soccer matches you'll find between 150 and 200 Honduran fans climbing over each other, eating, drinking and watching the game on one of their seven television sets. It's a pretty interesting place, off the beaten track, and good if you're into exploring. Check the soccer listings for Honduras.

- Chris Nelson

RITA'S MEXICAN RESTAURANT

1934 Rutland Dr. Ste. 100 78758
Phone: (512) 834-0999
Daily 7am-9pm
Breakfast 'till 10:45am
Credit Cards

Tucked into the low look-alike office buildings near Metric is Rita's — a little breakfast, lunch and dinner spot with an open dining room, typical bright blankets on the walls and taco options listed above the kitchen door. I recently stopped by and took one of every kind of their tacos to a bunch of guys working the line in an Italian joint, just before service on a Friday night. Guys who work in kitchens appreciate any kind of food they don't have to make themselves and descended upon the bag of tacos like wolves. One nice waitress and one guy on the line filled two enormous bags with carne guisada, beef and chicken fajita, ground beef, barbacoa and al pastor tacos which cost $2.25 a piece, pretty pricey for what we got. A bad start with crunchy edges to the tortillas, all of which were flour. The al pastor was the best according to the chefs, with lots of thumbs up for the queso as well. Chips were crisp and generous and the salsa, a thin puree, did have a good bit of spice. The most telling opinion on our first run with Rita's was offered by the dishwasher who is from Mexico and said dryly, "No bueno ni malo." So there you have it.

- Gracie Salem

Serrano's

12636 Research Blvd. 78759
Phone: (512) 250-9555
Sun-Thu 11am-10pm
Fri-Sat 11am-11pm
Breakfast all day
Credit Cards

Please see review on page 29

Other Locations: Central, South

Taco Cabana

12525 N MoPac Expressway 78727
Phone: (512) 310-0340
Sun-Thu 6am-1am
Fri-Sat 6am-2am
Beer, Margaritas & Piña Coladas
Breakfast
Credit Cards

8415 Research Blvd. 78758
Phone: (512) 832-0311
Sun-Thu 6am-1am
Fri-Sat 6am-2am
Beer, Margaritas & Piña Coladas
Breakfast
Credit Cards

9605 Research Blvd 78759
Phone: (512) 338-0345
Sun-Thu 6am-1am
Fri-Sat 6am-2am
Beer, Margaritas & Piña Coladas
Breakfast
Credit Cards

Please see review on page 30

Other Locations: All over the damn place

dlp

TACOS AND MORE

1325 Rutland 78758
Phone: (512) 272-5010
Mon-Fri 6am-1pm
Sat 6:30am-11:30am
Breakfast served until closing time

Authentic. The Real Deal. This ain't no Tex-Mex.

Ok. These people that ran the "Tow-Behind Kitchen" as I called it got real smart, real quick and they got a bonafied establishment. They now have a place not far from the original location on the Northwest corner of Parkfield and Rutland. The family as it turns out is the Morenos. Gorditas, tacos, menudo, quesadillas and many more menu items I haven't tried are on the extensive menu. I'm still stuck on the al Pastor tacos. There are around 6-8 tables inside the restaurant and it isn't too crowded outside of traditional lunch hours, so eating there is not out of the question. But, it's good for the food on the go also.

A handful of people work there now who remember me getting food when they were all cramped in the small tow-behind kitchen trailer making some kickass dishes. I've gone in there before, 75 cents short, but wanting three tacos. And there wasn't a single second of hesitation. Business was going to get done, and I'd walk away full.

- Paul Jacobs

TACO SHACK

12439 Metric Blvd. 78758
Phone: (512) 873-7977
Mon-Fri 6am-2:30pm
Sat 7am-1pm
Breakfast Mon-Fri 6am-11am

Please see review on page 32

Other Locations: Central, North

dlp essay

AUNT GAYLE'S SALSA

by Gayle Erickson

For the best salsa around, follow this simple recipe. It will be famous someday.

3 lb.	*can whole tomatoes (or equivalent fresh tomatoes)*
5	*large onions*
6	*jalapeños*
1	*bunch cilantro*
1 cup	*vinegar*
1/8 cup	*salt*

Blend the vegetables together in a blender (small batches at a time) until chopped and mixed but not pureed. Pour vegetables into large pot on stove and add vinegar and salt. Stir occasionally until mixed and bubbly (it does bubble). Chill and serve. If you can't finish it all, pour it into pint jars that have been heated and top the jars with a heated jar lid and ring and stick in the fridge. If you don't want to keep salsa refrigerated, get a canning kit and follow those instructions.

dlp

TRUDY'S NORTH STAR

8820 Burnet Rd 78757
Phone: (512) 454-1474
Fax: (512) 454-0592
Mon-Fri 11am-2am
Sat-Sun 10am-2am
Credit Cards

Please see review on page 33.

Other Locations: Central, South

VASQUEZ TACOS

9063 Research Blvd 78758
Phone: (512) 837-2753
Mon-Fri 6am-5pm
Sat 7am-5pm
Sun 9am-4pm
Breakfast all day
Credit Cards

From humble beginnings comes this family run and staffed taquería in North Austin. Señor and Señora Vazquez appeared on the taco radar several years ago when we noticed constant lines in front of their trailer that began appearing on a vacant lot just north of 183 on Burnet. Pulling the trailer and several family members up to their location by 6am every morning from South Austin and packing everything back up for the return home after lunch every day, the Vazquez family built a loyal following among the office workers, Dell legions (pre-Round Rock), landscapers, and assorted other miscreants who inhabit the area during normal business hours. The succulent food tubes that masqueraded as simple breakfast tacos were excellent (best bacon taco ever), but the coup de grace is the hot sauce. The red chunk-less fluid is so addictive and flavorful you'll swear somebody has been pureeing smack. The inherent inconsistency that results from homemade hot sauce in terms of heat and viscosity is just a bonus.

Following a move to a more permanent trailer location next to Buddy's Place, the Vazquez family opened a sit-down restaurant just east of IH-35 on Braker a few years ago and completed the second establishment at Burnet and 183 last year, retiring the trailer. The unparalleled

mexican food in austin

breakfast tacos are supplemented by the Al Pastor ($5.75 for a plate including fresh cilantro, onions, rice, and their lovely lard-infused refried beans), but the menu contains all the favorites plus a few surprises that make this the best inexpensive breakfast and/or lunch in this part of town. Not open Sundays and only 6am-3pm weekdays and opening a little later on Saturdays. Call in your order for pickup and be a hero at the office.

- Jordan Actkinson

Z Tejas Grill

9400 Arboretum Blvd Ste. A 78759
Phone: (512) 832 9952
Mon-Thu 11am-10pm
Fri 11am-11pm
Sat 10am-11pm
Sun 10am-10pm
Credit Cards

Please see review on page 35

Other Locations: Central

photo by Derek Hatley

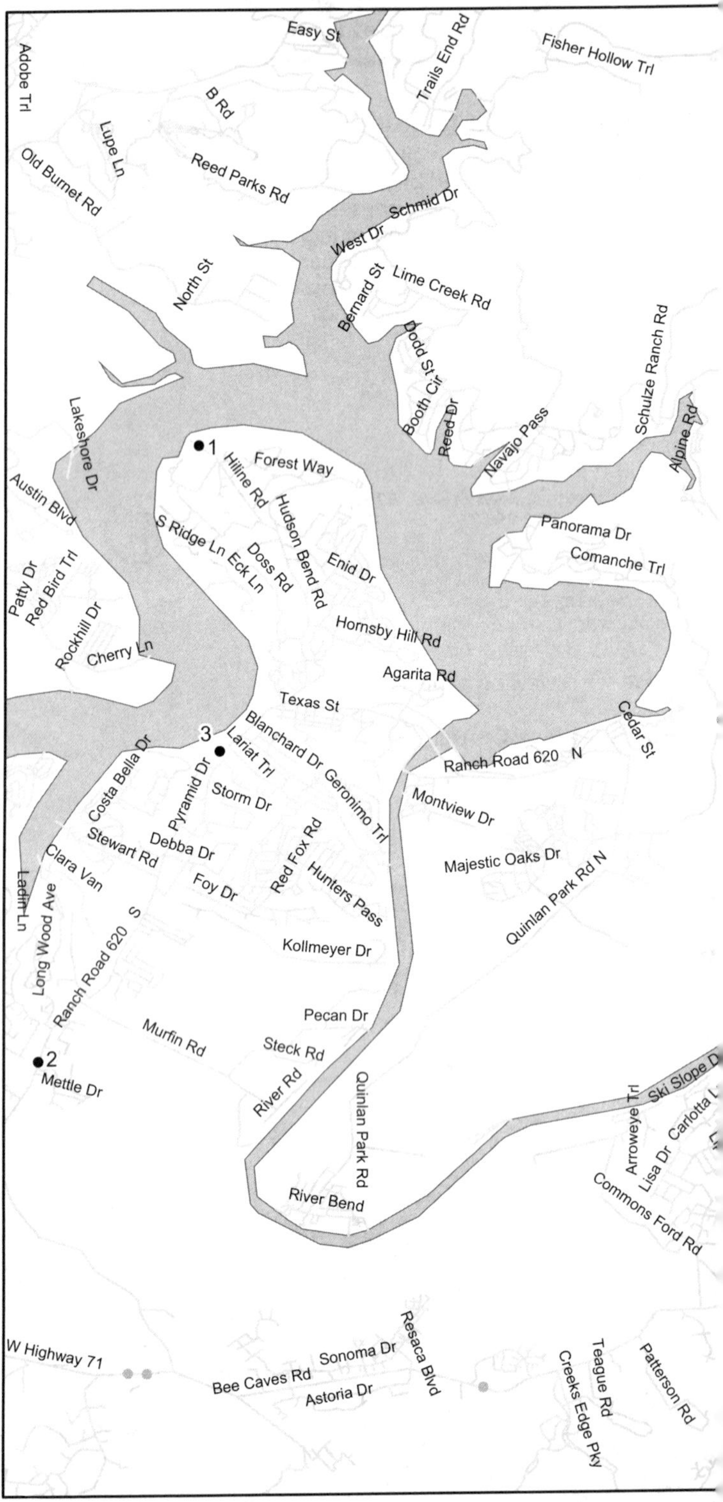
Easy St
Trails End Rd
Fisher Hollow Trl
Adobe Trl
B Rd
Lupe Ln
Old Burnet Rd
Reed Parks Rd
Schmid Dr
West Dr
Bernard St
Lime Creek Rd
North St
Dodd St
Booth Cir
Reed Dr
Schulze Ranch Rd
Alpine Rd
Navajo Pass
Lakeshore Dr
1
Forest Way
Hiline Rd
Austin Blvd
Hudson Bend Rd
S Ridge Ln
Eck Ln
Doss Rd
Enid Dr
Panorama Dr
Comanche Trl
Patty Dr
Red Bird Trl
Rockhill Dr
Cherry Ln
Hornsby Hill Rd
Agarita Rd
Texas St
Cedar St
3
Blanchard Dr
Lariat Trl
Geronimo Trl
Costa Bella Dr
Pyramid Dr
Storm Dr
Ranch Road 620 N
Montview Dr
Stewart Rd
Debba Dr
Red Fox Rd
Majestic Oaks Dr
Clara Van
Foy Dr
Hunters Pass
Quinlan Park Rd N
Ladin Ln
Long Wood Ave
Ranch Road 620 S
Kollmeyer Dr
Pecan Dr
Murfin Rd
Steck Rd
2
Mettle Dr
River Rd
Quinlan Park Rd
Ski Slope D
Arroweye Trl
Carlotta L
Lisa Dr
Commons Ford Rd
River Bend
W Highway 71
Sonoma Dr
Resaca Blvd
Bee Caves Rd
Astoria Dr
Creeks Edge Pky
Teague Rd
Patterson Rd

mexican food in austin

Lake Travis is one of the many man-made Texas lakes constructed in the 30's. It dams the Colorado River to create hydro-electric energy and provide a place for central Texans to jet ski and drink beer. All the requisite lake stuff is here — the restaurants, bars, ski shops, condos, fishing outposts and such. A top weekend destination for Austinites, Lake Travis provides fun in the sun (and some Mexican food places as well).

1 Carlos n Charlie's

2 Flores

3 Iguana Grill

4 The Oasis

Carlos n Charlie's

5973 Hiline Road Austin, Texas 78734
Phone: (512) 266-1683
Daily 11:30am- 10pm

If you like frat parties, hard bodies, Pat Green and the tastiest chicas on Lake Travis, then wax your chest, grab your Luchenbach koozie and head down to Carlos n Charlie's. This Austin outfit is the first US location for the formulaic and highly profitable Señor Frogs empire that stretches all the way down to Brazil, making pit stops wherever there are drunk college kids and bloated bar tabs. Spring and summer bring outside concerts featuring KGSR-sanctioned bands and all the usual suspects keeping "Austin Weird." The menu is extensive, well-prepared and affordable, but if you can taste the food, it probably means you just arrived at the lake or got out of an AA meeting. Have a margarita, or five, because Carlos n Charlie's is about the types of good times that come in a bottle, bikini or ski boat.

- Chris Nelson

Flores Restaurant

1310 RR 620 S, Ste. A4
512-263-9546
Mon-Thurs 11am – 10 pm
Fri 11am – 10:30 pm
Sat-Sun 9am – 2pm
Breakfast Sat & Sun only
Credit Cards

I have been eating at this Lake Travis location for what seems to be ten years, happily and regularly. I think my lake friends eat here three or four times a week as we are always greeted with huge smiles followed up with impeccable service. I always get the poblano enchiladas with extra poblanos and a few margaritas, which I love. The margaritas are so good in fact that we usually ask our favorite waiter to come over and make them for our special occasions. It can get kind of crowded during the summers so be prepared to wait — but there is not another Mexican outfit for several miles either direction so sit tight. But here's the rub ... I'm not a fan of the other locations. Oh well.

- Allison Walsh

Other Locations: West, North

IGUANA GRILL

2900 Ranch Road 620 North, Austin, TX 78734
Phone: (512) 467-8776
Sun-Thurs 11am-9pm
Fri-Sat 11am-10pm

This outfit is as famous for their incredible sunsets overlooking Lake Travis as for coining the term "Lake-Mex." Their chipotle pepper salsa always ranks at the hot sauce festival and compliments almost everything on the menu especially the carnitas and the flautas. A favorite of mine is the ceviche al estilo Yucateca—yellowfin tuna marinated in lime served with pico de gallo—consistently fresh and appetizing. In my opinion their food has been hit or miss over the years. Regardless, they have maintained a loyal, albeit sunburned following because honestly there really isn't a more beautiful spot to sip on a margarita than here.

- Allison Walsh

THE OASIS

6550 Comanche Trail 78732
Phone: (512) 266-2442
www.oasis-austin.com
Spring and Summer Hours
(During Daylight Savings)
Mon-Thu 11:30am-10pm
Fri 11:30am-11pm
Sat 11am-11pm
Sun 11am-10pm
Fall and Winter Hours
(Central Standard Time)
Mon-Thurs 11am- 9pm
Sat 11am- 10pm
Sun 11- 9pm
Credit Cards
Music as scheduled

With an impressive view of the sunset high above Lake Travis and the ability to accommodate multiple busloads of hungry, thirsty people at any given time, the Oasis is repeatedly voted a top area attraction by various Hill Country tourism boards. But don't get me wrong this place is ready for you to let loose and won't try to break up an impromptu conga line. From what I can see this place has two main personalities: Spring Break Fort Lauderdale minus the beach complete with beer-gutted frat boys and their overly tanned bikini clad counterparts chuggin' margs and catchin' rays. Or, the back end of a Pacific Princess cruise ship; multistoried with over forty lakeside Aledo decks, wedding chapel, restaurants, nightclub and gift shop full of sunburned tourists with cameras and Cocolocos with umbrellas disoriented enough to try to disembark in Puerto Vallarta.

It is an immense operation suitable for every occasion from a small child's birthday to a bachelorette party. The menu is exactly what you would imagine: nachos, fajitas, burritos, chicken sandwiches, chicken this and that; a big outdoor TGIF Friday's. If this is your cup of tea, don your Hawaiian shirt and your OP shorts and get ready to mingle. Hey…do me a favor and drink responsibly and if you haven't already gathered, don't go if it's raining.

— *Allison Walsh*

Sunsets:	Amazing
Margaritas:	Pretty Good
Food:	Stick to the margaritas

— *Ann Tucker*

dlp essay

MEXICAN CUISINE *continued from page 178*

sonings in the mole poblano include onion, garlic, tomato, cinnamon, and cloves. There are regions even within the State of Puebla, and as it is a state known for its cuisine, many of these regions boast of their own traditional dishes including tlacoyas, blue corn dough filled with refried beans, grilled on a hot comal and topped with chopped onions, cheese and your choice of red or green salsa; and mole verde, a stew made with tomate verde, cilantro, epazote, green chiles, garlic and onion simmered with shredded chicken or pork and the accompanying stock, served with rice and beans. Puebla by far is the land of varied and vast cuisine.

Gulf States

Here again is a region that enjoys the bounty of the sea, or in this case, the gulf where the coastal waters offer up a variety of fish and shellfish. Shrimp, black snapper, octopus, pampano, and cazon (baby shark) are typical of dishes throughout the region. Native Mayan ingredients as well as Afro-Cuban and Spanish influences reveal themselves in the relaxed culture and cuisine of the Gulf States. Native herbs and spices are supplemented by tropical fruits used in both the food and drink of this region.

Vera Cruz

The rich culinary tradition here stems from the heavy mix of influences; the indigenous, the Spanish and the Cuban all combine to create a thriving cultural melting pot. The use of corn, beans, squash, and indigenous herbs like hoja santa, a variety of tropical fruits, in combination with chiles, avocados, papaya, mamey, as well as the Spanish influence of cilantro, and bay laurel create a flavorful regional cuisine. Other influences of the region, plantains, yucca and sweet potatoes are all reflections of the West African culinary influence in the area. Local favorites include empanadas, picaditas and garnachos æ both of which are versions of bean-stuffed corn cakes æ arroz a la tumbada, a rice dish baked with a variety of seafood; pollo encacahuatado, chicken in peanut sauce, and caldo de mariscos, the hangover-curing seafood soup famous to the region. However, the most characteristic and probably most well known dish of

dlp essay

the region is the huachinango a la veracruzana, red snapper in a spicy tomato sauce seasoned and prepared with olive oil, garlic and capers. Vera Cruz encompasses the heart of the gulf coastal culture and cuisine in the region.

Yucatan Peninsula

The Yucatan peninsula maintains a long standing history of fine dining, sophisticated dishes and possibly the most distinctive regional cuisines in Mexico. Much of the areas' indigenous agriculture is still used today in most of the regions dishes. Corn has been a staple since the early days of the Maya as well as native fowl like turkey, which is still utilized today, although in some areas it has been replaced with chicken. Fruit and honey are other influential factors in the regional cuisine, and of course seafood is indispensable here too as most of the region shares a border with the Gulf.

Campeche

Known for its easy going people, Campeche is an ideal place for any one wishing to take it slow for a while and enjoy the finer things in life. Seafood abounds here, but they have their own breed of chicken as well as a white skinned chicken specifically bred to withstand the heat that typifies much of the Yucatan area. One will encounter not the typical snack foods of the central regions, like gorditas or chalupas, but rather the local favorites, panuchos and salbutes, which are similar corn dough-based snacks filled with black beans and either shredded fish or chicken depending on what you like. Many dishes of the region utilize the indigenous herb achiote, originally used by the Mayans, which is combined with the exotic fruits and other Spanish herbs that characterize the area. Sweet, flavorful juices and ice creams are found abundantly throughout the villages of Campeche and reflect the tropical geography of the region that has influenced the cuisine.

Yucatan

Hot chiles, seafoods and a wealth of indigenous fruits, vegetables and meats characterize this state's cuisine. Pumpkin and

dlp essay

squash seeds, a Mayan ingredient still heavily relied upon to this day, are used in many sauces including the sauce for papadzules, a common enchilada-like dish. Queso relleno, a whole Edam cheese hollowed out and filled with picadillo, (spiced ground meat), chilmole, turkey covered in a black sauce, and pollo ticul, Yucatan style chicken that uses bitter oranges and banana leaves for flavor are regional favorites that can only be found in the State of Yucatan. The achiote seeds, used in the recado rojo sauce which coats the cochinita pibil, a baked marinated pork dish; the peppercorns, cinnamon sticks, cloves, coriander seeds and the allspice berries that are used in the sauce for chilmole are among the multitude of spices at the Yucatan chef's disposal. Regional favorites include pollo ticu-leno, chicken baked in banana leaves, sopa de lima, sopa de mariscos, pork empanadas, pescado tikin-xic, fresh grouper seasoned with the typical Yucatan achiote paste, baked in banana leaves and chivitas, small river snails made into ceviche.

best dishes

SALSA

El Azteca
Habanero's
El Regio
Evita's Botanitas
Angie's
Tacodeli
San Juanita

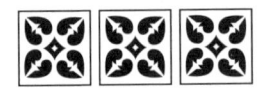

SEAFOOD

Polvos
Los Jaliscienses
Marisco Grill
Manuel's
Jardin Corona
Bejuco's # 2
Janitzio
Curra's

best dishes

TACOS

La Michoacana
Arandas
Taco Sabroso
taco cart across from Emo's
Nuevo Leon
Maria's Taco Xpress
Julio's
Tacodeli

TORTILLA SOUP

Al Pastor
Güero's
Mexico Lindo
Camino Real
El Chile
Nuevo Leon

best dishes

BREAKFAST TACOS

Mi Madres
Ruby's
Taco Shack
Curra's
Arturo's Bakery Café
Foodheads
Nueva Onda
Maria's Taco Xpress
Rosie's Taco Stand

MIGAS

Tamale House
El Meson
Trudy's
Juan in a Million
El Sol y La Luna
Enchiladas Y Mas

best dishes

MARGARITAS

Four Seasons
Fonda San Miguel
Baby Acapulco's
La Reyna
Güero's
Curra's
Trudy's
Ranch 616

FAJITAS

Las Cazuelas
Los Comales
Habaneros
Mama Ninfa's
El Chile
La Feria
El Rancho Grande

best dishes

Most Popular (for Gringos)

Juan in a Million
Güero's
Maudie's
Chuy's
Taco Shack
El Mercado
Hula Hut

Best Non-Mex Mex

Foodheads
Chumikal's
Ranch 616
Dartbowl
Z Tejas Grill

best dishes

BEST FOR YOUR MONEY

El Meson
Arandas
Azul Tequila
Tamale House
Taco Cabana
El Regio

ENCHILADAS

Aus Tex-Mex
Luviano's
Polvos
Las Manitas
Little Mexico
Angie's
Dario's
Ranch 616
Dart Bowl
Enchiladas Y Mas

best dishes

CONCHINITA PIBIL

Curra's
Fonda San Miguel
Azul Tequila
El Meson

TEX MEX

Angie's
Dario's
Jaime's Spanish Village
Maudie's
El Gallo
Mama Ninfa's

helpful phrases

General

Yes	Sí
No	No
Good/OK	Bueno/a
Bad	Malo/a
Better	Mejor
Best	Lo mejor
More	Más
Less	Menos
Very little	Poco/a or poquito/a
Where is…?	¿Dónde está…?
Taxi	taxi
Restroom	el baño
How far is…?	¿A qué distancia está…?
How much time?	¿Cuánto tiempo?

Greeting and civilities

Hello/Hi	Hola
Good Morning	Buenos días
Good Afternoon	Buenas tardes
Good Evening/Good Night	Buenas noches
Pleased to meet you	Mucho gusto
How are you?	¿Cómo está usted?
I'm fine	Estoy bien.
See you later	Hasta luego.
Good-Bye	Adiós
Please	Por favor
Thank You	Gracias
You're Welcome	De nada
Excuse Me	Disculpe / Perdóneme

helpful phrases

Buying and ordering

How much?	¿Cuánto es?
How much does it cost?	¿Cuánto cuesta…?
I would like…	Quisiera…
I would not like…	No quisiera…
Give me…	Déme
Do you have…?	¿Tiene usted…?
Is/are there any…?	¿Hay…?
May I have another…	Me puede dar otro/otra
This isn't what I ordered.	Esto no es lo que ordené.
What is this?	¿Qué es esto?
This is delicious.	Esto es delicioso/a.
I would like salt on my margarita.	Qusiera sal en mi margarita.
One more shot of tequila please.	Otro shot de tequila por favor.
Beer for all my friends.	Cerveza para todos mis amigos.
Drinks all around.	Bebida para todos.
What do you recommend?	¿Qué recomienda usted?
What is the most popular dish?	¿Cuál es el plato más popular?
What is your favorite?	¿Cuál es su favorito?
On the side	A parte
rare	Poco cocido/a
medium	A su punto
well-done	Bien cocido/a

Language

I do not speak Spanish.	No hablo español.
Do you speak English?	¿Habla usted inglés?
I understand.	Entiendo.
I don't uderstand.	No entiendo.
Do you understand?	¿Entiende usted?
What did you say?	¿Mande?/ ¿Como?
Please speak slowly.	Por favor hable despacio.
How do you say in Spanish?	¿Como se dice en español?

glossary

abulón	abalone
aceite	oil
aceituna	olive
achiote	annato tree seed used to make a seasoning paste of the same name
acitrón	candied cactus fruit
acocil	small, fresh water crustacean
adobo	paste used for cooking meats, poultry and fish
agua	water
aguacate	avocado
aguamiel	century plant juice
aguas frescas	a type of soft drink made by infusing water with various flavorings
aguayón	sirloin steak
aguja	a cut of beef that is one of the favorite char-broiled specialties in northern Mexico
ahumado	smoked
aji ayucllo	wild pepper
ajo	garlic
ajonjoli	sesame
a la parrilla	grilled over charcoal
a la plancha	grilled on a hotplate or griddle
a la tampiqueño, veracruzana, etc.	Tampico style, Veracruz style, cooked over charcoal or wood coals
al carbón	
al horno	oven-baked
al vapor	steamed
alambre	shish kebab
albahaca	basil
albaricoque	apricot
albóndiga	meatball
almejas	clams
almendra	almond
almíbar	syrup
almuerzo	lunch
anaheim	mild pepper
ancho chile	dried poblano pepper
añejo/a	something that is aged like cheese or liquor
anís	aniseed
anona	sugar apple
anticuchos	spicy beef kabobs
antojitos	hors d'oeuvres or appetizers
aperitivos	appetizers
apio	celery
arrachera	skirt steak
arroz	rice
arroz con leche	rice pudding
asadero	a soft and mild cheese
asado/a	broiled

glossary

ate	jam
atole	hearty corn or rice drink
atún	tuna
aves	poultry
ayocote	a large type of bean
azafrán	saffron
azúcar	sugar
bacalao	dried fish
balché	Mayan alcoholic beverage made with bark of the balché tree and honey
bañar	to immerse in liquid
barbacoa	barbecued meat
báscula	scale
batata	sweet potatoes
batir	to whisk or beat
betabel	beet
birria	soup from Jalisco made with lamb or goat
bistec	beef steak
bizcocho	flavored poundcake or cookie
bocadillo	sandwich
bolillo	crusty rolls for sandwiches
bonito	Latin American sweet potato
borracho/a	drunk, or cooked with wine
borrego	sheep
botana	snacks or appetizers
brasear	braise
brocheta	shish kabob or skewer
budín	pudding
buelo	deep-fried sweet pastry
burro/burrito	large tortilla wrapped around a filling
cabrito	young goat
cacahuate	peanut
cacerola	casserole dish
café	coffee or a café
café americano	black coffee
café con crema	coffee with cream served separately
café con leche	coffee with steamed milk or half and half
café de olla	Mexican style coffee made in a clay pot
caguama	large bottle of beer literally meaning turtle
cajeta	a confection made by simmering goat's milk and sugar to a thick paste
calabacita	squash
calabaza	squash or pumpkin
calamar	squid
caldo	soup or broth
caliente	Hot to the touch
camarones	shrimp
camote	sweet potatoes
campechano	seafood cocktail
canela	cinnamon

glossary

cangrejo	large crab
capulín	fruit resembling a wild cherry used for medicine or ornamentation
caramelo	caramel or hard candy
carne	beef
carne asada	broiled beef
carne de res	beef
carne guisada	beef stew served over rice or tortillas
carne molida	ground beef
carnero	mutton
carnitas	shredded pork
carta	menu
cayenne	pepper used in many hot sauces
cazón	shark
cazuelitas	a thin tortilla molded into a shallow bowl and deep fried before being filled
cebolla	onion
cebollitas de cambray	green onions or scallions
cecina	thin pieces of dried or partially dried meat infused with chiles and other seasonings
cedazo	strainer or sieve
cena	dinner or supper
cerdo	pork or pig
cerveza	beer
ceviche	seafood or fish cocktail marinated in lime juice
chabacano	apricot
chalupas	open faced tortillas fried and topped with shredded meat, cheese and other fillings
chambarete	shank of beef
champiñon	mushroom
champurrado	chocolate atole
charal	minnow-sized dried fish
chayote	squash
chícharo	pea
chicharrónes	fried pork rinds
chilaquiles	fried chips mixed with chile sauces often with chicken and cheese, served at breakfast
chile	chili pepper
chilatole	atole flavored with ground broiled tomatoes and chiles
chile con queso	melted cheese dip seasoned with chilis
chile relleño	chili peppers stuffed with meat or cheese then baked or fried
chili con carne	chili with meat, diced or ground beef, chilies and chili powder
chilocuil	red century plant worms
chilorio	a meat filling made with pork that is boiled, shredded then fried with chiles and spices
chilpachol	soup made with crab meat and tomato

glossary

chimichanga	deep fried burrito
chipotle	dried chilies fermented in vinegar
chivo	goat
chorizo	spicy pork sausage
chuleta	chop or cutlet
churros	deep fried pastry sprinkled with sugar
cilantro	fresh coriander
ciruela	plum
ciruela pasa	prune
clavo de olor	clove
cocer	to cook, boil or simmer
cocido/a	cooked
cocina	kitchen
cocinar	to cook
coco	coconut
cóctel	cocktail
cochinita	suckling pig
codillo	elbow or knuckle
codorniz	quail
col	cabbage
coladera	colander, sieve or strainer
colonche	alcoholic beverage made by fermenting the nopal cactus
coma	griddle made originally from clay, but now more usually from iron, steel, or tin
comal	round griddle used to cook tortillas
comida	food, or referring to the large meal eaten in the mid or late afternoon
comino	cumin
conejo	rabbit
confitar	to crystallize, to sweeten or to cook fruit in syrup
copa	wine glass or coctail
cordero	lamb
cortar	to cut
corunda	a trangle shaped tamal
costillas chuletas	rib steaks
cotija	hard cheese or queso añejo
crema	cream
crepas	crepes
cuchara	spoon
cucharada	tablespoon
cuchillo	knife
cuenta	check or bill
cumin	ground coriander
desayunar	to eat breakfast
dasayuno	breakfast
datíl	date
derretir	melt
deshuesar	debone

glossary

destapador	bottle opener
diezmillo	chuck steak
dinero	money
dorado	dolphin fish or browned
dulce	sweet or candy
durazno	peach
ejotes	green beans
elote	corn on the cob
embutido	cold meat, sausage and sausage making
empanada	pastry turnover filled with either meat or fruits and other sweets
empanizar	to bread or to fry meat or fish coated with bread crumbs
en su jugo	meat or poultry cooked in its own juice
enchilada	a corn tortilla rolled around various fillings then topped with sauce and cheese
enchilado	meat, cheese or other foods coated with chili paste or powder
enfrijoladas	corn tortillas filled, folded in half and topped with thinned frijoles before baking
enrollado/a	rolled
ensalada	salad
entomatadas	enchiladas made by dipping the tortillas in a sauce before they are wrapped around a filling
entrada	main course
envueltos	fried tacos
escabeche	pickled
escamoles	ant eggs
espaghetti	spaghetti
especialidad de la casa	house special
espinaca	spinach
espinazo	spine
estofado	a stew
estragón	tarragon
exprimidor	juicer
exprimir	to squeeze
Fajita	skirt steak
falda	refers to the flank steak rather than the skirt steak
farina	wheat flour
fécula	starch
fiambre	mixture foods like fruits, vegetables, meats or cheeses marinated in a dressing, served cold
fideo	vermicelli noodles
filete	filet
flamear	to flame, as in a flaming dessert
flan	baked custard with caramel coating
flauta	deep fried, stuffed corn tortillas
flor	flower
flor de calabaza	squash blossom
fonda	eating booth in a market or a small restaurant

glossary

fondo	broth made from soup bones or a reduced stock
frasco	jar
freír	to fry
fresadilla	tomatillo
fresas	strawberries
frijoles	beans
frijoles colados	beans that are cooked and strained before frying
frijoles refritos	refried beans
frito/a	fried
fruta	fruit
fundir	to melt
galletas	cookies
gallina	hen
garbanzo	chickpea
gazpacho	cold, spicy tomato soup
golosina	candy or sweet
gordita	deep fried thick tortilla stuffed with filling
granada	pomegranate
granadilla	passion fruit, parcha and maracuya
grasa	grease or fat
guacamole	mashed avocado condiment often served as a dip
guajolote	turkey
guava	tropical peach-tasting fruit
guisado/a	stewed
gusanos de maguey	fried century plant worms
haba	large, yellowish broad beans
habanero	hottest spicy pepper available
hamburguesa	hamburger
harina	flour
harina de maíz	flour for making cornmeal for tortillas and tamales
harina de trigo	wheat flour
helado	ice cream
hervir	to boil
hielo	ice
hierbabuena	mint
hierbas	herbs
higado	liver
higo	fig
hongos	mushrooms
horchata	drink made with melon seeds or rice with added fruits, coconut, almonds and sugar
hornear	to bake
horno	oven
huachinango	red snapper
huesos	bones
huevos	eggs
huevos cocidos	hard-boiled eggs
huevos fritos	fried eggs
huevos motuleños	tortilla topped with ham, fried eggs, peas and red sauce

glossary

huevos poches	poached eggs
huevos rancheros	fried eggs on tortillas covered in red salsa
huevos revueltos	scrambled eggs
huitlacoche	black, mushroomlike corn smut used as a filling for antojitos or an ingredient in soups
huicoy	thick winter squash
jaiba	small crab
jalapeño	small and spicy green pepper
jalea	jelly or marmalade
jamón	ham
jamoncillo	candy made from sugar and milk or from fruits and pumpkin seeds
jarabe	syrup
jarra	pitcher
jengibre	ginger
jícama	a crisp, white, edible root
jitomate	tomato
jugo	juice
jumil	insect that is eaten both alive and dried
kahlúa	coffee-flavored liqueur made in Mexico
langosta	lobster
lata	can
leche	milk
leche de enco	coconut milk
leche quemada	burnt milk candy
lechuga	lettuce
legumbres	legumes
lenguado	tongue
lenguado	flounder
lentejas	lentils
licor	liquor
licuadora	drink made from blended juice, water and sugar
liebre	hare
lima agria	Yucatan sour lime
limón	lime
limonada	limeade
lomo	loin
longaniza	sausage flavored with chiles and other spices
maguey	century plant
maíz	corn
mango	mango
malanga	potato or bean-flavored root
manioc	yucca
manitas	pigs feet
manjar	delicacy
mano	piece of volcanic rock used to grind food against another rock
manteca	lard
mantequilla	butter
manzana	apple

glossary

maracuya	round, lime size fruit
margarina	margarine
margarita	tequila based cocktail generally made with lime juice and triple sec
mariscos	seafood, usually shellfish
marquesote	sweet bread made with wheat, rice or corn flour and eggs
masa	dough or cornmeal
masa harina	masa processed with lime
mejorana	marjoram
melaza	molasses
melón	melon
menudo	soup or stew made with tripe and flavored with chiles, believed to cure hangovers
meocuil	white century plant worm
merienda	a light meal or snack eaten between lunch and dinner
mermelada	marmalade
mero	grouper
mesero/a	waiter
metate	rectangular stone grinding bowl
mezcal	distilled liquor made from the juice of various agave cactus plants
mezclar	mix
miel	honey
milanesa	breaded, fried cutlet of veal, beef or pork
miltomate	fresadilla tomatillo
mixiote	sliced lamb stew
mojo de ajo	garlic sauce
molcajete	volcanic rock shaped with which food is ground
molde	mold
mole	thick sauce or paste made from unsweetened chocolate
molido/a	ground
molotes	cornmeal for tortillas
molusca bivalvo	scallops
mora	lightly smoked jalapeño often used for canned chipotles, salsas and sauces
morcilla	entrails, cooked in blood or stuffed into intestines and grilled or broiled
mostaza	mustard
muslo	thigh
names	yams
naranja	orange
naranja agria	sour orange
nata	cream
natillas	custard
nixtamal	hominy
nogada	sauce made from ground nuts
nopales	edible cactus

glossary

nuez	pecan or nut
nuez moscada	nutmeg
NuMex	Big Jim Pepper
oja	cornhusk, used to wrap tamales
olla podrida	stew of meats and vegetables
orégano	oregano
ostión	oyster
ostionería	small café specializing in oysters and seafood
Palomitas de maíz	popcorn
pan	bread
pan dulce	sweet rolls
panela	crumbly cheese
panocha	unrefined sugar sold in small, very hard cones
papa	potato
papadzules	hardboiled egg enchiladas or soft tacos filled topped with tomato and pumpkin seed sauces
papas fritas	French fries
parrilla	cast-iron grid or grate used for grilling or making tortillas
pastel	cake
pato	duck
pavo	turkey
pay	fruit pie
pechuga	breast, as in chicken breast
pejelagarto lepidoseus viridis	alligator gar
pepino	cucumber
pepitas	pumpkin or sunflower seeds
perejil	parsley
pescado	fish
pibil	meat prepared in a barbaque pit used in the Yucatan
pica de Gallo	minced salsa
picada	gordita
picadillo	meat hash
picante	spicy and hot to the taste
pierna	leg, as in leg of lamb
piloncillo	pressed, unrefined dark brown sugar
pimentón dulce	paprika
pimienta	black pepper
piña	pineapple
pinole	flour made from roasted, dried corn
pinon	pine nut
pipián	sauce made from pumpkin seed, chile and spices
piquin	chile pepper often used to flavor vinegars
plancha	griddle
plantain	creamy cousin to the banana, often fried
plátano	banana
platillo	small plate
plato	plate or prepared dish
poblano	popular chili pepper for chile relleños

glossary

pollo	chicken
ponche	punch, made with liquor such as brandy or rum and fruit, and usually served hot
postre	dessert
pozole	soup made with meat (usually pork) and hominy and flavored with chile
propina	tip
puchero	large dish, or stew
puerco	pork
pulpo	octopus
pulque	mikly alcoholic drink made by fermenting aguamiel, the juice of the century plant
quesadilla	melted cheese between two tortillas sometimes with additional fillings
queso	cheese
queso añejo	hard cheese
queso asadero	string cheese
queso fundido	melted cheese served with tortillas
queso fresco	fresh cheese
queso panela	fresh cheese similar to feta
quinoa	tiny, round, ivory colored grain
rábano	raddish
rajas	fried poblano slices
rallar	to grate
raspada	shaved ice flavored with syrup
recado or recaudo	Yucatan style seasoning pastes
recipiente hondo	bowl
refresco	soft drink
refrigerador	refrigerator
relleño/a	stuffed
remojar	to soak
repollo	cabbage
repostería	confectionary
requeson	curd cheese
res	beef
riñon	kidney
ristra	string of dried red chiles
robalo	sea bass
romero	rosemary
rompope	Mexican style eggnog
ropa vieja	stew made with shredded meat
sábana	tenderloin steak pounded paper thin and briefly seared on a comal or parilla
sal	salt
salbutes	small, thick tortillas, fried until crisp and topped with shredded meat and vegetables
salchicha	sausage
salmón	salmon
salpicón	finely chopped or shredded ingredients
salsa	sauce

glossary

salsa cruda	uncooked salsa
salsa fresca	uncooked salsa
salsa Mexicana	uncooked relish made with diced tomato, onion and fresh chile
salsa roja	red salsa made with tomatoes
salsa verde	green salsa made with tomatillos
salsera	sauce boat
salvia	sage
sandía	watermelon
sangría	drink made of red or white wine, sugar, oranges, lemons and lime
sangrita	cocktail made of orange juice, grenadine, chile and tomato juice served on the side of tequila
seco/a	dry
serrano	type of pepper
servilleta	napkin
sesos	brains
sierra	mackerel
sin sal	without salt
sopa	soup
sopa seca	rice or pasta dish
sopera	soup bowl
sopes	gorditas
taco	corn or flour tortilla folded over a filling
tacos a la plancha	tacos made from meats cooked on a comal or griddle
tacos al carbón	tacos filled with charbroiled meats
tacos al Pastor	pork tacos
tacos al vapor	tacos with steamed meat filling, often from a cow or goat's head
tacos de barbacoa	tacos made from barbacoa
tacos de carnitas	tacos made from carnitas
tacos de cazuela	tacos filled with ingredients, usually a stew of some sort, cooked in a cazuela
tacos de harina	tacos made with flower tortillas
tacos de maíz	tacos made with corn tortillas, usually doubled up
tacos dorados	tacos with a crisp-fried corn tortilla, filled with shredded meat
tacos sudados	sweated or basket tacos
tamal	singular of tamales
tamales	choice of filling surrounded by masa and steamed in a corn husk
tamarindo	tamarind
tapas	appetizers or bar snacks
taquería	a place, either large or small, to buy tacos
taquitos	small flautas
taza	cup
te or thé	tea
tejano	Spanish word meaning Texan
tejocote	tree that produces a fruit resembling a crab apple
tejolote	pestle

glossary

telera	type of wheat flour roll usually used to make tortas
tenedor	fork
tepache	alcoholic beverage made from pineapple and sugar, or cane juice and other juices
tequila	distilled liquor made from agave cactus or century plant
tesguino	beer made from corn
tiburón	shark
tlacoyos	tortilla dough enclosing a simple filling and grilled on a comal
tocino	bacon
tomatillo	small tomato with a husk
tomillo	thyme
toronja	grapefruit
torta	sandwich served on a roll
tortas compuestas	Mexican version of the sandwich
tortilla	flat Mexican bread made of cornmeal or flour
tortuga	turtle
tostada	fried flat corn tortilla topped with a layer of beans, shreddedbeef or chicken, lettuce, tomatoes, cheese, avocado and salsa
totoaba	endangered fish with delicately flavored flesh
totopos	fried tortilla chips served as appetizers and snacks
trigo	wheat
tripas	tripe
trucha	trout
tuba	alcoholic beverage made from fermented palm juice
tuna	fruit of the nopal cactus
uchepos	tamal that is a specialty of Michocán, made from fresh rather than dried corn
uva	grape
uva pasa	raisin
vainas de vainilla	vanilla beans
vainill	vanilla
vaso	drinking glass
venado	venison or deer
verdolaga	purslane
verdura	vegetable
vinagre	vinegar
vino	wine
vino blanco	white wine
vino tinto	red wine
xnipec	type of chile sauce
yuca	yucca
zacahuil	gigantic tamal, often filled with a suckling pig or whole turkeys, and cooked in a pit
zanahoria	carrot
zapote	sweet fruit, best blended with juice or Kahlua
zumo	juice

contributors

Jordan Actkinson
Jordan has been consuming copious amounts of Tex-Mex and other Mexican food for his entire thirty years. He is overeducated and underemployed, having recently retired from nine years of wino-hood in Austin and currently resides somewhere in America—probably on somebody's couch.

Kenneth Adkins
Growing up in Houston, I've always been interested in food and the food business. After school at the Hilton School for Hotel & Restaurant Management at the University of Houston, I made my way to Austin to work the restaurant circuit here. I haven't been able to get away from my H-Town roots, however. I currently sell coffee beans for my brother who owns Fontana Coffee Roasters, based in Houston. My night job? You can find me at Vespaio — definitely one of our non-Mexican food favorites.

Jennifer Braflaadt
A former environmental educator turned alcoholic-beverage salesperson, Jennifer has three dogs and is obsessed with snake, bear and Mt. Everest stories. She has lived in Austin for eight years. She sometimes eats Mexican food for five meals in a row and has been know to get tipsy on pitchers of margaritas at Jaime's. $21 for a pitcher of top-shelf margaritas during happy hour — and it's a big pitcher.

John Buchanan
Born and raised in Texas, I inherited my passion for food from my grandmothers. They were both accomplished in the kitchen and taught me the basics and baking. My father taught me steak and potatoes and my mother taught me how to order out. Ten years in New Orleans had a tremendous impact on me as a cook and bartender (I will always have a place in my heart (and liver) for the Crescent City). I've cooked professionally in several restaurants, but have never had any formal training. However, that doesn't seem to bother my guests at my home on Lake Austin, where Stacey and I entertain frequently.

Catherine Ann Bower
I know food because I study addiction — no comment from the peanut gallery! I grew up in Houston and graduated from high school as soon as possible to get out! I have lived in Alabama, South Carolina, Washington and California and am currently a graduate student at Texas

contributors

State University pursuing a doctorate in Clinical Psychology. I hope this book, compiled by someone who loves food even more than myself, will serve you well. Happy eating in Austin and please support the unique small businesses that abound here!

Kevin Burns
Kevin is a young, skittish, wide-eyed doe that is lost in the wild and caught in the headlights of a slammed Cadillac (on dubs of course). This man-child goes to 11 and is not afraid to turn it up. If awake after midnight or doused with tequila, El Burnso should be approached with caution.

Shazza Calcote
Shazza is an Austinite, friend, advocate, neighbor, pedestrian, voter, fan, listener, patron, goer, viewer, citizen, reader, lover, confidant, passenger, enthusiast and a talking ZZZhead.

Patricia Campos
This Brazilian, raised in the Amazon, physical education teacher loves guacamole and quesadillas. She got so into Mexican food and culture that she's marrying a Mexican whose mom cooks the best fajitas ever.

Brady Dial
Brady is an Austin-based filmmaker, but was born in South Texas and bottle-fed habanero salsa as an infant. He considers Tex-Mex and barbecue to be among society's greatest achievements, ranking just above the moon landing and second only to the Dallas Cowboy Cheerleaders.

Todd Erickson
Don Todd is a seasoned Mexican food buff with the distinction of once having successfully eaten "all he could eat" at a Mexican food buffet. He has sampled fine (and not so fine) Tex-Mex on three continents and numerous islands and has lived to tell about it. When not eating Mexican food, Todd has advised hedge funds and mutual funds on investment strategy and managed teams while living in New York, Tokyo and Chicago as a Vice President with Credit Suisse First Boston. His next stop is down home in Houston. So, if you're a money manager with a penchant for Tex-Mex, dinner's on CSFB.

Marc Ferrino
Marc Ferrino is a Jack of all trades to say the least. Never

contributors

sinking his teeth into something long enough to draw blood. He plays music with a popband, draws animated crazy cartoons and is a graphic designer by day. With an eye for the unique and different, Marc jumped at the chance to design a guide for his stomach's favorite past time - Mexican Food.

Jeff Fraley
Jeff understands the importance of self-promotion. In his short life, Jeff has produced a top-ten soundtrack, ridden a bull, started a national youth education program, produced several award-winning documentaries, water skied on an oar, taught at two distinguished prep-schools, waited tables, turned down a job from Karl Rove, known poverty, co-founded a film production company, delivered a commencement address, shot a deer and been Allison's friend since the fifth grade. Allison introduced herself to Jeff on the first day of school with a swift kick to the shin that made Jeff cry — they've been best friends ever since. Born in Fort Worth, Jeff is Director of New Business and Producer at Trinity Films in Austin.

Lucrecia Gutierrez
Translator/Research
Like many Austinites, Lucrecia is a California transplant to this exciting and down-to-earth city. Currently she is an elementary school teacher, a broadcast journalist for the U.S. Army Reserves and an occasional translator for those who are bilingually challenged. Additionally, she is engaged to one of the last great guys on this planet. One of her most recent accomplishments was running the Los Angeles Marathon and finishing in 5 and a half hours…without training. She just woke up one morning and decided she wanted to run a marathon, went and did the late registration thing and showed up bright and early the next morning. As soon as her knees recover from this idiotic stunt she plans on actually training for the next one.

Stephen Graham
Maps
Steve grew up in Austin and has enjoyed many Mexican food restaurants — including many that have long since disappeared. He received his PhD from UT at Austin and now does research and development with GIS and web technologies as well as hydrology and climate modeling.

Chad Hamilton
Chad was born and raised in Dallas, Texas where the

contributors

Wednesday night enchilada special at El Fenix was a family staple — he and his father once shared five enchilada dinners in a single sitting. He is a staunch believer that the cheese enchilada is the fundamental menu item on any self-respecting Tex-Mex restaurant. He maintains that "Corn or Flour" is a much more important than "Republican or Democrat" and that refried beans should be jarred like peanut butter. He now spends many of his off hours cycling in and around Austin. Mi Madre's migas tacos, Maudie's Enchiladas Perfectas and Curra's Enchiladas Curras are a few of his post-ride favorites.

Derek Hatley
Photographer
Derek is a long time resident of Austin, Texas. He is blessed with intelligence, good looks and the most beautiful wife in South Austin. His photographs invoke a direct connection to "the MAN" who spiritualizes the visual "beachfront property of internal creativity". His pictures are fast, obsessed with the underclass and leave the taco shacks loving the limelight. The tripas and lenguas are waiting ...

Leanne Heavener
Research / Fact-checker
An Oklahoma native and nine year resident of Austin, Leanne is a lover of all food, wine, music, musicians, smoky honky-tonks, upscale restaurants, Barton Springs pool and anything Texas. A self-proclaimed expert from haute cuisine to chicken-fried; Leanne spends herdays as a professional event planner, or more to the point, anything that results in folks having a good time.

Juliana Hoffpauir
Hoffpauir moved back to Austin several years ago after living in the Colorado mountains (where she had various jobs) and a warehouse in Brooklyn (where she co-founded a theatre company). Back in Austin after 10 years, she is making up for lost time in local Tex-Mex establishments and live music venues. In addition, she apprentices at The Garden Room, a local woman's clothing boutique, and shoots/edits wedding videos.

Paul Jacobs
I am a 28 year old father of a wonderful 5 year old boy named Asher. I develop Legislative software systems for the State of Texas, and I am an avid mountain biker. Aside from working and playing I like to eat and cook. Mexican food is a staple of what is cooked and where I eat. I've

contributors

lived in Austin for 5 years but grew up in Southern California before being transplanted to Houston.

Aaron Kirksey
Aaron recently moved away from Texas after living there since he was a baby. He dropped out of college three classes short of graduating and is currently working his third season on a trail crew in the Frank Church River of no Return Wilderness in central Idaho. In his spare time he enjoys painting, playing music and spending time in the woods fly-fishing and mountaineering. After living in Austin for five years, he feels qualified to contribute to this book. He'll miss Mexican food in Texas, but he's moving to Idaho for good. There just isn't enough snow in Texas.

Shelly Lamont
Shelly, a Yankee at birth and an Oklahoman for a spell, has settled nicely here in her true home, Texas. In the service, and I mean the service, industry for a mere eighteen years, she has lived in Austin for eight. Her hobbies include sports, drinking and boys. She is excellent at all three.

Clay Langdon
Originally from up north — Fort Worth, Clay is an advertising genius and a retired smooth-talking ladies man. He moved to Austin a year ago from New York City where he spent ten years searching for decent Mexican food in vain. He currently lives in Austin with his wife and new daughter and works as a Planning Director for GSD&M.

Stephen Levay
Poet, cowboy, philosopher, full of baloney. May be reached for comment or evening out inquiries at stephenlevay@hotmail.com

Stephen Malina
Native to Austin, Texas, Stephen enjoys a complex routine of soccer, coffee, bicycles and cheap beer. After graduating with a BA in English from Michigan State University, he fled the North to repatriate to his much warmer and more enjoyable homeland in Austin. Fishing and household cat herding are his art, while writing is his job. Currently Stephen is a staff writer for *INsite* magazine where he covers food, music, art and film, among other things.

contributors

Wes Marshall
Wes is a food and wine writer published widely in Texas and the author of *The Wine Roads of Texas*.

Kevin Martin
Kevin has been a friend of Allison's for many years. Together, they have been globetrotting adventurers. He now leads a dual life. He works in New Haven, Connecticut as a paramedic. Working on the ambulance, he spends a lot of time eating take-out. He estimates that last year he only cooked two meals — both pasta with tomato sauce. His other job is as Sheryl Crow's stage manager. He's been on the road on and off for the last five years and has been to every state and to over forty countries. He gets to eat great cuisine all over the world, but the Mexican food in Austin, Texas has a special place in his heart. He lived in Austin during most of the 90s and he now misses the Mexican food the most. He wrote his review while on tour in Dublin and after just a week of pub food he really could use some chicken fajitas. He can't wait for his next trip back to town!

Pat McIntyre
Originally from Oklahoma City, Pat spent the 70's studying Jazz Guitar, and spent the 80's playing everything else to make a living. Since the mid 90's he has languished in high-line sales gigs. Famous quotes: "I'm sorry but I won't apologize."; "The greatest crime in history is its revision."; "The highest level of technique is nuance." He enjoys Formula 1 racing, drinking, poker, and Italian Opera — not necessarily in that order. Contrary to popular myth, he did not invent crack. Available as distinguished escort.

Cile Montgomery
Copy Editor
A life-long Austinite, Cile is the queen of queso. She has been known to force friends through the late-night Taco Cabana window for some warm tortillas and hot queso. If given the chance, she would gladly swim in the soft sauce. She is often spotted around town on her cruiser and being absolutely charming to everyone she meets.

James Moody
Marketing
Moody is a vagrant and an entrepreneur who is very fond of gold, flamingos and mescal. You can usually find him at the gym working out or downtown waxing his Cougar. He dabbles in pharmaceuticals and bocce ball.

contributors

When it comes to food, he is an experienced Tex-Mex troubadour ... and that's the bottom line. His lineage can be traced to the likes of Don Quixote and Eric Estrada. Moody's knowledge of Mexican food was born in Merced, fostered in Germany and mastered in Louisiana. Add it all up and you've got an enchilada aficionado. When Moody talks Mexican — listen up amigo. Moody's life-long dream is to get a spot working for Steubine+Media. This is a top-tier multi-national media giant that is now almost impossible to break into. He is hoping to leverage this literary masterpiece of a book by the Dirty Lowdown Press to gain exposure and catch the attention of Steubine+Media CEO Billeam J and his team. B.J. if you're reading this, Moody is your man. Pull the trigger — you won't regret it.

P.S. Ladies, Moody is now single and currently scheduling interviews in Austin. Buckle up.

Christopher Nelson
Editor/Layout
Chris hails from the northern parts of Texas and wears #22 on his jersey. Hobbies include: European fashion, private jets, horse drugs, fur and discotecas. At Georgia Tech he double majored in Lasers and Corporate Malfeasance and triple minored in Sexual Healing, Taxidermy and Crunk Studies. Chris sings lead in the turbo-gangster-country band the FMCKB ("FoMoCoKiBo" in Japan), serves on the board of Steubine+Media and drills in the Alaskan wilderness. He is happily unmarried with three children.

Will O'Connell
Will, a self- professed jackass and Austin native, can be found nightly at various local pool tournaments swilling beer and placing second. By day, Will is the door greeter and expert hair colorist at Wet Salon on South Congress. Hobbies include playing pranks on his friend and fellow "not gay" hair stylist Eric, and superimposing his picture alongside that of his longtime love, Drew Barrymore. Will breaks routine to attend any event requiring a backstage laminate or a secret password. He is often accompanied by his lovely and tolerant girlfriend, Michelle. They're the ones with the matching dreds.

Cory Plump
Cory plays music with various legendary bands including the Awesome Cool Dudes, FMCKB and Los Laundry Boys. He's a vegetarian who loves girls, beer and Jesus.

contributors

Doug Prince
Doug moved to Austin in the early 90s. He has fourteen years experience working professionally as an artist and animator. He has spent the last nine years creating computer games primarily for Electronic Arts and Microsoft. Doug currently works in his new art studio when not spending time with his fiancée and two dogs, Poly and Theo.

Jesse Proctor
Jesse has been drug through every bean and beer joint between Houston, Acuna and points way farther south. His experience is a moot point. He's just eaten more Mexican food than you. How 'bout that?

Butros Puchachos
Known simply as "The Boutros" he is a cock-strong young man from Rancho Putenango, Mexico. His hobbies include private islands, amphetamines and cricket. He is a founding member of the Foggy Mountain Cop Killin' Boys and a patron saint in Austin's Turbo Gangster Country music scene. He is currently exiled in Washington, DC, pursuing an advanced degree in "Authoritarian Regimes and the Politics of African Strongmen". He misses Texas and the last time he tried to eat Mexican food, he got hit on by an old Laotian dude; afterwards, he cursed the day he ever wrote the "Fast Food Miscegenation" essay.

Amy Rogers
Amy is a fifteen year Austin local who once dated the brains out of a Tex-Mex restauranteur whose restaurant is featured herein. Today she is an avid golfer with a 50 handicap, the only girl allowed at her weekly all-boy poker game and is casually in search of her next restaurateur, but only interior Mexican this go 'around.

Tomas Salas
When he is not writing, acting, or painting, Tomas is a handyman. He repairs leaky faucets, builds walls or tears them down, installs ceiling fans, and fixes broken hearts. If you need an actor, a writer, a painter, or some home improvement he can be reached at (512)445-6928.

Gracie Salem
Gracie is the food writer for *Tribeza* magazine.

contributors

Tony Sanchez
Tony spends his time selling Coors beer, playing poker and fly-fishing. He has few complaints.

Edmund Schenecker
Edmund is not a writer, but having discovered the perfect taco, he will take pen in hand when fed properly. ¿No hay comida? If you have tequila, he has a glass. He has contributed to *Brilliant Magazine, Cowboys and Indians Magazine, Tastevin Magazine* and *The San Antonio Express-News*.

Susan Shields
Copy Editor
Susan is a writer who has lived in Austin since 1997, when she entered the Master's program in Creative Writing at the University of Texas at Austin. She was previously a reporter for the *Daily Variety* in New York City and has penned a food column locally since 2001. Her story "Demolition" won The Austin Chronicle Short Story Contest in 2000. She is also a waitress at the best Italian joint in the city. She loves all food — including Mexican.

Scott Staab
Advisor
Scott spends his time avoiding nihilists, Robert Novak, and Shepard's Pie.

Stacey Stoddard
Stacey is a native Texas who loves the outdoors, her man and Mexican food.

Trent Tate
Trent is an artist who paints in what he calls, "the radically traditional manner of the ancient monks." His formal training came under the careful guidance of an obscure manuscript (which had been lost for a couple hundred years) holding the lost secrets of the methods and materials of 14th century painting in the almost forgotten medium of egg tempera. Trent lives in Austin and in various other locations near trout streams throughout New Mexico, Colorado and Montana.

Caroline Tinkle
Caroline was brought up by a Mexican grandmother who taught her the secrets of Mexican cuisine at an early age. She is an Arabic-speaking MBA-holding Texas who is vastly underemployed as a high school teacher. Certain government agencies have expressed interest in her Arabic language skills.

contributors

Michael S. Thomson
Chef and restaurateur, Michael is a recognized leader in the Texas food movement and the force behind Fort Worth's successful Michael's Restaurant. Michael founded the restaurant a decade ago after an early career with several well-known Texas hotels and restaurants. For eight years, he was the corporate consulting chef for the Burlington Northern Railroad, and he has been a regional chef for Delta Air Lines since 1994. Michael also serves as an ambassador for the Texas Beef Council and the U.S. Meat Export Federation, training foreign chefs in the mysteries of Texas cuisine. His innovative cookery reaches a national audience through his column, "C.P. Express" in *Chile Pepper Magazine* as well as through frequent television appearances and cooking classes. Michael's Restaurant & Ancho Chile Bar 3413 W 7th Street, Fort Worth, Texas, 76107 www.michaelscuisine.com

Ann Tucker
Copy Editor
Ann is a graduate student in Architecture at UT, a freelance designer, an editor for the Dirty Lowdown Press and currently preparing a nation-wide launch of a line of textiles and furniture. With all that free time on her hands, she can be found eating Mexican food with friends and tearing it up on the dance floor.

Fay Wallace
Fay knows what a good meal should be, and she isn't afraid to let you know when it's not. A talented cook, entertainer, event party planner and connoisseur of all the finer things, Fay is sure to fill the void created by Martha Stewart when she tried to apply her decorating techniques to the legal system. Fay currently spends her time studying Literature at St. Edwards University and sending her drinks back at bars around town. She lives in Austin and the Little Blanco farm.

Allison Walsh
Publisher, Editor
Allison is the founder of The Dirty Lowdown Press. A well-traveled native Texan, she is positive that Austin, though landlocked, is *the* greatest place to live. Regardless, she looks forward to being able to spend part of the year swinging on a hammock with a book and a beer right on the magnificent ocean. She is blessed with amazing friends and an incredible life. Current projects include the revival of the answer "yes."

contributors

Shayna Weeden
Shayna likes Mexico, Mexicans and Mexican food. When she isn't eating Mexican food, she can be found in Taxco, Mexico hanging out with Mexicans where she makes original jewelry from semiprecious stones and the native silver. www.shaynajewelry.com

Fleetwood Fay Wilson
Fleetwood is not named after Fleetwood Mac. Fleetwood is not named after the Cadillac either. Sometimes when she meets people for the first time, they think they are really funny when they ask her where her "Mac" is. Fleetwood thinks those people are stupid. Fleetwood knows one other person named Fleetwood in the world. She enjoys Bruce Lee, Lonestar, Homestar, uprooting her life and dark chocolate.

Virginia B. Wood
Virginia is the Food Editor for the *Austin Chronicle*.

restaurant index

A
A la Carrera 184
Abarrotes 38
Abuelo's 144
Al Pastor 82
Alonzo's 82, 128, 158
Amaya's 38
Ancho's 2
Angie's 29
Antonio's 158, 184
Arandas 39, 98, 128, 159
Arandinas 40, 83, 185
Arturo's Bakery Café 2
Arturo's Taqueria 41
Aus Tex Mex Café 3
Azul Tequila 98

B
Baby Acapulco 84, 99, 159, 185
Baja Fresh 3, 128
Bejuco's 42
Berryhill Baja Grill 144

C
Camino Real 186
Cancun 186
Carlos'n Charlies 206
Casa Garcia 100, 129
Casa Maria 129
Chango`s Taqueria 4, 100
Chapala Jalisco 46
Chaveros Chicken Bowl 5

restaurant index

Chipotle 6, 130, 145, 187
Chulita's 46
Chumikal's 130
Chuy's 101, 187
Cisco's 47
Copa 7
Costa del Sol 48
Curra's 102

D
Dario's 48
Dart Bowl 163
Dina's 134
Dos Hermanos 49

E
El Arroyo 8, 145, 164
El Azteca 50
El Caribe 164
El Charrito 50
El Chile 51
El Flaco 104
El Gallo 104
El Jacalito 84
El Mercado 8, 105, 165
El Meson 85
El Nopalito 105
El Paraiso 165
El Patio 9
El Rancho Grande 166
El Regio 52, 86, 134
El Rey 109
El Sol 135

restaurant index

El Sol Y La Luna 109
El Sumbido Grill 86
El Tacolote 190
El Tripaso 52
Elsi's 166
Enchiladas Y Mas 167
Evita's Botanitas 135

F

Flores 146, 168, 206
Fonda del Sol 55
Fonda San Miguel 168
Foodheads 12
Freebirds 12

G

Garibaldi's 136
Güero's 110

H

Habanero 112
Hacienda 89
Happy Taco 89
Hula Hut 146

I

Iguana Grill 207
Innocente's 55
Iron Cactus 13, 190

J

Jaime's Spanish Village 14
Jalisco's 112
Janitzio 90

restaurant index

Jardin Corona 191
Jefes 170
Joe's Bakery & Coffee Shop 56
Jorge's 170
Jovita's 113
Juan in A Million 57
Juanita's 14
Juarez 191
Julio's 16

L

La Bahia 58
La Casita 60
La Casuelita 90
La Cocinita 60
La Feria 114
La Fuentes 136
La Mexicana Bakery 114
La Michoacana 61
La Morada 192
La Morenita 62
La Palapa 62
La Parrilla 193
La Playa 137
La Posada 138
La Regiomontana 91
La Reyna 115
La Salsa 150, 172
La Tapatia 92, 116
La Terraza 92
Las Cazuelas 63
Las Colinas 171

restaurant index

Las Manitas 16
Las Palmas 64
Las Palomas 150
Little Mexixo 116
Los Altos 65
Los Comales 65
Los Jaliscienses 66
Los Portales 194
Luvianos 69

M

Mama Ninfa's 19, 174
Manuel's 20, 194
Maria's Taco Xpress 117
Marisco Grill 25, 172
Mariscos Seafood 93
Mary's Bar 173
Matt's El Rancho 118
Maudie's 120, 138, 151, 195
Mesa Rosa 195
Mexico Lindo 120
Mi Madre's 69
Mi Rey 70
Moe's Southwest Grill 70
Morelia 71
Mr. Natural 71, 121
Mr. Pollo 197

N

Nueva Onda 123
Nuevo Leon 72

restaurant index

P
Pancho's 25
Papa Pancho's 72
Pappasito's 73
Polvos 123
Porfirio's 75, 93

R
Ranch 616 26
Rico's Tamales 75
Rincon Catracho 197
Rita's 198
Rosie's Tamale 124, 151, 152
Ruby's BBQ 27

S
Sabor a Mexico Tipico 174
San Juanita 139
Santa Rita Tex-Mex Cantina 28
Santiago's 175
Serrano's 29, 124, 152, 175, 199

T
Taco Cabana 30, 95, 125, 139, 179, 199
Taco More 200
Taco Sabroso 76
Taco Shack 32, 179, 200
Tacodeli 153
Tamale House 179
Texican Café 140
The Oasis 207
Tia's Tex Mex 154

restaurant index

Tierra Caliente 180
Tres Amigos 77, 140, 154
Trudy's 33, 125, 202

U
Un Rincon de Mexico 77

V
Vallarta Jalisco 95, 141
Vasquez Tacos 202
Vivo 78

W
Whole Foods 34

Z
Z Tejas Grill 35
Zunzal 78
Zuzu 181

To order books or t-shirts visit our website at:

www.thedirtylowdownpress.com

The Dirty Lowdown Press
P.O. Box 1972
Austin, Tx 78767

Look for our new title coming soon:

The Dirty Lowdown Press Presents... **Austin: The Guide**